CONTINUING EDUCATION
LIBRARY
MICHIGAN STATE UNIVERSITY
EAST LANSING, MICHIGAN

D1253934

MICHIGAN STATE UNIVERSITY
LIBRARY
WITHDRAWN

PERSONALITY
AND ORGANIZATION

CONTINUING EDUCATION
LIBRARY
MICHIGAN STATE UNIVERSITY
EAST LANSING, MICHIGAN

PERSONALITY
AND ORGANIZATION

*The Conflict Between System
and the Individual*

by CHRIS ARGYRIS

Associate Professor of Industrial Administration, and Research
Project Director, Labor and Management Center, Yale University

HARPER & BROTHERS: NEW YORK

PERSONALITY AND ORGANIZATION

Copyright © 1957, by Harper & Brothers

Printed in the United States of America

All rights in this book are reserved.
No part of the book may be used or reproduced
in any manner whatsoever without written per-
mission except in the case of brief quotations
embodied in critical articles and reviews. For
information address Harper & Brothers
49 East 33rd Street, New York 16, N. Y.

Library of Congress catalog card number: 57-11116

To my Parents
Stephen and Sophia Argyris
With Deepest Appreciation.

CONTENTS

CONTENTS

PREFACE

The increasing acceptance and use of the behavioral sciences as integral parts of the teaching and research curricula (in schools of engineering, business, and public administration) and the realization by practitioners of the importance of understanding the *why* of human behavior in organizations represent a significant trend in the field of organization and administration.

During the past six years I have helped to establish behavioral science curricula in an engineering and business school. As a result, I became increasingly aware that my colleagues were unsure of the scope, depth, and potential contribution of the behavioral sciences (e.g., psychology, sociology, anthropology, and political science). Likewise, many of my students expressed frustration in finding that few of the traditional courses in psychology or sociology, for example, focused in the areas of their interests. Many would ask if it were not possible to integrate the contributions of the behavioral sciences, keeping in mind the interests of students in an engineering or business school.

At the same time, through my research and consulting interests, I became aware that although many practitioners were accepting the importance of the behavioral sciences, and some were even creating their own research departments, few seemed to have a clear view of the uniqueness of these disciplines and their potential contribution.

I began to wonder if it would not be helpful for someone to attempt the necessary first step of assembling as much of the existing empirical research as possible, preferably on some sort of framework, in order that more meaningful patterns could emerge.

This book represents my first step at integrating the existing research literature relevant to understanding human behavior in on-going organizations. The result of such an integrated review will produce, I hope, a few basic foundations for what may some day develop into a systematic framework for the field of organizational behavior. This study does not attempt to present a mature theory. The latter objective is unattainable for three reasons. First, a whole mature theory is beyond the capabilities of one individual researcher. Second, the available empirical research from which one can build a theory is itself not mature, since many of the studies reported are admittedly exploratory. Not one area of inquiry presently being studied has been explored to the minimum limits required by scientific standards. Third, there are a number of areas of inquiry that are crucial to the formulation of a theory, but which apparently have not yet been explored.

The reader may wonder why a book like this is attempted if the field is in such an underdeveloped state. The answer is inescapable. No science matures until it has developed at least one workable theory that may be used to make sense of existing knowledge and at the same time points to areas that require further exploration. Someone has to make such an attempt and I am interested and willing to try.

The task of creating the foundations for a theory is difficult, and it becomes even more formidable when one desires to create a scaffolding upon which to hang and interrelate as much of the existing literature as possible without doing violence to the basic results of each individual study.

There are at least two modes of operation for such an endeavor. One is to limit attention to a narrow band of the literature and focus on developing a theoretical model from which to elicit logical derivations (preferably in mathematical language) that illustrate, predict, and/or expand the results within this narrow band of research. Another is to try to cover a maximum portion of the literature by the use of a theoretical scaffolding whose logical limbs are not as developed and interrelated as the ones in the previous approach.

The latter approach is chosen for a number of reasons. First, to my knowledge no one is taking such an over-all point of view. Second, examination of the fruits of the former approach by scientists suggests that the results are not as logically sound and empirically fruitful as the complex formulas could lead one to believe.[1] * Third, if no one takes the over-all approach, there is the danger that the many contributions in the field will remain scattered, and their possible collective impact might never be ascertained. Fourth, by taking the over-all approach it is possible to arrive at some inventory of the number and kinds of areas that are presently being researched and the areas that remain untouched. Finally, as Lewin suggests, one can, by successive approximations, make finer and finer differentiations, which will impart to the over-all approach the depth required by scientific standards. Experience suggests that this is not as feasible if one begins with the limited but "depth" approach and attempts to expand his scope later.[2]

This book is intended for advanced undergraduates and beginning graduate students, especially those in engineering, business, public administration, and public health schools, who tend to have a relatively weak background in the behavioral sciences. I hope that the human relations researchers in the universities and the human relations and personnel specialists in industry will find the book of value. Finally, the book should be of some help to line and staff executives who are tired of those analyses of human problems that purport to provide simple answers but which, when stripped to their essentials, are gimmicks. Human beings are not simple and they deserve the consideration of not being manipulated by trick or specious methods.

Most of this book, therefore, focuses on the question of *why* people behave the way they do in organizations. Wherever possible, concrete practical applications are included in order to make the book more useful to those on the "firing line." Chapters II and VIII, and parts of VII, provide such examples.

Another reason that the *how* answers are not prevalent is the plain and simple fact that little of the present research effort is focused on such questions. There is a lack of competent scientific research in the more applied questions. Much more develop-

* References are listed by chapter at the end of the book.

mental research has to be done if the already known findings are to be applied with any high degree of confidence. This explains why the analysis of what is wrong with management practice is stronger here than the discussion on constructive action.

The developmental research should perhaps be conducted by competent individuals within action-oriented organizations in industry or the Armed Services. However, behavioral scientists should not overlook the lesson the physical scientists learned years ago, namely, that developmental research can feed back upon and raise important questions about pure research.

This book tries to focus on such questions as: What are the basic components of organization? How does organization tend to evolve? How does it tend to maintain itself internally? However, these questions are not answered completely, and a number of important ones are not even raised. For example, one will not find here a systematic discussion of the problems an organization faces in order to integrate itself with the socio-economic-political environment within which it is embedded. The environment does have important influences upon the internal organizational system, and a valid theory of organization must await their being made explicit. Wherever possible, studies are noted that focus on these important problems. However, a thorough analysis must await another research project.

Another important topic not discussed is organizational change. How do changes arise? How are they carried through? What are their influences? These unanswered questions represent an important gap in existing knowledge. However, the omission may not be as crucial as the first because, before one can understand and measure change, one must have some reference point of "stability" or "steady state" (quasi-stationary state, to quote Lewin). Another difficulty with studying organizational change is that many events which, on the manifest level of observation seem like changes, are shown by depth analysis not to be changes in the basic makeup of the organization. Clinical psychologists and psychiatrists long ago learned to differentiate between skin-surfaced (phenotypical) changes and the more basic underlying (genotypical) change. When is a change not a change becomes an important subject for study if useful progress is to be made in this area. For example, many administrators would defend the position that the recent emphasis on human relations programs represents a basic change in management behavior. This claim is examined in this book and its validity questioned.

Since the basic topic of change is not discussed, one will not find a discussion regarding the decision-making process within an organizational context. However, even if change were discussed, an examination of the literature reveals a meager amount of research on decision-making. There is too little known as to how a decision is first created and how it travels through the organization in order to have its intended effects.[3]

I am greatly indebted to Professor E. Wight Bakke, the Director of the Labor and Management Center, who not only concurred with the necessity for this project but gave the kind of professional, moral, and financial support that made it possible. Largely through his efforts, a generous grant was made available by the Foundation for Research on Human Behavior, for which I am extremely grateful. Professor T. T. Holme, chairman of the Department of Industrial Administration, also made available financial and clerical help without which the book would never have been finished on time. Mrs. Mary B. Clark, Mrs. Nancy Babcock, Mrs. Susan Henry, Mr. James A. Staley, and Mr. Robert Bjorn are to be thanked for their hard work in helping to translate a mountain of scribbled handwriting into clear typewritten manuscript. The book could never have been written without the help given to it and to me by my wife Renée.

PERSONALITY
AND ORGANIZATION

I
Basic Assumptions and Viewpoints of the Book

A. INTRODUCTION

In order to enter the Medical Library at Yale, one must walk through a corridor on whose walls are hung many old cartoons having to do with the medical profession. Many give the impression of "panning" the doctor for claiming that he really can cure human diseases. In those days, people felt that diseases could not be understood, much less cured, by scientists. For the most part, people turned to spiritualists, witches, "bleeders," clergymen, barbers, and even blacksmiths for treatment. Of course, as medical science progressed, the doctor became viewed increasingly as the correct source for medical treatment.

The medical profession is not the only one to go through the stage of being damned. Most professions have been criticized by the public during their formative years, and some are still being panned. Psychiatrists and psychologists are good examples, although here again, as these professional people prove their worth, the panning seems to be decreasing. To be sure, criticism has useful effects, for as long as the underdogs see criticism as a challenge, it obliges them to become more accurate and to redouble their efforts to become more effective. Criticism keeps the scientist alert.

The use of the behavioral sciences in administration is in these same early stages. No doubt, if practical people put into cartoons their true feelings about "experts" in human relations, these could fill up several long corridors. A big difference, however, between medicine and human relations is that in the latter case *everybody* tends to feel that he is an expert. People tend to believe that "experience is the best teacher about human nature," an attitude which is understandable because millions of people would be unhappy if they could not view themselves as being competent in living with their fellow men. But, even if this were not the case and the layman turned to the scientist for advice, he would find it difficult to obtain concrete, valid advice because of the immature state of scientific research and the lack of well-trained experts.

A primary motivation for this book is to suggest that "human relations" is becoming a scientifically rooted field, as evidenced by the increasing use of the behavioral sciences to understand *why* people behave the way they do. By bringing together some of the present behavioral science research results, a systematic picture of a basic and useful field of knowledge emerges.

This observation is not intended to imply that human relations is ready to (or should) become a profession and a closed shop open only to those with graduate training in the behavioral sciences. However, the use of these sciences to understand human behavior in organizations has now come of age. The time has arrived when the training of a skilled individual in human relations requires more than that he "like people."[1] In the hands of qualified people, it can be a useful addition to the administrative process as well as a further advancement toward basic knowledge of human behavior.

B. The Viewpoint

The first objective of this book is to help the reader understand some of the basic causes (i.e., the why) of human behavior in ongoing human organizations such as industrial plants, banks, insurance firms, trade unions, and government bureaus. No one research center or individual scientist has all the answers. In fact, if all the research from all the centers were combined, it could not produce as much help as the practitioner desires or as valid knowledge as the scientist requires. However, after conducting a preliminary survey of the research in human relations,[2] I am convinced that if the work of the many research centers were brought together in a systematic manner, it could provide the basis for a better understanding and, consequently, a greater degree of practical help than is now possible in its scattered form. Thus we come to the second objective of the book—to bring to the reader a systematic and integrated picture of some of the current research of human relations in on-going organizations.

The frequent use of the words "systematic" and "integrated" is intentional. "Systematic" work is work which passes minimum scientific standards set by scientists of today. The qualification "of today" is used because it is well known that in all science the values as to what is "good" science change as the science matures.[3]

The layman may wonder why this review should be limited to literature exhibiting minimum scientific standards. "For his own protection" is the best answer. Scientists' primary reason for using, and demanding that others use, scientific standards is to protect the layman who some day may be using this information to influence others. Also, they want to protect the layman from the scientist! Yes, that is true. They want to make certain that no scientist releases inaccurate information.

The word "integrated" simply means that only those research results that are truly interrelatable will be presented, so that the reader may gain an organized picture of the field "behavioral sciences and organization." Integration is one of the primary objectives of any scientist. It is his dream to see his field some day begin to have some order. He gains as much satisfaction from seeing that someone has integrated hitherto seemingly discrete information as the reader might receive from reading a novel, seeing an exciting movie, or going to the World Series.

The scientist also has an ideal as to how the field should be integrated. The ideal is to derive logically all the known results from a few "basic" statements (usually called postulates) that any scientist will accept as true. This is what Euclid did for geometry. He said if you accept this basic axiom (postulate), then I can show you how a whole host of theorems follows logically (i.e., their truth is inherent in the axiom). Newton did the same for physics. After stating a few postulates which most scientists of his day accepted, he then showed how he could derive logically many of the seemingly discrete results current in physics during his time. (Of course, he found he had to create calculus to help him with the job, but it is the basic desire we are trying to document.) Einstein, by reorganizing the basic statements and adding a few new ones, brought Newton's work up to date; at the same time he brought into the integrated picture research results that up to this time could not be fitted into the jigsaw puzzle of physics.

Euclid, Newton, and Einstein did most of this work using their minds as the primary research instrument. This is called theory building and it is crucial in the development of all sciences. One of the most important signs of the maturation of a social science is the degree to which its theory (1) can actually be used to understand (and then predict and control) human behavior, (2) incorporates within it the known results based upon scientific investigation, and (3) provides the basis for further explorations into unknown territory.

Why all this attention to theory? Why do we place such an emphasis on theories that integrate what is known? One part of the answer is that scientists' personal needs are fulfilled by doing this. It is not unlike the executives who gain personal satisfactions by working hard and earning high salaries or the ministers who fulfill their personal needs by preaching and attending to the spiritual development of their congregations. Another part of the answer is that the fundamental task of science is to understand and comprehend nature—not to invent atomic bombs, radar, and guided missiles.[4] The process of comprehending is something like solving a jigsaw puzzle. We increase our chances of finishing it as we find how the pieces fit together and study those which we have not yet been able to fit into the total picture.

Einstein describes both of these reasons when he states:

. . . What, then, impels us to devise theory after theory? Why do we devise theories at all? The answer to the latter question is simply: Because we enjoy "comprehending," i.e., reducing phenomena by the process of logic to something already known or (apparently) evident. New theories are first of all necessary when we encounter new facts which cannot be "explained" by existing theories. But this motivation for setting up new theories is, so to speak, trivial, imposed from without. There is another, more subtle motive of no less importance. This is the striving toward unification and simplification of the premises of the theory as a whole (i.e., Mach's principle of economy, interpreted as a logical principle).[5,6]

Administrators also have similar needs in their work. As management becomes a mature profession, there is an increasing desire for administrators to see the "whole" picture. They desire administrative practices that increase their degree of understanding about the total process of administration and that relate sales, finance, manufacturing, and so forth into one integrated picture in order that management may become more free to create bigger organizations, newer products, more effective distribution schemes, and so on.

In many ways the administrator's goals are similar to those of the scientist in studying human problems. This may be one sign of the increasing maturity of the profession. In the more mature sciences—medicine, physics, biology, chemistry, engineering, and so forth—intimate contact between the scientist and the practitioner is common. Let us examine, therefore, in more detail some of the common tasks of administrators and scientists.

C. COMMON TASKS OF THE ADMINISTRATOR AND THE SCIENTIST

The administrator and the scientist are basically interested in the same question, namely, *why* people behave the way they do in organizations.

Once they *understand,* it is an easy matter to *predict* and *control* behavior. Predictions and control of behavior are the fruits of understanding. Too often administrators *and* scientists try to take short cuts and go directly to predicting and controlling. For example, the latter create such techniques as intelligence tests to try to predict how to control human beings without knowing what intelligence is. (E.g., you're smarter; you can stay out of the Army. Or, you're dumber; you had better go into a slow class. Or, you have social interests so don't be an engineer.) The former develop complex production records and budgets which, within reasonable limits, predict how much the company will produce and at what costs but lack understanding of *why it is so*.[7]

Because they want to understand why people behave the way they do, both types of individuals must be able to *diagnose* human problems in organizations. The sharper and more systematic their diagnostic procedures, the more accurate their predictions and controls will be.

A valid diagnosis of human situations requires *knowledge of ourselves*. The administrator as well as the scientist must be aware of, and ideally be able to measure, the impact he has on the situation he is diagnosing. Fundamentally, this requires *self-awareness*. We shall see later that *it is impossible to understand others unless we understand ourselves and we cannot understand ourselves unless we understand others*.

The scientists working in the natural sciences have the same problem, but to a lesser degree. For example, in using their electron microscope to study electrons, they find that the light of the microscope affects important aspects of the electron they are studying.[8] Bridgman describes the dilemma as follows: "In order to think about a system or situation, we apparently always have to imagine ourselves as an observer standing on the outside, whereas when we try to do it, we find that we always end inside the system we try to stay outside of."[9]

Being aware of ourselves is not an easy or necessarily a pleasant task. It is much easier to study *others* than to study ourselves. One student of science points out that those sciences that developed first required the *least* amount of self-study among men. Man tends to shun the behavorial sciences because they ultimately will coerce him to take a closer look at himself.

There is one advantage to this "natural tendency" to resist self-understanding. Only those who are sincerely interested in understanding themselves and others will succeed in understanding human behavior. It would be dangerous indeed if anyone could become competent in analyzing and controlling other people without first focusing on himself. Psychologists or psychiatrists are not licensed if they have not gone through counseling or psychotherapy. Fundamentally, this requirement is made to safeguard the patient from the power the clinician has over him. This is *not* implying that all administrators must be psychoanalyzed. It is implying, however, that a certain amount of self-awareness ought to be required as a matter of respect for the human beings who are to be their subordinates.[10] Although years ago management would reject this requirement, research shows clearly that there is an increasing acceptance by management of the importance of such factors.

A valid diagnosis of human situations also requires *knowledge of the best principles available*. Although self-awareness is necessary, it is not sufficient. Both an administrator and a scientist must know something about the nature of what they are studying. A bridge-builder knows something about the strength of the materials he uses. A car mechanic knows something about the functioning of mechanical and electrical systems. A medical doctor learns physiology, biochemistry, and anatomy so that he may understand the workings of the human body.

Why should not this requirement hold for people who are trying to understand "human nature"? Most individuals know more about automobiles, boats, liquors, fishing, hunting, and sports than they know about human beings.

The latest available research suggests that, basically, all human behavior in an organization is caused by any one or a combination of:

1. *Individual factors*—requires an understanding of personality factors and principles.
2. *Small informal group factors*—requires understanding principles of social psychology, one aspect of which is group dynamics.
3. *Formal organizational factors*—requires understanding of traditional principles of organizing people (staff-line, chain of command, specialization of tasks; production layout and control, and so forth).[11]

Each of these three factors has its own principles. Thus the principles for understanding the individual are different from those of the group, and both are different from those of the formal organization. In some cases the "correct" principles of one (i.e., individual analyses) are antagonistic to the "correct" principles of the other (i.e., organization).

Organization as a whole. The reality a manager and a scientist face when trying to diagnose human behavior in organizations is *all* the above three factors combined. They try to understand what happens when these three factors are thrown together in creating an organization. Thus a fourth level of analyses results from the *mixture* of individuals, groups, and formal organization. Each level has its own principles, and the principles of the other three levels do not necessarily apply to the fourth.

It is as if there were on a table one glass of whiskey, one of ice, and one of soda. So long as these glasses are separate, there are three different components. The components of soda are different from the components of ice. Now, if the three are put together, a "highball" is obtained. A highball is different from soda, whiskey, and ice.

Although the analysis of the first three levels has a respectable history, the analysis of the organization as a whole is a new emphasis. It has had to wait until enough was known about the other three. Recently there have been more and more signs of people focusing on the organization as a whole—a focus which we shall call, for the want of a better term, *organizational behavior.*

But diagnosing the problems is only half the battle. The next stage is to do something about them. Technically, the plan of action may be called a *prognosis.* It is the use of all available knowledge to solve the problem in the most effective way known. Self-insight and principles must be put into action. Many social scientists would say that this is where scientist and administrator part ways. They believe that a scientist's role is primarily a diagnostic one. The scientist tries to answer the question *why* and is satisfied when this occurs.

Scientists try to find generalizations as to *why* people behave the way they do, but this does *not* necessarily prevent them from entering the stage of action. It is the essence of science that a diagnosis which has not been fully tested is not acceptable. For example, I once made a diagnosis of what I thought were the critical factors and how they interconnected to create the "problems"[12] as the management of a bank saw them.[13] Management then asked, "So what? What do you recommend that we do? What concrete action can be derived from your systematic picture?" Although it is not part of the role of the *researcher* to tell the management what to do, I could on the basis of my analyses help to predict the possible impact of any plan for corrective action that the management should decide to create. The researcher could say, "*If* you decide to do such and such, then on the basis of the research, I predict that the organization will respond as follows. But *you* must decide what action to take."

The administrators decided what courses of action to take and in what sequences. Observations were made during this phase to see whether the researcher's predictions were confirmed. The results showed that some of the predictions were accurate and others were not. Parts of the diagnosis had to be reexamined. In other words, studying the prognosis gave the researcher important insights into his diagnosis. When human behavior in organizations is studied, it is difficult to separate the diagnosis from the prognosis. This procedure is not new in the physical and biological sciences. For example, in the medical profession no one would dream of separating the creation of a new vaccine from the laboratory control testing of the new drug.

Successful administrative action requires "skills" that are derived from, and therefore deeply rooted in, systematic research. These "action skills" are not of the gimmick type. As Sheviakov and Redl point out:

Sometimes we discover two or three nice little tricks that work. Then we develop the delusion that, if we just keep on sticking to those tricks, the rest of the problems of life will dissolve themselves kindly into so much smoke. Well, it won't wash.[14]

The word "skill" may cause difficulties if it is understood to represent a vocational activity or to imply the manipulation of people. Neither of these meanings is intended. Skill is used to represent the human being *as a whole* responding to his environment.[15] The kind of "skills" psychologists usually speak of, such as intelligence, manual dexterity, and depth perception, are of a different order. As Roethlisberger points out:

Under this conception skill becomes something to be learned, a technique rather than a way of learning. Our version of skill (singular) as a process of balanced growth and learning disappears and skill is broken up into a multiplicity of discrete and separate skills (plural) to be used for different occasions. But our "skill" cannot be atomized. If it is, it becomes immediately manipulative and ineffective.[16]

Roethlisberger defines skill to include:

a. *Skill* deals with the concrete and not the abstract; through skill one relates himself directly to concrete phenomena.
b. *Skill* is a way of learning; it is the elementary way one learns to improve his relations to the external environment.
c. *Skill* is a process of balanced growth. Through skill one develops a growing awareness of the complexity of relationships in concrete phenomena as well as a growing confidence in his capacity to deal with them.
d. *Skill* is thus an organic, evolving, growing system of capacity for response which allows a practitioner to respond more effectively to a particular point in a given situation.
e. *Human relations skill* in particular is the capacity of a person to communicate his feelings and ideas to others, to receive such communications from others, and to respond to their feelings and ideas in such a fashion as to promote congenial participation in a common task.[17]

Roethlisberger emphasizes the individual's capacity to integrate himself with the environment. This he calls the individual's "skill in living." He assumes that the personality is an organism (a whole) and maintains this idea when he tries to understand how one individual relates himself to others. All this may become more meaningful after the chapter on the human personality, where it can be shown that Roethlisberger's conception of "skill" fits with the latest conceptions of the structure of the human personality.

The point to emphasize now is that an administrator requires human relations skill to put into effective action his self-awareness and the principles that he has learned. Perhaps Roethlisberger would place self-awareness and principles as part of "skill in living." To be sure, these aspects are highly interdependent. However, keeping them separate points out that it is possible to gain one without the other. There are numerous clinical cases where the patient has obtained self-insight (intellectually and emotionally) but still lacks principles for, or a skill in, living with others.

No one is capable of acquiring all the self-insight, principles, and skill that he requires in his everyday living. An administrator therefore, needs to have a *philosophy of life* (and of leadership) upon which he can base his action when the above capacities fail.

He needs to have a philosophy of life to judge the "goodness" and "badness" of his self, the principles, and the human relations skill. Science can never tell an administrator what is right or wrong or what is good or bad. These fundamental decisions are up to the administrators (and scientist) as individuals.

Science can tell the administrator such things as, "If you are directive in your leadership, your subordinates will tend to behave as follows . . ." Or, "A collaborative leader has the following impact upon his subordinates . . ." Or, "The principles of task specialization and chain of command tend to have the following impact upon the employees . . ." This is as far as science can go. It cannot tell the administrator which of these impacts is "good" or "bad." For example, a series of studies of top executives suggests that most of them feel that pressure is good. They feel it keeps them and the employees on the ball. On the other hand, research shows that pressure can cause some difficult problems in an organization.[18] However, the researcher cannot conclude that pressure is "bad." That value judgment depends on the individual's own ethics and values.[19]

To develop a philosophy of life, one must know the basic characteristics of our society—and how they have evolved. Thus an administrator must be familiar with American history, customs, mores, ethics, and goals. He would have a deeper basis for his philosophy if he knew the roots of American culture. This may take him back to men like Locke and even further back into the classics.[20, 21]

This is expecting much from an executive or a social scientist.

After all, how much can a person learn in his lifetime and still accomplish the job for which he is being paid? None of us is a Superman. The administrator especially may really become skeptical.

One answer is that we all lead busy, problem-filled lives. However, the executive may want to consider that as an executive he has power assigned to him to influence others in such a way that the organization's demands are fulfilled. Consequently, whether he likes it or not, in the course of leading he is also influencing others. Such influence is not to be taken lightly. Why, therefore, should it be easy to be a leader? Is it not safer for all concerned to know that the leaders have spent, and continue to spend, much of their time learning how to be more effective leaders?

Another consideration is whether the executive really has the alternative of being an average or mediocre leader. Albert Nickerson of Socony Vacuum Oil Company states that "A survey of 76 American Coporations revealed that a lack of specific skills accounted for only a shade over 10 per cent of the (executive) discharges, while character traits accounted for virtually 90 per cent."[22]

The task of learning to be an effective leader has been eased somewhat as a result of behavioral science research. This research has developed to the point where there now exists a body of knowledge to guide us in choosing the relevant information much more quickly and effectively and to specify the skills required to put this new knowledge into action. This is not to say that social scientists have learned everything there is to know. In fact, they have just begun to scratch the surface. But enough has been done to make future research much more economical and useful.

This in turn is now actually having effects on the educational opportunities available for administrators (in the form of executive development programs) and for students (in the form of a college education). One reason universities have not been more effective in providing programs that develop future leaders is that they simply did not know what was necessary for effective leadership. If we at universities can overcome such activities as interdepartmental jealousies (executives are not the only ones affected by these problems), we can eventually "field" an excellent, scientifically based curriculum on leadership. Some schools have already taken important steps in that direction.

D. The Objectives of the Book

The objectives of the book are to begin to set the foundations for a framework, which as it matures should be able to: (1) bring together the best research results available through the use of (2) a systematic framework which (3) will integrate the available research (or show the steps necessary for integration) (4) into one coherent systematic picture which (5) will explain (i.e., give better and better approximations) within its present range of application *why* people behave the way they do and (6) provide new hunches to understand behavior which is presently not understood (i.e., is outside the present range of application of the systematic framework) and (7) provide concrete practical advice (within the range of problems it purports to understand) or (8) show the degree of lack of valid action-advice that is available.

How do we begin? Looking out into the world of reality, we see that people are organized into activities called banks, hospitals, bureaus, stores, plants, refineries, insurance companies, and so forth. No organization, it seems, has "life" without people. If so, then it might be useful to know something about people. What are they made up of? What do we mean by human nature? How does it develop? Why does it develop? Why are some people better workers than others?

E. The Need for Common Sense and Experience

"Now just a minute," asks one executive, "what are you trying to do? Make psychoanalysts out of us? If you want my opinion, and I know the fellows who've been out working like I have for years, common sense is what we need—good old-fashioned-down-to-earth-horse-sense."

"That's right." "If you ask me, experience is the best teacher," adds another executive.

"All right," I reply, "let's talk about common sense for a while. May I ask you, in your experience, do all people show equal amounts of common sense?"

"Hell no!"

"Have you ever experienced a situation in which Joe and Bob make the same error? Joe seems to learn from his fault while Bob does not."

"Happens all the time."

"Then are you saying that it is possible that two people can go through the same experience and learn differently?"

"I don't know what you are driving at, but so far all you've said is obvious."

"Sometimes science is characterized as trying to understand the obvious. If Joe and Bob experience the same error, and they come out differently, then it *isn't* experience that teaches Joe or Bob, it is what Joe and Bob *do* with (or how they view) their experiences that counts."

"O.K. so far; I'll go along."

"Then we can change your principle that 'experience is the best teacher' to read, 'experience is the best teacher *when* the *individual* is capable of learning positively from what he experiences. This changes the emphasis. Experience is no longer the thing to focus on. The important question, *what has the individual done with experience?* leads to the question 'Why does Joe learn and Bob not learn?' in order to provide an answer, we have to know something about Joe's and Bob's personalities, thus bringing us right back where we started. In short, if we try to explain something by 'chalking it up to experience,' we have explained nothing."

"That's an interesting point. However, I still feel experience is important."

"You seem to feel that it is better to emphasize the role of 'experience' rather than the individual. Is that your feeling?"

"Yes, I can't help but feel that experience is a damn good educator."

"I agree with you—if you would permit me to add *if the individual wants to learn.* May I ask you, why do many operating executives tend to take your point of view, that is, experience is the best teacher?"

"Because most of us have come up the hard way. Whether you have gone to college or not, most of us have learned that it is our experience that counts," replies the executive.

"To be consistent with the position that you have just accepted, may I rephrase your reply to read, 'Most of us have learned that it is possible to profit from experience . . .'? This places an emphasis not on experience *per se* but on you as an executive, that is, your *skill to learn* from experience. One reason that some operating executives do not agree with this position may be that they feel it would force them to focus on how capable or incapable they are."

Let us stop here[23] and follow the assumptions of the book by postponing the answer to the question *why* this may be true until we know something about the human nature (personality) of people. To summarize the points made above, we can say:

Experience *per se* teaches nothing.[24]

The way in which the individual *uses* experience is the crucial factor.

All people learn something by experiencing events. Some learn lessons that we call good. (And we say, "That man learns from experience.") Some learn lessons that we call bad. (And we say, "That blockhead never learns," which of course is not true.)

Roethlisberger describes the limits of experience well when he states:

Let us explore more carefully this idea of learning from experience. One of the interesting things about experience is how personalized it becomes, how important to each of us our own personal experience is, and how difficult it is to communicate this importance to others. What does this personal experience teach us? Astonishingly enough, it seems to teach different people different lessons. It often teaches the 'wrong' as well as the 'right' lesson. The 'school of hard knocks' makes criminals as well as businessmen.[25]

It seems fair, therefore, to ask the question, "Is common sense all we need to understand why people behave the way they do?" Let us try to arrive at an answer by examining how other people try to explain the behavior of things they are trying to understand. We might start with the behavior of something that is admittedly easier to explain than the behavior of a human being. Let us take a watch. We might ask, "Why does a watch work?" The answer is not easy. To understand a watch one must be able (1) to take it apart, (2) to recognize all the parts and know their particular tasks, and (3) to know how each part is connected with every other part.

Or, how about an automobile? If we listen to a mechanic, he will tell us the same thing. He must learn the individual parts of the motor and then he must know how each part dovetails with the other parts. We can continue these examples into other fields, such as chemistry, biology, physics, and medicine.

Do we follow the same rules in order to understand why people behave as they do? Do we know all the parts of the human personality? Do we know how these parts dovetail with each other? Understanding why people behave is therefore not an easy task. To make matters more difficult, the parts of the human personality are not as easy to observe as are the parts of the body, the parts of a watch, or the parts of a car motor. For example, can we observe a need or an ability in the same way a doctor can point to a heart? The answer is clearly "No." In order to understand people, therefore, we have to work by the method of inference. We are not as lucky as the doctor or the mechanic.

If we picture a watchmaker trying to understand why a watch works, without ever being able to open the watch, we have an idea of the difficulty of understanding human behavior. In our case, the "watch" is the human personality. It is always closed to us. We cannot conceive of its ever being opened. The most we can do is to observe it and try, through experimentation and experience, to build up a picture (theory) of what we think the personality is like. Based on this picture, we make predictions and if these predictions are verified, we can begin to have more faith in our picture. Finally, after many years of constant experimentation, we are able to present a picture which might account for the workings of the human personality.

"What mysterious methods these human relations fellows use to understand personality," someone might remark. But are they mysterious? A moment's reflection on the history of physics will remind us that this is the very method the physicist must use. We can safely say that the character of modern physical science is that nothing is ever directly observable in immediate experience; it is always observable by inference. Einstein makes this point when he writes:

In our endeavor to understand reality we are somewhat like a man trying to understand the mechanism of a closed watch. He sees the face and the moving hands, even hears its ticking, but he has no way of opening the case. If he is ingenious, he may form some picture of a mechanism for all the things he observes, but he may never be quite sure his picture is the only one which could explain his observations. He will never be able to compare his picture with the mechanism and he cannot even imagine the possibility and meaning of such comparison.[26]

What does all this add up to? Simply this. If human beings are at least as difficult to understand as are watches, atoms, and car motors, then is it not clear that something more than common sense is necessary to help build a sound, systematic way of looking at social life?

This is not to say that common sense cannot be a method which may be of value in answering questions. Common sense may fall short of what is required by sound, systematic explanation for at least three reasons:

1. Common-sense answers are answers based primarily upon one individual's attempt to explain certain problems, largely in terms of his own experience. But since his individual experiences are never enough to sample anywhere near what is required by scientific standards, his answers are limited.

In order to believe that common sense is adequate, it is necessary to assume that social and psychological answers can be found simply because we live. Such an attitude is similar to the one expressed by the people back in the Middle Ages concerning the physical world. They felt that since they lived in the physical world they knew what it was all about. The history of science gives us many examples of the results that this common-sense approach obtained. For example, the people used to believe that the earth was the center of the universe and that motion was due to some characteristic within and inherent in the material.

Let us take an example of how vague and inaccurate common-sense "truth" can be. Below are some "truths" used so often that people always introduce them with, "Well, as the old saying goes. . . ." By doing this, people imply that the lesson expressed by the phrase is something of an enduring truth. For example:

Repeat a lie frequently enough and people will believe it.

Clothes make a man.

You can't teach an old dog new tricks.

Out of sight, out of mind.

You have all heard these phrases used as arguments at one time or another. They express "truths" that have weathered the years. But, and this is what seriously limits knowledge based on common sense, for every "truth" above, comon sense provides us with a contradictory "truth." For example:

The truth will always prevail.

You can't make a silk purse out of a sow's ear.

Never too old to learn.

Absence makes the heart grow fonder.[27]

The question arises, which is correct? The experienced person upon reflection is forced to say both may be correct because each may hold "truth" under given conditions. At this point we leave common sense and enter the world of science. For science is the attempt to describe phenomena under defined conditions.

2. The second reason for the limitation of common-sense answers may be best understood by an examination of the following scientifically tested statements concerning human beings, some of which have already been mentioned.

We tend to look at our social world through a set of colored spectacles.

We have a habit of wanting practical results rather than objective data in any situation.[28]

We affect the very situation which we want to observe just as a physicist affects the electron which he is trying to observe under an electron microscope.

In other words, common sense answers, when examined more thoroughly, are observed to be exactly what a person wants to believe are the correct answers for a given problem. This is true because the individual's personality acts to color the way he looks at the world. The coloring is always in line with the desires of the individual.

3. The final limitation of the common-sense approach is actually an extension of the limitation stated above. Since we all tend to see the world through our own set of colored glasses, and since this coloring is created by us in order to keep our own personality in a healthy balanced state, it follows that common sense is in reality our own personal framework with which to understand life. This framework (i.e., common sense) is a theory. It is a way of looking at and trying to make sense out of the world in which we live. And that, after all, is the ultimate aim of any science.

It can be said, therefore, that common-sense proponents are actually using a theoretical framework with which to understand the world. It is their own personal, private, prejudiced framework created to keep themselves in a relatively happy state with their environment. The difference between a common-sense theoretical framework and a scientific theoretical framework is that the latter attempts to be public, not private; it is systematic, not random; it does not permit prejudices to enter; and finally, it is continuously tested not by one case but by many.

II

The Human Personality

How does one begin to analyze organizational behavior? It is obviously complex, it exists on multi-levels, and it is multi-caused. One way is to begin with the fact that all organizations which this analysis purports to consider originate with the attempt to fuse two basic components, the individual and the formal organization. The formal plan is the "grand strategy" which the individual participants are supposed to follow as accurately as possible.

The participants, however, are human beings who are themselves living organisms with their own "grand strategy" as exemplified in their abilities, needs, and goals. As organisms, they will always be striving for self-actualization while behaving as agents of the organization. The nature of the human personality, therefore, is an important component in organizational behavior. What are the properties of this basic component? What problems will tend to arise as the individual interacts with and transacts upon aspects of the organization? In this chapter, the focus is upon the human personality.

A thorough discussion of the theories and the empirical research regarding the human personality would require volumes. Instead, the literature was examined in order to discover those basic properties of personality with which most students would agree.[1] These would be the basic "givens" with which the administrator or the scientist must cope. Especially for the information of the latter, some practical implications are presented with the discussion of each property.[2] The practical hints are useful in understanding individuals as individuals. However, they may have serious limitations in dealing with individuals as agents of the organization. This is a limitation unfortunately forgotten by those who define human relations as "treating employees as individuals." This definition misses the reality of the organization.

A. The Parts of Personality Maintain the Whole and the Whole Maintains the Parts

The parts of the personality, no matter what they are, plus the way they are related to one another, constitute the "whole" that all personality theorists would call personality. Whatever we try to understand personality we must not only understand the parts, but also how these parts are related to each other. Personality, therefore, is never simply the sum; nor is it greater than its parts. Personality is something different from the sum of the parts; it is an *organization* of these parts. The example of the highball mentioned previously as something that is different from its parts also applies to personality. The administrator must always deal with personality as a highball. He cannot conceive of an individual only as one with an itemized list of characteristics (e.g., honesty, loyalty, and initiative).

Let us say we approach a foreman and suggest in our best human relations manner, "Joe, if you would only give the other fellows a chance to speak, you would be one of the best foremen in the plant." This advice is misleading and may cause Joe to feel worse. The undesirable behavior mentioned above exists as an *integrated* part of Joe's personality. In other words, the "bad" behavior exists because it is integrated with the "good," and conversely, the "good" behavior exists because it is integrated with "bad." Therefore, a suggestion to Joe to change "only one" aspect of his personality is in reality asking him to change the very organization of his personality. Maybe Joe does not give others a chance to speak because he does not feel confident about himself as a leader and therefore prevents any embarrassing suggestions or questions by simply not permitting them to arise. Or Joe may act as he does because he has the notion that a good leader directs his men and issues the orders. By finding out how these parts are related to each other effective help can be given to Joe.

Such a line of reasoning carried into the field of human relations training suggests that the effective training of foremen in new techniques of human relations may actually require that they change their general, or total, behavior. Thus, training in human relations, no matter how simple, is not only a matter of "getting the subject matter across clearly," but it is also a matter of understanding how to help the foreman to incorporate the subject matter as part of his personality.

B. Organization Manifests Simultaneous Dynamic Internal-External Balance

The parts of the personality stick together because each part "uses" one or more other parts in order that it may exist. In the process of using each other (by feeding back on each other) the parts form the whole. *Internal* personality balance exists when the parts of the individual's personality are in equilibrium or balance with each other. People whose personalities are internally balanced are called *adjusted*. *External* balance exists when the personality as a whole is in equilibrium with the outside environment. People whose personalities are externally balanced are called *adapted*. Total balance occurs when the internal balance "jibes" with the external balance (i.e., when a person is adapted and adjusted, which some call *integrated*).

To put it another way, adjustment indicates the soundness of the internal arrangements of an individual's personality. Adaptation indicates the arrangements a person has worked out to adapt to his environment (e.g., his job). It is possible for a person to be adapted but not adjusted. Witness the many executives who are successful but who also have ulcers, or the people on the assembly lines who are internally tense but who nevertheless produce. It is also possible for a person to be adjusted but not adapted (e.g., a criminal). He may be internally adjusted, but his relationships with the environment are not healthy.

One practical implication of all this has to do with attempts to define "happiness" or "morale" of people. Does happiness in the industrial world mean adjustment? Or does it mean adaptation?

Or can it mean both? Another practical implication is related to assigning people to perform certain jobs. Are the people chosen those who will adapt (and thus produce) even if they cannot adjust? Is adequate attention paid to the adjustment problems that jobs tend to create?

Returning to the notion of equilibrium, since the parts of the personality are in balance (equilibrium), a change in one part tends to affect the other parts. The change may be so small that the balance is restored without affecting the total balance. But if the change or disturbance is above a certain point, the balance is upset and *disequilibrium* occurs. Disequilibrium, therefore, means no balance among the parts of the personality.

The amount of change necessary to upset the balance differs with different people and even differs with the same person in different situations. Generally speaking, the higher the "tolerance" a personality can exhibit for disturbance, the healthier it will tend to be.[3]

In summary, equilibrium of parts is a "steady state" which the parts of the personality achieve in the course of an individual's life experience. Total personality balance occurs when the parts are in balance and when the personality as a whole is in balance with the world. Equilibrium is the "solution" that the personality arrives at so that it may adapt to the world in which it exists.

Practically speaking, this means that the balance (equilibrium) an employee exhibits in his personality is not a static affair. It is quite the opposite. The balance is maintained through active behavior, which ceases only when the individual dies. To put it another way, the individual personality is continually working hard to maintain itself in its present basic state. It works hard *not* to change. Therefore, the basic parts of the human personality are stable. This inherent tendency to maintain itself is called a basic trend toward self-actualization, which guarantees the constancy of personality. In fact, the individual's specific personality is inferred partially from the constancy his behavior exhibits.

Employees who tend always to look for a fight; to avoid a fight at all costs; to feel continually sorry for themselves; to "buck" continually are simply examples of the different kinds of behavior patterns different people may exhibit in an attempt to keep their personality (and its parts) in balance.

This proposition, along with the first one, raises some fundamental questions about any procedure that tries to evaluate an individual trait by trait. If an individual's personality is different from the sum of the parts, what meaning is there to merit ratings that attempt to score an individual's personality by adding up the parts to get an over-all score? Can these parts be added? How about the relationship among the parts? If someone receives a score of 80 and someone else a score of 40, what does this mean?[4]

C. Personality Manifests Energy

An analysis of the research literature suggests substantial agreement on the assumption that personality manifests some type of energy. Most personality theories assume this to account for the growing, moving, living characteristics of personality. Note that the word *assume* is used. Although there is agreement that personality manifests energy, no researchers have ever been able, nor do they feel it is necessary, to show exactly where energy is located or how it arises. They postulate that it exists.

They observe in everyday life people behaving in an infinite number of ways. The question arises, "Where do they acquire this energy, strength, or drive to behave in such a manner?" In order to account for this movement (this life), students of personality postulate that the personality has its own energy which, generally speaking, seems to have these four characteristics:

1. It is energy which (scientist's postulate) exists "in" human beings. Some psychologists place its source deep in the parts of personality (e.g., libido, birth trauma). Others simply say they do not know where it comes from. They begin by assuming that it exists.

2. The first group believes that the amount of energy is fixed by the instinctual systems developed in early life. The second group believes the amount of energy is determined by the state of the mind of the individual at any given time. Presumably, if the person feels in "tiptop shape," he has much energy available. If he feels "down in the dumps," he has little energy available.

Both groups admit that conflict, frustration, and anxiety use the psychological energy that an individual has available.

3. Both groups believe that energy is indestructible.

4. Both groups believe that the energy is changeable so that a need not fulfilled in one way will some day and somehow find expression in some other way.[5]

For the administratior, the following ideas seem important: (1) All people have psychological energy. (2) Psychological energy is indestructible. (3) The amounts of energy people express vary with their states of mind. (4) If the expression of people's energies is temporarily blocked, these energies will eventually try to find expression in some other way. (5) If the expression of people's energies is channeled (for example, by the administrator) in directions not equally satisfying, the people will some day try to obtain expression elsewhere.

Some examples of psychological energy may help to clarify the point: Four college seniors play tennis all day. By the rules of physiological energy, they should be dead-tired. Yet they go out on dates the same night. The same four men go to bed one night at eight o'clock and wake up twelve hours later. By the laws of physiology they should be rested. Yet they say, "Never again; we feel dead-tired after sleeping so long."

When administrators express discouragement over the fact that their people do not work hard or that they are lazy, the problem is one of psychological energy. Another example common in the plant is the employee who complains he is too tired to work harder or longer but who plays basketball all evening. The difference is the psychological energy the worker draws upon as he leaves the plant because he does something he enjoys much more.

Using the above principles, the administrator could say to himself, "I know the employees have energy. I know its expression varies with their states of mind. What is 'in' their working world and/or in the world outside the plant that creates this state of mind?" Such a diagnosis leads the administrator to examine the question, "What is causing this particular state of mind? Could it be I, certain policies, or misunderstandings? Could it be a combination of all these factors?" Asking these questions tends to prevent the administrator from rationalizing and explaining away the difficulties by simply placing the fault in the people. "Human beings are inherently lazy," or "People expect something for nothing," are examples of this type of rationalization.

Some administrators believe they can solve basic human relations problems by channeling people's feelings in other directions. Or they may grant certain concessions which admittedly solve nothing but which, as one administrator put it, "keep peace in the family." Temporary "cures" or organizational gadgets for releasing energy do not solve problems. A medical analogy may help make the point. Aspirin stops headaches but never cures them. If headaches are to be cured, the cause must be found. Similarly, human relations problems have to be understood in their full complexity. The administrator who does not take into account principles #4. and 5. above, will find that "new problems keep arising" no matter what he does. He will soon think, as one administrator experienced it, that "People are never satisfied. I comply with their requests in one area and grant concessions, only to find two days later that a new problem has cropped up."

There is no necessary one-to-one relationship between physiological and psychological energy in a human being. It is possible for a person to play tennis all day and dance all night. It is also possible for the same person to go to sleep early and wake up feeling tired. Another example of the differences in physiological and psychological energy may be observed when employees, a few moments after having coffee, may be heard to remark, "Now I feel better. That coffee hit the spot." The coffee actually couldn't have "hit the spot" (physiologically), because it takes much more time before it can affect the body.

The alert administrator attempts to know those jobs in the plant which require primarily physiological energy and those which require primarily psychological energy. He also learns the factors that help to rejuvenate an employee who is physiologically tired (these are different from the factors that help an employee who is psychologically tired to recover). Thus a secretary or an executive who complains of being tired may not be helped at all by being told to "go home and take it easy."

D. The Source of Psychological Energy Is in the Needs

The energy that most researchers postulate is pictured as being located in the need systems of the personality.

People behave. They love, hate, eat, cry, fight, work, strike, study, shop, go to the movies, play bridge, bring up children, go to church. The psychological energy to behave in all these ways comes from the need systems that exist in our personalities.

Let us note one question that is bound to arise, namely, "Where do need systems come from?" This is a difficult question to answer. The physicists have the same problem in their science. For example, there are at least two general theories about what electricity is and where it comes from. The fact that two different theories exist to explain electricity has not prevented the physicist from making basic and practical contributions toward the use of electricity. The physicist merely starts with the fact that there is electricity. Thomas Edison, when asked "What is electricity?" is reported to have answered "Electricity *is;* just use it." Since no one disagrees with the notion that personality manifests energy, let us also follow the lead of the scientists, accept this as a postulate and move on.

Personality has energy; and the energy is located in the need systems. The energy in every need system is always ready to release itself, to bubble over. But so long as the boundary of the need system is strong enough, the energy will not release itself. When the energy bubbles over, the need system is in *action*. Need systems that are quiet and not in action are *inert* needs or *potential active needs*. This is similar to the pressure in a boiler. So long as the pressure does not become too great, the boiler will not burst.

The amount of energy in every need system differs. Briefly, the deeper (i.e., the more important) a need, the more potential energy it has to release. By watching people behave we can infer from their behavior what need system is in action. An employee cuts down production to follow the informal shop rule of "no speed-up"; we may infer that there is a need in *action* for group belongingness and/or partial dependence upon the group. After observing thousands of cases of people's behavior, the psychologists have been able to categorize many of the needs that the people in our culture seem to express.

Why is a need always described as being in action or not in action? Because all our needs are rarely in action at the same time. Personality scientists call this action—this bubbling over of energy —*tension*. Therefore, a need that is in tension is a need in action.

There are those who believe that the basic reason for life is to seek "reduction of tension." Recent researchers, beginning to be critical of this point of view, point out that people who seek only tension reduction may be neurotic or psychotic. These people are preoccupied with their own irritations and are continually trying to seek relief. There is not much that is creative about their interests. They cannot take suffering or delay or frustration. Psychologically healthy people, on the other hand, usually have certain goals of self-actualization or enhancement. They are willing to accept temporary frustration if it will help them in the long run. Thus they may at times be more interested in sustaining and directing tension than in escaping from it.[6]

In line with this, Goldstein points out that it is important to distinguish between "pleasure by release of tension" and the active "feeling of enjoyment."

The two emotions of joy and pleasure play essentially different roles in regard to self-realization; they belong to different moods. Pleasure may be a necessary state of respite. But it is a phenomenon of standstill; it is akin to death. It separates us from the world and the other individuals in it; it is equilibrium, quietness. In joy there is disequilibrium, but it is productive disequilibrium, leading toward fruitful activity and a particular kind of self-realization.[7]

Let us ask, "So what?"

What is the advantage of saying that people have needs in tension in relation to goals? Why go all through this fuss? To answer the question let us imagine that there are two foremen. Mr. A. is hard-working, does an exceptional job, and is up for promotion. Mr. B., on the other hand, is slow, is lax on the job, has many problems which he does not seem to care about, and is being considered for a demotion.

Common-sense answers to *why* these two foremen behave the way they do usually go like this:

"Well, that's human nature."

"I guess Mr. B. just doesn't give a damn."

"Mr. A. is really loyal to our company. Looks like Mr. B. isn't."

"Mr. A.'s attitudes are better; that's why he works harder."

"Maybe B. has been having some 'off days.' "

Tackling the same question by using the scheme above, we would have to say:

"Mr. A. has a need in tension which is directed at certain goals. He *needs* to be hard-working."

"Mr. B. had a need in tension which is also directed at a certain goal. He *needs* to be slow."

Examining both sets of answers, we note that the practical set jumps immediately to such vague, high-sounding conclusions as "human nature," "doesn't give a damn," "loyalty." None of these conclusions provides a jumping-off point for *constructive* action. Every one of them immediately implies there is something wrong with Mr. B.

The second list, on the other hand jumps to *questions*. It forces the person to find out more facts. For example, "What need is in tension?" "At what goal is it directed?" "Why does Mr. A. have a certain need and why does Mr. B. have a different need in action?" The second list points out one of the most important rules in trying to understand human behavior. The real causes of human behavior are rarely found in the observable behavior. It is important to ask, "What is behind this behavior that we see?"

The second list does not immediately classify someone as "bad" and someone as "good." People who truly respect others will try their best to respect all human beings, not just the ones with whom they happen to agree. Therefore, the second list is more useful, in that it does not automatically condemn Mr. B. or praise Mr. A. Perhaps Mr. B. is a poor supervisor because he is so involved in his job that he does not feel worthy of it, whereas Mr. A. works excessively hard in order to escape from some other problem. Probably one of the greatest weaknessees in trying to understand others is the immediate attempt at labeling them "good" or "bad." Once this is done, it is impossible to think objectively about a person.

The second list, in short, creates an understanding, questioning attitude. Understanding behavior is not a simple one-two-three proposition, as some would have us believe. The task is not easy. Some people seem to feel they can understand human beings more quickly than they can understand their own car carburetor or their watch. No one would give a lay person ten easy steps for taking apart his watch, or the "golden rules" for taking apart and putting together a carburetor. Why do we do it with human beings?

The attitude, therefore, that the second list provides is the important result. It is one of inquiry, finding out, asking, searching, listening, being patient, understanding, being warm, and being friendly. And if we reflect for a moment, are not the above ways of behaving characteristic of an effective leader?

Before returning to listing the various kinds of needs, it is necessary to discuss one important mistake people usually make in thinking about needs.

Many people use the word "need" in such a way that it has a meaning different from the one above. For example, a partial list of "needs" that a group of experts compiled is given below. They felt:

1) Foremen need basic skills in their jobs.
2) Foremen need to know company rules.
3) Foremen need to be leaders.
4) Foremen need to feel integrated.
5) Foremen need to have opportunity for success in their work.
6) Foremen need to have a feeling of being wanted and of belonging to some group.

The "need" in the first three sentences differs from the "needs" in the last three sentences.

The first three sentences refer to something that foremen *should* have if they are to be "good" foremen. Thus he ought to know the basic skills in his job *if* he is to be the kind of foreman these experts desire. This is the same as saying, "The child needs discipline." What is really meant is that the "child should be *given* discipline *if* he is to become the kind of boy *we want* him to become." There is no implication that the boy has an urge within him to be spanked, that he desires disciplining. The word "needs" therefore in this sense means that *someone else needs* to discipline the boy if he is to become the boy that this *someone else needs* him to become.

Similarly, the first three statements do not imply that there are inner urges for foremen to know their jobs; to know company rules; to be leaders. They are not needs *in* the foremen simply because they are called needs. These are needs that management has in relation to their goal of having what they feel are effective foremen. In short, they are not as yet needs in foremen but paths which, if the foremen follow, will lead to successful foremanship. Therefore, the more accurate way of writing these first three statements is:

1) Management feels that foremen *should* need basic skills in their jobs.

2) Management feels that foremen *should* need to know company rules.

3) Management feels that foremen *should* need to know how to be leaders.

Turning to the last three statements, the word "need" refers to something that exists within a person which requires a particular behavior to occur. The needs to be integrated, to feel successful, to feel wanted, and so on are felt by people in our culture and come from within their personalities. No one has to attempt to instil these needs into adults. These needs are real *psychological* needs. Both of these types of "needs" are important but it is important to differentiate between them.

Summary Definition of Need. A need (psychological) in tension is therefore something that (1) exists "in" the personality of the person; (2) is related to all other needs; (3) initiates and guides behavior until the goal is reached, which destroys the tension, or until the tension is released in some other way.

Kinds of Needs.

Since we acquire many needs during our lifetimes, it might be useful to present a classification of needs. In doing this, we should recall that classification schemes of needs represent simply an individual's attempt at trying to unify, and to put into some order according to some characteristic, the kinds of needs the personality exhibits. The difficulty lies in the fact that every need has more than one characteristic and therefore could be classified under more than one heading. The list presented is not perfect; it is merely indicative and suggestive.

Inner needs and outer needs. Every human being has certain needs which are at the very heart, or very depth, of his personality. One of the most important inner needs is the need to maintain adjustment of the self in relation to the world in which it exists. Inner needs can be inferred to be active when a person is observed to be upset, or expressing much emotion, or working doggedly at a task without letting up. All inner needs, as we mentioned before, have large amounts of energy, and once they bubble over, they call forth strong emotional or persistent behavior. If a person, to our surprise, "blows his top" at a suggestion, it may be that we have set into action an inner need.

The outer needs are closer to the surface of the personality. Little emotion is created if these needs become active. They are skin-surface needs. The inner needs are more basic and vital. Whereas the inner needs give us a cue as to what the person *is;* outer needs tell us what the person *does.*

Conscious and unconscious needs.[8] People are never aware of all their needs. Some needs, usually the most inner ones, are unconscious. Thus the simple question, "Joe, why do you behave the way you do?" may be impossible for Joe to answer accurately.

Social needs. Another way of classifying inner-outer needs and conscious and unconscious needs is according to whether or not the culture helps instill them into people. Needs vary from culture to culture. There are societies in which the people do not care for money, success, or a great many friends.

Physiological needs. There are needs that are imperative if the

body is to keep healthy. Food, shelter, and movement are but a
few examples. It should be pointed out, however, that the way
these needs become fulfilled varies. Thus the Japanese have a
different diet from our own diet, and ours differs from that of the
people of South America.

E. Personality Has Abilities

Bordering the needs, and in most cases evolving from them, are
the abilities. Abilities are the tools, so to speak, with which a
person expresses and fulfills his needs. Abilities are the communications systems for the needs to express themselves. Once
the energy bubbles over from the needs, it goes "through" the
appropriate ability designed to express the need. A difficulty sometimes arises because the channel between needs and abilities
is not direct or may be distorted. Thus it is possible for a person
to have a set of defenses which exist between his needs and abilities and which act to modify his behavior. For example, an
employee may want to be an excellent lathe worker and he may
have the necessary abilities. But if he is placed in a test situation,
to be observed while working, it may call forth some defenses
which upset him. The resulting tension acts to reduce the efficient
expression of his abilities and the person may not be considered
capable.

As far as is known to date, needs are developed first. Then as
the child tries endlessly to express them through hard work and
learning, he creates and sharpens his abilities to express his needs.
One of the big tasks of a parent (and, later, of administrators) is
to help the individual learn and develop appropriate abilities to
express his needs.

Interests are usually a product of a fusion of several needs.
This fusion usually comes about at an early age and is unconscious. Interests, therefore, are indicators of the kinds of needs
people have. For example, a person with a strong need to be independent, to achieve, and to know things, might make a good
scientist.

The skills that are given to us by inheritance are such skills
as finger dexterity and other manual and manipulative skills.

Few abilities are inherited. The majority of the more important abilities are learned and developed in interaction with others. This is especially true for such abilities as leadership. *There are no born leaders.* The personality of a leader is developed, probably during early home life and by the situations in which this personality finds appropriate expression.

Abilities, in summary, function between needs and the environment, thus providing the line of communication for needs.

Kinds of Abilities. There are, briefly, three main types of abilities. Although they are listed as separate abilities, they are not independent. Each kind of ability affects the others greatly:

1) Knowing (cognitive) abilities: The abilities which we use to know our world (e.g., intelligence).

2) Doing (motor) abilities: The abilities which permit us to do things physically (e.g., seeing, working with our hands, smelling).

3) Feeling abilities: The ability to experience the many complex feelings in life and to be sensitive to other people's feelings.

Since most psychological tests are associated with measuring some sort of ability, it might be useful to digress for a moment and say something about the usefulness of tests.

Generally speaking, the tests that are most accurate and will give the most reliability and validity are the tests that are related to the *knowing*, and especially the *doing*, abilities.

But since abilities are interrelated and continually affect one another, it is difficult to think that a test of "intelligence," for example, is not also being affected by the person's doing, and especially his feeling, abilities. A test can never be arranged to test just one type of ability. If, for example, an intelligence test, or a test of the ability for problem-solving is given, the person's frustration tolerance, the person's ability to control his feelings of anxiousness, and the person's level of aspiration may simultaneously be tested. Thus a test score really becomes a statement about the person's intelligence or problem-solving ability, *as we try to "measure" it under a specific set of internal and external conditions.* The person's intelligence has not really been measured.

A specimen of it under particular conditions has simply been taken.

It is difficult, therefore, to place confidence in individual tests. A battery of tests should be used. Recent research indicates that if a person's interest is high in a certain area, *that* is the best criterion as to whether or not he will succeed.[9] In other words, if a foreman receives a low score on some sort of "ability to supervise" test but he has a lot of motivation to become a foreman, the chances are that he can be helped to become one. Since abilities are partially determined by needs, the administrator would find it useful to be cautious in the interpretation of test scores of an individual's abilities.[10] He might also examine in relation to these test scores the individual's motivation or desire to do a specific job. Thus a high test score may not necessarily mean a highly efficient worker. Conversely, a low score does not necessarily mean a poor worker. It may well be, for example, that the employee with high abilities may have such low motivation that his abilities are never used to their potential.

F. PERSONALITY ORGANIZATION IS CONCEPTUALIZED AS "THE SELF"

It has been found convenient to label the unique personality whole created by the specific interrelationships of the parts, *the self*. To put it another way, the basic parts of the personality are all the same (needs and abilities). However, the way these parts are organized may differ for each individual and even within the same individual as he develops. The self is a concept used by the scientists to focus on the unique integration of the parts of the personality for any given individual.

To introduce this concept, let us consider the growing infant. As soon as he discovers his physical body (his hands, feet, face), he turns to the task of discovering who *he* is, i.e., his self. He becomes aware that there is a "me" that exists. From the day this awareness begins, the child will throughout his life be discovering and rediscovering, changing, and adding new parts to the picture he has of himself. This marks the beginning of awareness of the *self*.

The *self* is more than just the physical body. It includes the child's unique organization, conscious and unconscious, of his needs, goals, abilities, and the resulting feelings, values, and prejudices. It includes how he evaluates his abilities (e.g., the confidence he has in them). Finally, it includes his sensitivity for understanding himself and others. This sensitivity is called "empathy." A person who has empathy usually has a lot of *insight* (understanding) into people's feelings.

The self is seldom built up by the person by merely reflecting about himself. It is built through his social contacts (interaction) with others. We cannot become "whole" by ourselves. We need contact with others.

Once the picture of the self is formed, it serves as a framework or a guide with which to make sense out of experience. All future experiences are either (1) accepted and integrated with the picture one already has of the self, (2) ignored because the experiences do not make sense to the person in terms of his self concept, and (3) denied or distorted because the experience is inconsistent with the picture of the self.[11] Those ways of behaving are adopted that are consistent with, or in agreement with, the self picture. Because individuals tend to see only that which agrees with their concept of self, it is difficult to be a truly objective observer. There is in fact no objective world for the individual; rather, it is always his *picture* of the objective world. It is always his "private world."

G. Defense Mechanisms Maintain Self Against Threat

Generally speaking, there are at least two ways to reduce feelings of threat. One is to change the self so that it becomes congruent with whatever is causing the difficulty. This involves "accepting" the fact that one is "wrong." It involves admitting the limitations associated with the difficulty and a willingness to change the self so that the difficulty will not arise again. The second approach is to defend the self by somehow denying or distorting (consciously or unconsciously) what is threatening and clinging to the present self concept. This behavior is called a defense reaction. A defense reaction, therefore, is any sequence of behavior in response to a threat whose goal is to maintain the present state of the self against threat.[12]

A defensive reaction may create difficulty if it happens that the individual, instead of the situation in the environment, is "wrong." A defense reaction reduces the awareness of threat but never affects that which is causing the threat. For example, let us say that supervisor A is threatened because he "knows" his boss does not think that he (supervisor A) is doing a good job. Let us assume that he defends his self by placing the blame on the boss. This will not in any way stop the boss from feeling the way he does about supervisor A. Soon the supervisor will have to justify his defensive reactions to himself. He may do this by saying that the boss is "out to get him." Each of these defenses is a distortion which in turn will require further justification and further defense. After some time supervisor A has built up deep layers of defense, all of which will have to be uncovered if he is to understand the cause.

Freud was the first to study systematically the different kinds of defense mechanisms. Although much is available describing examples of defense mechanisms, little is known about exactly why people pick the defense mechanisms they do pick. Part of the difficulty lies in the way in which defense mechanisms are defined. Most of them do not have operationally clear-cut definitions, and thus they tend to overlap in meaning. Nevertheless, it is possible to say that (1) past experiene is an important factor in determining the choice, and (2) anticipation of the punishment involved may influence the choice.

Defense mechanisms are therefore developed to be used any time that the self feels threatened. All individuals have a set of defenses. This set of defenses is not to be viewed as necessarily being "bad" or "good." It is best to view them as simply the individual's way of defending himself from threat. The four most frequently threatening experiences are anxiety, conflict, frustration, and failure.

Since defense mechanisms are primarily related to experiences of anxiety, conflict, frustration, and failure, it may be wise to define these experiences before the defense mechanisms are listed.

ANXIETY. Anxiety is an emotional state that resembles fear and anger in that it is aroused by something that is threatening to the individual. Anxiety is a response to nothing particular in the environment, while fear is always a response to a genuine threat, which clearly requires some sort of escape or attack. When we are in a state of fear, we have something before us that we can see, that we can try to remove, or that we can run away from. We can point to it and say, "This is what makes me fearful." Anxiety, on the other hand, "attacks from behind." We experience it, but we cannot figure out where it is coming from or what causes it. Thus, we do not know whether to run or to attack.

Some specific symptoms of anxiety are:

. . . sleeplessness, stage fright, headaches, stubbornness, stomach upsets, and prejudice. Anxiety usually appears as a symptom, that is to say, it makes itself as some specific form of behavior, using that word in its broadest sense; but in its 'pure' form it usually appears as a vague sort of uneasiness; a feeling of panic, discomfort, or helplessness; or an awareness of tension with no identifiable cause. We usually do not experience anxiety in the latter form, because we are likely to look for some 'reasonable cause' for such a feeling. Thus one person might attribute his feeling of tension to something his brother said, in which case anxiety would be masked as anger or irritation. A woman might attribute her feeling of tension to the way her husband drives their automobile, in which event she might think of her anxiety as fear.

Stage fright is a good case in point. On the surface, stage fright looks like fear because the individual who is suffering from its symptoms thinks he is afraid of the audience. But suppose he is a capable speaker who knows his subject. What does he have to fear? His appearance before the group he will address is no threat to his safety or even his stature. It does not take much to locate the source of his trouble—he is afraid that he will not live up to the expectations he has for himself and which others have for him. He is afraid that he is 'not good enough.' Perhaps he is thinking: 'What am I doing on this lecture platform? There are dozens of others who could do a better job.' If, on the other hand, he had never spoken before or knew nothing about the subject on which he was to speak, we would say that he would have a valid reason to be afraid of the situation he is about to face. Most cases of stage-fright, however, are more or less colored by anxiety which the victim usually tries to explain away as reasonable fear.[13]

CONFLICT. Conflict, generally speaking, refers to the event which occurs when a person is not able to act in a specific situation. All conflict involves opposite needs being in action (tension) at the same time. The conflict may be due to indecision over doing something, or it may be due to wanting to do two things simultaneously which cannot be done simultaneously.

Behavioral scientists have analyzed four types of conflict.

Conflict will tend to exist when the person desires to do two things which he likes equally well but it is possible to do only one. A child tries to decide whether to buy a vanilla cone or a candy bar, both of which he likes equally well.

Conflict will tend to exist when a person has the choice of doing two things, each of which he dislikes equally. It is being, so to speak, "between the devil and the deep blue sea." For example, there is the person who hates his job but has not found another one and therefore risks unemployment if he quits.

Conflict will tend to exist when the person has the choice of doing something he likes, but runs the risk of punishment or loss. For some people, gambling provides this conflict.

Conflict will tend to exist when the person has the *alternative* choices of doing something he likes but running the risk of some loss or punishment. For example, there is the investor who has before him three or four equally good investment possibilities, each with an equal possibility of failure.[14]

Many people have been brought up to think that conflict is bad. This is not necessarily so. True, conflict can be uncomfortable, but it is even more true that conflict harms a person's personality *when the personality uses incorrect ways of dealing with the conflict.* Conflict when dealt with correctly, is an experience of growth for the personality. In fact, without conflict (psychologists suggest) there would be little need for us to develop new ways of behaving. The old ways would merely be sharpened up a bit, but there would be little reason to try something new. Odd but true, conflict can be used to help build the personality as well as to distort and even destroy it.

FRUSTRATION. Coupled with, and perhaps a special case of, conflict is the problem of not being able to overcome some barrier in order to arrive at a goal. If the goal is not reached, the person will become emotional, uneasy, antagonistic—he will show signs of being frustrated. The person under frustration does release emotions, whether he shows these emotions in his observable behavior or not. These emotions act like a sleeping pill, so to speak, on the person's whole personality (especially his abilities) and reduce his efficiency.

For example, if prior to frustration the person's efficiency is said to equal ten, under frustration it is usually reduced (e.g., to five) without the person's realizing it (i.e., unconsciously). The person therefore cannot figure out what is wrong with himself. "Why can't I overcome these barriers? I was certain I could. What's wrong with me?" All these are typical questions. This worry only increases the emotional imbalance, which increases the action of the emotions on the efficiency of the personality, and down goes the efficiency some more. It is like quicksand; the more he struggles the deeper he sinks. The thing that makes frustration most destructive is that a person may not know why he is less efficient.

The reduction of psychological efficiency is called *regression*. Regression means that the personality has returned to a more primitive, childlike state, where efficiency is much lower. The important property of regression is that while the person becomes more like a child, he is *not* a child; he is still an adult.

Every person has developed his own tolerance against frustration. Some people have little tolerance and become easily frustrated. Others have developed a high resistance and therefore it takes quite a bit to frustrate them. The individual's ability to withstand frustration is known as *frustration tolerance*. The higher the frustration tolerance, up to a point, the more adaptive life will be. We emphasize "up to a point" because a person who never becomes frustrated, no matter how difficult the situation, is not necessarily a healthy personality.

FAILURE. Perhaps the easiest way to explain psychological failure is to define what is not failure. Psychological success, the opposite of failure, occurs when the individual is able to direct his energy toward a goal that *he* defines, whose achievement will fulfill *his* inner needs, and which cannot be reached without overcoming a barrier strong enough to make him "put up a fight" but just weak enough to be overcome. (In other words, the individual has a realistic level of aspiration.)

Failure occurs when an individual lives in a world in which he is not able to define his own goals in relation to his inner needs and whose barriers are either too great to overcome or so small that no success is derived in overcoming them.[15]

DEFENSE MECHANISMS.

1. *Aggression.* One of the common results of regression is aggression. Aggression means trying to injure or hurt the person, group, or object that is acting as the barrier or as the cause of conflict. By the words "injure" and "hurt" we include all types of injuries, including social and psychological injury, such as name-calling, insults, and cheating.

2. *Guilt.* If the "block" is due to the limitations of one's own personality (e.g., the individual who desires to become a supervisor but does not have a good enough record), then the aggression can be turned toward the self. The person usually feels guilty criticizes himself, or may even go so far as to hurt himself. Guilt is, therefore, aggression from ourselves to ourselves.

3. *Continuation.* Sometimes the conflict is not resolved but the person continues to live by making another choice which is "second best." For example, a student who becomes a businessman but still wishes he could have gone to medical school is in a sense continuing his conflict.

4. *Discriminatory decision.* At times, a conflict is resolved by sitting down and writing the reasons for and the reasons against doing something. We try to make a list of the reasons and then pick out (discriminate) the best one. This mechanism almost always occurs on a conscious level. In general, it may be used when the personality is healthy and the conflict is not strong. For example, an executive, in order to choose between foreman A and Foreman B for a new promotion, may sit down, list the "goods" and "bads" of each foreman, and then pick (discriminate) one.

(Such behavior, of course, violates the first principle discussed under agreements in personality.)

5. *Denial.* An easy course to follow when threatened is simply to remain unaware of the facts which could create one side of a conflict. An example that is particularly annoying to supervisors occurs when employees apparently do not seem to hear instructions concerning a new regulation or a forthcoming change. Although the supervisor may speak clearly and concisely, the employees will insist "they didn't quite hear what he said" or "they had difficulty in understanding what he said." Actually, what happens under denial is that the employees do not allow what has just been said to penetrate into their consciousness. (Denial, it should be pointed out, is a different thing from deliberate pretense, in which the individual knows something but decides to make believe that he does not.)

6. *Repression.* When the threat is due to factors active within ourselves, we often forbid ourselves to recognize them. Repression is thus forcing down into the unconscious that part of a threat which we do not like. Repression almost always occurs unconsciously. It is usually a response to an inner threat. For example, a patient once complained of a great fear of running water. She could not go near a drinking fountain. A careful analysis brought out the fact that as a young child she fell in a lake near a waterfall and nearly drowned. The incident had been repressed, all except the noise of running water. Once the patient was able to recognize and accept the fact, progress could be made in therapy.

7. *Suppression.* Suppression is somewhat like repression. Whereas in repression we push things into the unconscious without realizing it, in suppression we push things into the unconscious and generally know it. Suppression is hardly ever permanent, while repression is usually permanent.

8. *Inhibition.* Inhibition is like repression but it most often occurs on a conscious level. In inhibition the person purposely and knowingly refrains from doing something. For instance, an inhibited person would be one who never speaks up in a conference because he fears he may say something wrong or he fears

what he has to say is not important.

9. *Conversion.* Conversion occurs when a person fears he will not be capable of meeting an unusual situation and converts this fear into some bodily trouble. An example would be the child who because he fears to take an examination in school, suddenly develops some kind of illness. Or the newly elected foreman, feeling inadequate, becomes "run down" after the first week in his new job. Finally, the foreman, who is afraid to see the boss in the boss's office suddenly becomes ill (e.g., gets a splitting headache) and has the meeting postponed. He may actually be converting his difficulty into a physical problem (i.e., headache).

10. *Overcompensation.* Sometimes a person resolves his fear of not being able to do something by working so hard that he accomplishes his goal and usually goes way beyond it. The person who thinks that he is incapable of doing something tries to make up for his limitations and in fact makes up too much or overcompensates for these limitations. A typical example is the hardworking executive who accomplishes his goal, does better than expected, but never seems to relax once the goal is achieved.

11. *Rationalization.* Rationalization occurs when we knowingly invent some acceptable excuse (acceptable to our own personality) to cover up a failure or to cover up an inability to accept something. Rationalization occurs when an alibi is created for otherwise untenable behavior. For example, a person might walk to the drug store to buy some cigarettes. On arriving at the drug store he finds it is closed and remarks, "Oh well, I didn't want to smoke anyway." Or the employee who, upon finding out he did not become a foreman (although he was hoping he would be) remarks, "Who wants all that responsibility anyway?" Rationalization can also occur unconsciously. For example, some multimillionaires who feel guilty about their wealth try to cover up these feelings by giving away huge fortunes to charity.

12. *Identification.* Identification refers to the desire to be like someone else or to identify with other people's experiences. We have identified with someone when we act in a situation as we feel that person would act. Top management men usually have some subordinates who tend to identify with them.

13. *Projection.* The concept of projection has two meanings. Colloquially, it is usually used to mean any attempt we make to avoid blame for, or to ascribe to others, ways of behaving, feeling, and thinking which we really have ourselves. Some employees, for example, continually "get into trouble" and, despite all evidence to the contrary, really believe the other fellow is always to blame.

In the true psychological sense, projection is a mechanism whereby we "see" in other people a quality which would embarrass us greatly if we were to admit it is our own. For example, a person might be watching someone go up to a stage to make a speech and remark, "I bet he (the speaker) is scared." Actually, it is the person watching the potential speaker who is frightened. Another example is the well-behaved employee who continually "squeals" on the other employees who break the rules. The employee is actually pointing to something happening outside of him (e.g., the other employees breaking the rules) as a way of denying his own desire to break the rules. The employee who does this is usually sincere and does not feel he is a hypocrite.

14. *Vacillation.* At one time people in conflict may decide in favor of solution A, then a minute later reject it and accept solution B. This constant rejection and acceptance and never coming to a conclusion is called vacillation.

15. *Ambivalence.* People attempt to resolve some conflict situations by hating and liking the same person who is the focus of the threat. For example, a foreman working for an autocratic boss once said, "The s.o.b. I hate his guts, but you know, I really admire him. He's a pretty good egg." This contradictory statement is hardly ever seen as contradictory by the person who makes it. In this case, the ambivalence is probably due to the fact that an autocrat never permits real freedom, but is always quick to do personal favors to keep the subordinates happy, and thereby keep them dependent on him.

16. *Slips of the tongue.* Every slip of the tongue has some meaning. It does not happen accidentally. Slips of the tongue are usually expressions of thoughts or feelings which are in our unconscious, and sometimes (at the oddest times at that) quite

without warning, they come into our consciousness.

In psychoanalysis, slips of the tongue, like dreams, are used as clues for understanding the unconscious. Some people, upon hearing this, remark that psychoanalysts are "making mountains out of molehills." Yet many sciences approach their data by this method. A detective looks for the smallest clue to build up his case. During a war, the intelligence service tries to pick up every bit of news, no matter how small, and fits it into a picture which may be used to move entire divisions of troops.

One resultant of defense mechanisms is that they make it difficult to differentiate between an individual's underlying motivations and the skin-surface ones.[16] We observe Mr. A. and Mr. B. while we interview them for a job. Mr. A. talks so much that we cannot speak. Mr. B. hardly says a word. These two bits of behavior at the immediately observed "manifest" level seem to be different. But on the "latent" or deeper level—the level to which we must learn to go—both people may really have the same self-concept and, as a result, may feel insecure in and fear unknown situations. But they make up for their fear in different ways. Mr. B. adapts by doing little talking. Mr. A adapts by talking so much that no one else is able to say a word.

Or it may be that the personalities of supervisor A., who "works himself to death," and supervisor B., who "hardly lifts a finger," are basically similar. Both may feel they are not competent. One works hard and overcompensates for limitations he senses in himself. The other does very little for fear of doing something wrong.

The basic characteristics of an individual's personality may be hidden by defensive behavior and thus may not be observed directly. What is usually observed are the methods an individual has developed to express the basic aspects of his personality. Only by inferring from this symptomatic defensive behavior can we assess the basic motives of an individual.

The practical implications are that a clear distinction between "manifest" and "latent" must be made if we want to predict how individual supervisors, for example, will react to frustration, conflict, and anxiety. The same is true if changes are to be made.

If the changes made satisfy only manifest behavior, then the underlying latent reasons will not be satisfied. We can predict that the complaining will continue but probably shift to another area. It is similar to taking an aspirin to relieve migraine headaches. The headache will be relieved but not cured.

Ball parks, athletic teams, company picnics, and company lectures are programs that fulfill the skin-surface or manifest needs of the workers. Company newspapers, slogan schemes, and pep talks are also in the same category. If so, increased benefit and communications programs will not tend to decrease the company's human problems. Moreover, since these programs tend to focus on skin-surface needs, they tend to leave the employees' important needs unfilled (e.g., the need to be led by effective leaders). The employees, not truly satisfied and therefore still requiring need-fulfillment, ask for more. Soon management begins to feel that the quality of the employees is going down. "All the employees want is more. How much do they expect us to give them?" According to this analysis, the management *trains* the workers to focus on material satisfactions (e.g., ball teams, pictures in the newspaper, and so on) and then complains when the workers want more. (More on this in Chapter IV.)

An interesting example of the impact of defense mechanisms was reported recently by a medical doctor who discovered that patients were distorting their explanations of their problems to their own doctors. For example, they seemed to say different things to the general practitioner and to the psychiatrist. After careful research he found that the patients' answers were at times biased by the very "set" they had before they went into the office of the psychiatrist or general practitioner. To the latter, they would emphasize something physical; to the former, they would emphasize something mental.

For example, here are the reasons several patients gave to the interns (I) and then to the psychiatrist (P) about the "same" problem.

PATIENT 1: I : Pain over heart brought on by exercise.
　　　　　 P: Pain over heart when nervous.

PATIENT 2: I : Stomach pain and bloating.
P: Vague fears keep stomach in knots.

PATIENT 3: I : Headaches, occasionally relieved by alcohol.
P: Alcohol's big problem—occasional headaches.

PATIENT 4: I : Backache won't let him work.
P: Dislikes business; has bad headaches since he opened his store.[17]

H. GROWTH MEANS AN INCREASE IN PARTS AND IN OUR "PRIVATE WORLD"

Most personality theories are in agreement that as the individual matures, he not only acquires more parts (i.e., more needs, abilities), but he also deepens many of them.[18] As these parts are acquired, they are also integrated with the already existing parts of the personality. Every part which is added must be added so that the balance (organization) is not upset. Simultaneously with the personality growth of the individual is the expansion of the individual's private world or environment. Every time a new part is created "in" his personality, a new part is also experienced in his own private world. The world of experience is called "private" because it can never include the total objective world. It is impossible for the individual to experience everything, no matter how long he lives. Furthermore, every experience is colored, as we have seen, by the self-picture. Therefore, one individual's world may not necessarily be the world of another individual. Every individual lives in a private world.

Education (i.e., training) must not only give the pupil an increase in his "private world" but it must simultaneously help the person increase the parts of his personality and at the same time help the person integrate these new parts in the already existing personality make-up. A part added to the private world without being integrated with the personality make-up will never be effective and will always tend to be a source of tension and anxiety.

Finally, most personality theories state that the personality becomes complete, organized, and integrated only when it interacts with other people, ideas, and social organizations. Growth cannot occur if the person exists alone. He must interact with others in order to understand himself and thereby develop. Thus *we cannot understand ourselves unless we understand others, and we cannot understand others unless we understand ourselves.*

To summarize, man, in his need-fulfilling, goal-directed behavior is to some extent: "like all other men, like some other men, like no other men."[19]

He is like all other men because some of his personality is derived from common biological roots. He is like all other men because he always lives in a culture and must adjust to the traditionally defined expectations of the culture. He is like all other men because he has to use other men to develop. Finally, he is like all other men in that he experiences both gratification and deprivations. These experiences accumulate and become a storehouse of learning which, in turn, he uses to adapt to the continual occurrence of new problems and situations.

Man is like some other men in that he shares common experiences with his own work group, social class, sporting club, or other cultural organization.

Personality cannot be understood without taking into account the culture in which the personality exists. Culture and personality are inseparable. It is actually not culture and personality, but culture in personality and personality in culture. As L. K. Frank has pointed out, human personalities are the individual expressions of our culture, and our culture and social order are the group expressions of individual personalities.

A top management executive who said that "the trouble with the workers today is that 5 per cent of them work, 10 per cent of them think they work, and 85 per cent of them would rather die than work," was asked to repeat the same sentence and add at the end of it the phrase "in my plant." The executive complied with the writer's request and obtained a new outlook on the problem of understanding human motivation. People complaining about workers in general (or other problems in general), might find it interesting to specify the setting (i.e., the plant or organization) in which their complaints seem to be true.

Similarly, the administrator may find it to his advantage to know the culture of his plant. Knowledge of the culture helps the administrator evaluate the locus of problems (i.e., "in" the people, "in" the machines, or "in" the plant culture). Knowledge of the plant culture can also be used to expedite different solutions which the administrator might find difficult in propagating through formal channels of an organization.[20]

Finally, man is unlike any other man because, due to his own personal and private way of seeing and experiencing the world, he behaves, feels, thinks in certain patterns unique to himself.

I. Basic Self-Actualization Trends of the Human Personality

All organizations may be said to strive to achieve their objectives, maintain themselves internally, and adapt to their external environment. This multidimensional process may be called self-actualization. In order to make more precise predictions about the problems involved when human beings are considered for employment by the formal organization, it is necessary to be more explicit, if possible, about the demands the former will tend to make upon the latter. Since the human personality is a developing organism, one way to become more precise is to define the basic growth or development trends "inherent" in it (so long as it remains in the same culture). One can then logically assume that, at any given moment in time, the human personality will be predisposed to find expression for these developmental trends. Such an assumption implies another, namely, that there are basic development trends characteristic of a relatively large majority of the population being considered. This assumption might seem strained, especially to the psychologists inclined to stress individual differences. However, individual differences need not necessarily be ignored. As Kluckhohn and Murray point out,[19] people tend to have some similar basic psychological characteristics because of their biological inheritance and the socio-cultural matrix within which they develop. This does not preclude the possibility that each individual can express these basic characteristics in his own idiosyncratic manner. Thus the concept of individual differences is still held.

So much for the logic behind the developmental trends listed below. It is assumed that human beings in our culture:

1. Tend to develop from a state of passivity as infants to a state of increasing activity as adults. (This is what Erikson[21] has called self-initiative and Bronfenbrenner[22] has called self-determination.)

2. Tend to develop from a state of dependence upon others as infants to a state of relative independence as adults. Relative independence is the ability to "stand on one's own two feet" and simultaneously to acknowledge healthy dependencies.[23] It is characterized by the liberation of the individual from his childhood determiners of behavior (e.g., family) and developing his own set of behavioral determiners. This individual does not tend to react to others (e.g., the boss) in terms of patterns learned during childhood.[24]

3. Tend to develop from being capable of behaving only in a few ways as an infant to being capable of behaving in many different ways as an adult.[25]

4. Tend to develop from having erratic, casual, shallow, quickly-dropped interests as an infant to having deeper interests as an adult. The mature state is characterized by an endless series of challenges, where the reward comes from doing something for its own sake. The tendency is to analyze and study phenomena in their full-blown wholeness, complexity, and depth.[26]

5. Tend to develop from having a short time perspective (i.e., the present largely determines behavior) as an infant to a much longer time perspective as an adult (i.e., where the behavior is more affected by the past and the future).[27] Bakke cogently describes the importance of time perspective in the lives of workers and their families and the variety of foresight practices by means of which they seek to secure the future.[28]

6. Tend to develop from being in a subordinate position in the family and society as an infant to aspiring to occupy an equal and/or superordinate position relative to their peers.

7. Tend to develop from a lack of awareness of self as an infant to an awareness of and control over self as an adult. The adult who tends to experience adequate and successful control over his own behavior tends to develop a sense of integrity (Erikson) and

feelings of self-worth.[29] Bakke,[30, 31] shows that one of the most important needs of workers is to enlarge those areas of their lives in which their own decisions determine the outcome of their efforts.

These dimensions are postulated as being descriptive of a basic multidimensional developmental process along which the growth of individuals in our culture may be measured. Presumably, every individual, at any given moment in time, can have his degree of development plotted along these dimensions. The exact location on each dimension will probably vary with each individual, and even within the same individual at different times. Self-actualization may now be defined more precisely as the individual's plotted scores (or profile) along the above dimensions.[32]

It may be helpful to add a few words of explanation concerning these dimensions of personality development.

1. They comprise only one aspect of the total personality. All the properties of personality described previously must be used in trying to understand the behavior of a particular individual. Much depends upon the individual's self-concept, his degree of adaptation and adjustment, and the way in which he perceives his private world.

2. The dimensions are continua where the growth to be measured is assumed to be continuously changing in degree. An individual is presumed to develop continuously in degree, from the infant end to the adult end of each continuum.

3. The only characteristic assumed to hold for all individuals is that, barring unhealthy personality development, they will be predisposed toward moving from the infant end to the adult end of each continuum. This is a model (a construct) describing the basic growth trends. As such, it does not make any predictions about any specific individual. It *does*, however, presume to supply the researcher with basic developmental continua along which the growth of any individual in our culture may be described and measured.

4. So long as one develops in a particular culture one will never obtain maximum expression of these developmental trends. Clearly, all individuals cannot be maximally independent, ac-

tive, and so forth all the time and still maintain an organized society.[33] It is the function of culture (e.g., norms and mores) and society (e.g., family, friends, schools, churches, and laws) to inhibit maximum expression and to help an individual adjust and adapt by finding his optimum expression.

A second factor that prevents maximum expression and fosters optimum expression is the individual's own finite limits set by his personality. Some people fear the same amount of independence and activity that others desire. Also, it is commonplace to find some people who do not have the necessary abilities to perform specific tasks. No given individual is known to have developed all known abilities to their full maturity.

Finally, defense mechanisms also are important factors operating to help an individual to deviate from the basic developmental trends.

5. The dimensions described above are constructed in terms of latent or genotypical characteristics. If one states that an individual needs to be dependent, this need will probably be ascertained by clinical inference because it is one that individuals are not usually aware of. Thus, if one observes an employee acting as though he were independent, it is possible that if one goes below the behavioral surface, the individual may be quite dependent. The obvious example is the employee who always seems to behave in a contrary manner to that desired by management. Although his behavior may give the appearance that he is independent, his contrariness may be due to his great need to be dependent upon management, which he dislikes to admit to himself and to others.

It may be said that an independent person is one whose behavior is not unduly dominated by the influence others have over him. Of course, no individual is completely independent. All of us have our healthy dependencies (i.e., those which help us to be creative and to develop).

One operational criterion to ascertain whether an individual's desire to be, let us say, independent and active is truly a mature manifestation is to ascertain the extent to which he permits others to express the same needs. Thus an autocratic leader may say that he needs to be active and independent; he may also say that he wants subordinates who are the same; however, there is ample research to suggest that his leadership pattern only makes him and his subordinates more dependent-ridden.[34]

The model of growth trends is a construct developed to help the researcher to understand the basic dimensions of growth and to measure any given individuals' growth at a particular moment in time. Nothing is included in the model that should be interpreted to mean that all individuals strive toward maximum expression of the adult end of the continuum.

To the extent that individuals who are hired to become agents of organizations are predisposed toward maturity, they will want to express needs or predispositions related to the adult end of each specific developmental continuum. Theoretically, this means that healthy adults will tend to obtain optimum personality expression while at work if they are provided with jobs which permit them to be more active than passive; more independent than dependent; to have longer rather than shorter time perspectives; to occupy higher position than their peers; to have control over their world; and to express many of their deeper, more important abilities.[35] These developmental trends may be considered as basic properties of the human personality. They are the "givens" that an administrator accepts the moment he decides to accept human beings as agents of the organization.

III

The Formal Organization

The purpose of the previous chapter as well as this one is to lay the groundwork for analyzing some of the causes of organizational behavior. The framework cannot be elaborated upon without knowing the properties of the two original basic components, the individual and the formal organization. Up to now, the focus has been on the individual. Some interesting insights have been obtained into the personality "givens" which the administrator or social scientist must understand if he is to explain human behavior in organizations.

The next step is to focus the analytic spotlight on the formal organization. What are its properties? What are its basic "givens"? What probable impact will these "givens" have upon the human personality? How will the human personality react to this impact? What "chain reactions" are probable when these two basic components are brought together?

A. FORMAL ORGANIZATIONS ARE RATIONAL ORGANIZATIONS

Probably the most basic property of formal organization is its logical foundation or, as it has been called by students of administration, its essential rationality. It is the "mirror image" of the planners' conception of how the intended consequences of the organization may best be achieved. The underlying assumption made by the creators of formal organization is that man within respectable tolerances will behave rationally, i.e., as the formal plan requires him to behave. Organizations are formed with a

54

particular objective in mind and their structure mirrors these objectives. Although an individual may not follow the prescribed paths and consequently the objectives might never be achieved, Simon suggests, that by and large, men do follow these prescribed paths. As he points out:

Organizations are formed with the intention and design of accomplishing goals; and the people who work in organizations believe, at least part of the time, that they are striving toward these same goals. We must not lose sight of the fact that, however far organizations may depart from the traditional description . . . nevertheless most behavior in organizations is *intendedly rational behavior.* By intended rationality I mean the kind of adjustment of behavior to goals of which humans are capable —a very incomplete and imperfect adjustment, to be sure, but one which nevertheless does accomplish purposes and does carry out programs.[1]

In an illuminating book, Urwick[2] eloquently describes this underlying characteristic. He insists that the creation of a formal organization requires a logical "drawing-office" approach. Although he admits that "nine times out of ten it is impossible to start with a clean sheet," the organizer should sit down and in a "cold-blooded, detached spirit . . . draw an ideal structure." The section begins with Urwick's description of how the formal structure should be planned. He then continues:

Manifestly that is a drawing-office job. It is a designing process. And it may be objected with a great deal of experience to support the contention that organization is never done that way . . . human organization. Nine times out of ten it is impossible to start with a clean sheet. The organizer has to make the best possible use of the human material that is already available. And in 89 out of those 90 per cent of cases he has to adjust jobs round to fit the man: he can't change the man to fit the job. He can't sit down in a cold-blooded, detached spirit and draw an ideal structure, an optimum distribution of duties and responsibilities and relationships, and then expect the infinite variety of human nature to fit into it. . . .

To which the reply is that he can and he should. If he has not got a clean sheet, that is no earthly reason why he should not make the slight effort of imagination required to assume that he has a clean sheet. It is not impossible to forget provisionally the personal facts—that old Brown is admirably methodical but wanting in initiative, that young Smith got into a mess with Robinson's wife and that the two men must be kept at opposite ends of the building, that Jones is one of those creatures who can think like a Wrangler about other people's duties but is given to periodic amnesia about certain aspects of his own.[3]

The task of the organizer, therefore, is to create a logically ordered world where as Fayol suggests there is a "proper order" and in which there is a "place for everything (everyone)."[4]

The possibility that the formal organization can be altered by personalities, as found by McGregor and Arensberg[5] and Stodgill and Koehler,[6] is not denied by formal organizational experts. Urwick, for example, in the passage below states that the planner must take into account the human element. But note that he perceives these adjustments as "temporary deviations from the pattern in order to deal with idiosyncrasy of personality." If possible, these deviations should be minimized by careful prior planning.

He should never for a moment pretend that these (human) difficulties don't exist. They do exist: they are realities. Nor, when he has drawn up an ideal plan of organization, is it likely that he will be able to fit in all the existing human material perfectly. There will be small adjustments of the job to the man in all kinds of directions. But those adjustments are deliberate and temporary deviations from the pattern in order to deal with idiosyncrasy. There is a world of difference between such modifications and drifting into an unworkable organization because Green has a fancy for combining bits of two incompatible functions, or White is "empire building"—a technical term describing smash-and-grab raids on other people's responsibilities—or Black has always looked after the canteen, so when he is promoted to Sales Manager he might just as well continue to sell buns internally, though the main product of the business happens to be battleships.

What is suggested is that problems of organization should be handled in *the right order*. Personal adjustments must be made, insofar as they are necessary. But fewer of them will be necessary and they will present fewer deviations from what is logical and simple, if the organizer first makes a plan, a design—to which he would work if he had the ideal human material. He should expect to be driven from it here and there. But he will be driven from it far less and his machine will work much more smoothly if he *starts* with a plan. If he starts with a motley collection of human oddities and tries to organize to fit them all in, thinking first of their various shapes and sizes and colors, he may have a patch-work quilt; he will not have an organization.[7]

The majority of experts on formal organization agree with Urwick. Most of them emphasize that no organizational structure will be ideal. None will exemplify the maximum expression of the principles. A satisfactory aspiration is for optimum expression, which means modifying the ideal structure to take into account the individual (and any environmental) conditions. Moreover, they urge that the people must be loyal to the formal structure if it is to work effectively. Thus Taylor[8] emphasizes that scientific management would never succeed without a "mental revolution." Fayol has the same problem in mind when he emphasizes the importance of *esprit de corps*.

However, it is also true that these experts have provided little insight into *why* they believe that people should undergo a "mental revolution"; or why *esprit de corps* is necessary if the principles are to succeed. The only hints usually found are that resistance to scientific management occurs because human beings are what they are, or "because it's human nature." But, *why* does "human nature" resist formal organizational principles? Perhaps there is something inherent in the principles which cause human resistance. Unfortunately, there exists too little research that specifically assesses the impact of the formal oragnizational principles upon human beings.

Another argument offered by the formal organizational experts is that logical, rational design in the long run is more human than creating an organization haphazardly. They argue that it is illogical, cruel, wasteful, and inefficient not to have a logical design. It is illogical because design must come first. It does not make sense to pay a large salary to an individual without clearly defining his position and its relationship to the whole. It is cruel because in the long run the participants suffer when no clear organizational structure exists. It is wasteful because unless jobs are clearly pre-defined it is impossible to plan logical training, promotion, resignation, and retirement policies. It is inefficent because the organization becomes dependent upon personalities. The "personal touch" leads to "playing politics," which Mary

Follett has described as a "deplorable form of coercion."[9]

Unfortunately, the validity of these arguments tends to be obscured in the eyes of the behavioral scientist because it implies that the only choice left, if the formal rational predesigned structure is not accepted, is to have no organizational structure at all, with the organizational structure left to the whims, pushes, and pulls of human beings. Some human relations researchers have unfortunately given the impression that formal structures are "bad" and that the needs of the individual participants should be paramount in creating and administering an organization. However, a recent analysis of the existing research points up clearly that the importance of the organization as an organism worthy of self-actualization is being recognized by those who in the past have focused largely upon the individual.[10]

B. Some Basic Principles of Formal Organization

In the past, and for the most part in the present, the traditional organizational experts have based their "human architectual creation" upon certain basic principles (more accurately, assumptions) concerning the nature of organization. These principles have been described by such people as Urwick,[11] Mooney,[12] Holden et al,[13] Fayol,[14] Dennison,[15] Brown,[16] Gulick,[17] White,[18] Gauss,[19] Stene,[20] Hopf,[21] and Taylor.[22]

Although these principles have been attacked by behavioral scientists, the assumption is made in this book that to date no one has defined a more useful set of formal organization principles. Therefore, the principles are accepted as "givens." This frees us to inquire about their probable impact upon people, *if they are used as defined.*

In introducing these principles, it is important to note that, as Gillespie suggests, the roots of these principles may be traced back to certain "principles of industrial economics," the most important of which is the basic economic assumption held by builders of the industrial revolution that "the concentration of effort on a limited field of endeavor increases quality and quantity of output."[23] It follows from the above that the necessity for specialization should increase as the quantity of similar things to be done increases.

Task (Work) *Specialization.* If concentrating effort on a limited field of endeavor increases the quality and quantity of output, organizational and administrative efficiency is increased by the specialization of tasks assigned to the participants of the organization.[24]

For example Davis, Canter, and Hoffman[25] suggest, and Marks[26] concurs, that the overwhelming influence in the design of industrial jobs is the criterion of minimizing immediate costs of producing. This criterion is satisfied, continue the authors, by specializing skills in order to reduce skill requirements which, in turn, decrease learning time. Inherent in these practices are three assumptions: (1) that the human personality will behave more efficiently as the task it is to perform becomes specialized; (2) that there can be found one best way to define the job so that it is performed at greater speed;[27] and (3) that any individual differences in the human personality may be ignored by transferring more skill and thought to machines.[28]

A number of difficulties arise with these assumptions when the properties of the human personality are recalled. First, the human personality we have seen is *always* attempting to actualize its *unique organization* of parts resulting from a continuous, emotionally laden, ego-involving process of growth. It is difficult, if not impossible, to assume that this process can be choked off and the resultant unique differences of individuals be ignored. This is tantamount to saying that self-actualization can be ignored. The second difficulty is that task specialization requires that the individual use only a few of his abilities. Moreover, as specialization increases it tends to require the use of the less complex doing or motor abilities, which research suggests is of lesser psychological importance to the individual. Thus the principle violates three basic "givens" of the healthy adult human personality. It inhibits self-actualization and provides expression for few, shallow, skin-surface abilities that do not provide the "endless challenge" desired by the healthy personality.

Wilensky and Lebeaux[29] correctly point out that task specialization causes what little skill is left in the job to become very important. Now *small* differences in ability may make enormous differences in output. Thus two machine-shovel operators or two drill press operators of different degrees of skill can produce dramatically different outputs. Ironically, the increase in importance of this type of skill for the healthy, mature worker means that he should feel he is performing self-satisfying work while using a small number of psychologically *unchallenging* abilities when in actuality he may be predisposed to feel otherwise. Task specialization therefore requires a healthy adult to behave in a less mature manner, but it also requires that he feel "good" about it!

Not only is the individual affected, but the social structure also is modified as a result of the above. Wilensky and Lebeaux, in the same analysis, point out that placing a great emphasis on ability makes "Who you are" become much less important than "What you can do." Thus the culture begins to reward relatively skin-surface materialistic characteristics.

Chain of Command. The principle of task specialization creates a plurality of parts, each performing a highly specialized task. However, a plurality of parts busily performing their particular objective does not form an organization. A pattern of parts must be formed so that the interrelationships among the parts create the organization. Following the logic of specialization the planners create a new function (leadership) whose primary responsibility shall be the control, direction, and coordination of the interrelationships of the parts and to make certain that each part performs toward objective, adequately. Thus the assumption is made that administrative and organizational efficiency is increased by arranging the parts in a determinate hierarchy of authority where the part on top can direct and control the part on the bottom.

If the parts being considered are individuals, then they must be motivated to accept direction, control, and coordination of their behavior. The leader is therefore assigned formal power to hire, discharge, reward, and penalize the individuals in order that their behavior be molded toward the organization's objectives.

The impact of such a state of affairs is to make the individuals *dependent* upon, *passive* toward, and *subordinate* to the leader. As a result the individuals have *little control* over their working environment. Concomitantly, their time perspective is *shortened* because they do not control the information necessary to predict their future. Martin[30] reports that "extension of time perspective in decision situations tends to vary directly with movement up the management hierarchy." Significant differences (at the .01 level) exist between the various levels of management in this respect, with the lower levels tending to deal predominantly with decision situations of relatively short time perspective and higher levels with situations of long time influence. These requirements of formal organization act to inhibit four of the growth trends of the personality; adults who are passive and subordinate, and who have little control and short time perspective, exemplify dimensions of immaturity, not adulthood.

The planners of formal organization suggest three basic ways to minimize this admittedly difficult position. First, ample rewards should be given to those who perform well and who do not permit their dependence, subordination, passivity, and the like to influence them in a negative manner. The rewards should be material and psychological. Because of the specialized nature of the job, however, few psychological rewards are possible. It therefore becomes important that adequate material rewards be made available to the productive employee. This practice can lead to new difficulties, since the solution by its nature does nothing about the on-the-job situation (which is causing the difficulties) but instead pays the individual for the dissatisfactions he experiences. The end result may be that the employee is paid for his *dissatisfaction* while at work and his wages are given to him to gain satisfactions *outside his* immediate work environment. Thus the management helps to create a psychological set which leads the employees to feel that basic causes of dissatisfaction are *built into* industrial life; that the rewards they receive are wages for *dissatisfaction* and that if satisfaction is to be gained, the employee must seek it *outside* the organization.

To make matters more difficult, there are three assumptions inherent in the above solution that also violate the basic "givens" of human personality. First, the solution assumes that a *whole* human being can split his personality so that he will feel satisfied in knowing that the wages for his dissatisfaction will buy him satisfaction outside the plant. Second, it assumes the employee is primarily interested in maximizing his economic gains. Third, it assumes that the employee is best rewarded as an individual producer. The work group in which he belongs is not viewed as a relevant factor. If he produces well, he should be rewarded. If he does not, he should be penalized even though he may be restricting production because of informal group sanctions.

The second solution suggested by the planners of formal organization is to have technically competent, objective, rational, loyal leaders. The assumption is made that if the leaders are technically competent, presumably they cannot have "the wool pulled over their eyes." This would lead the employees to have a high respect for them. The leaders should be objective and rational and should personify the rationality inherent in the formal structure. Being rational means that they must avoid becoming emotionally involved. As one executive states, "We try to keep our personality out of the job." The leader must also be impartial. He does not permit his feelings to operate when he is evaluating others. Finally, the leader must be loyal to the organization so that he can inculcate the loyalty that Taylor, Fayol, and others believe is so important in the employees.

Admirable as this solution may be, again it violates several of the basic properties of personality. If employees are to respect an individual for what he does rather than for who he is, the sense of self integrity based upon evaluation of the *total self* which is developed in people is lost. Moreover, to ask the leader to keep his personality out of his job is to ask him to stop actualizing himself. This is not possible so long as he is alive. The executive may want to *feel* that he is not involved, but it is a basic "given" that the human personality is an organism that is always actualizing itself. The same problem arises with impartiality. No one can be completely impartial. As has been shown, the self concept always operates when we are making judgments. As Rollo May has pointed out, the best way to be impartial is to be as partial as one's needs predispose, but to be aware of this partiality in order to "correct" for it at the moment of decision.[31] Finally, if a leader can be loyal to an organization under the conditions postulated above, there may be adequate grounds for questioning the health of his personality make-up.

The third solution suggested by many adherents to the formal organizational principles is to motivate the subordinates to have more initiative and to be more creative by placing them in competition with one another for the positions of power that lie above them in the organizational ladder. This solution is traditionally called "the rabble hypothesis." Acting under the assumption that employees will be motivated to advance upward, the formal organizational adherents add another assumption that competition for the increasingly (as one goes up the ladder) scarcer positions will increase the effectiveness of the participants. Williams,[32] conducting some controlled experiments, shows that the latter assumption is not necessarily valid. People placed in competitive situations are not necessarily better learners than those placed in noncompetitive situations. Deutsch,[33] as a result of extensive controlled experimental research, supports Williams' results and goes much further to suggest that competitive situations tend to increase tension and conflict and decrease human effectiveness. Levy and Freedman[34] confirm Deutsch's findings and go further to relate competition to psychoneurosis.

Unity of Direction.[35] If the tasks of every person in a unit are specialized, the objective or purpose of the unit must be specialized. The principle of unity of direction states that administrative and organizational efficiency increases if each unit has a single activity (or homogeneous set of activities) that is planned and directed by the leader.

This means that the work goal toward which the employees are striving, the path towards the goal, and the strength of the barriers they must overcome to achieve the goal are defined and controlled by the leader. Assuming that the work goals do not ego-involve the employees (i.e., they are related to peripheral needs), then ideal conditions for *psychological failure* have been created. The reader may recall that a basic "given" of a healthy personality is the aspiration for psychological success. Psychological success is achieved when each individual is able to define his *own* goals, in relation to his *inner* needs and the strength of the barriers to be overcome in order to reach these goals. Repetitive as it may sound, it is nevertheless true that the principle of unity of direction also violates a basic "given" of personality.

Span of Control.[36] The principle of span of control states that administrative efficiency is increased by limiting the span of control of a leader to no more than five or six subordinates whose work interlocks.[37]

Dale,[38] in an extensive study of the organizational principles and practices in 100 large organizations, concludes that the actual limits of the executive span of control are more often violated than not. Worthy[39] reports that it is formal policy in his organization to extend the span of control of the top management much further than is theoretically suggested. Finally, Suojanen,[40] in a review of the current literature on the concept of span of control concludes that it is no longer valid, particularly as applied to the larger government agencies and business corporations. Healey's findings based upon an intensive study of the practice of span of control in 620 firms representing most major industries does not agree with Suojanen's findings.[41] He reports that in practice the concept of span of control is used and that its use closely adheres to that advocated in theory. For example, when executives seem to have a choice they tend to limit themselves to five subordinates or less. In an interesting review of perception and small group experimental research Miller[41A] concludes that the human being may be "inherently" limited in the amount of information that he may receive, evaluate, store, and communicate. He shows that past the number of seven human situations become so complex that individuals must simplify by grouping, categorizing, evaluating, abstracting, organizing, and naming their information. Such results add indirect evidence to the probable validity of a concept similar to span of control.

In a recent article Urwick,[42, 43] criticizes the critics of the span of control principle. He notes that in the case of Worthy, the superior has a large span of control over subordinates whose jobs do not interlock. The buyers in Worthy's organization purchase a clearly defined range of articles, and therefore find no reason to interlock with others.

Simon criticizes this principle on the grounds that it increases the "administrative distance" between individuals. An increase in administrative distance violates in turn another formal organizational principle, "that administrative efficiency is enhanced by keeping at a minimum the number of organizational levels through which a matter must pass before it is acted on."[44] Span of control, continues Simon, inevitably increases red tape, since each contact between agents must be carried upward until a common superior is found. Needless waste of time and energy results.

Whisler[45] suggests that an increase of administrative distance between individuals and an increase of levels tends to create communication problems for the top executive of the organization. For example, it is unfortunate that although the top executive has the greatest amount of decision-making power—hence a greater need for information—the message-flow to him gets increasingly heavy, while he has proportionally less time available to digest the information. He soon must depend on briefed-down communications usually interpreted by his assistants.

Martin[46] reports similar results. He finds that the content of decision tends to become more abstract as one moves from lower to higher levels of administration. Reports on production, for example, consist of summaries prepared by subordinates or staff personnel; to a considerable extent, impressions of employee morale and sentiment come from subordinates, who in turn are interpreting from the views of their key personnel.

Another limitation of the principle is that it tends to decrease the amount of control and time perspective of the individuals who are at the bottom of the ladder. This again places individuals in a work situation which presupposes immaturity of the participants.

Although the distance between individuals in different units increases (because they have to find a common superior), the administrative distance between superior and subordinate *within* a given unit decreases. As Whyte[47] points out, the principle of span of control, by keeping the number of subordinates at a minimum, places great emphasis on close supervision. Close supervision leads the subordinates to become dependent upon, passive toward, and subordinate to the leader. Close supervision also tends to place the control in the superior. Thus we must conclude that span of control, if used as defined, to keep the number of subordinates at a minimum, will tend to increase the subordinates' feelings of dependence, submissiveness, passivity, and the like. Again, these are typical of a work situation which requires immature rather than mature participants.

C. A Basic Incongruency Between the Needs of a Mature Personality and the Requirements of Formal Organization

Bringing together the evidence regarding the impact of the formal organizational principles upon the individual, it is concluded that there are some basic incongruencies between the growth trends of a healthy personality and the requirements of the formal organization. If the principles of formal organization are used as ideally defined, employees will tend to work in an environment where (1) they are provided minimal control over their workaday world, (2) they are expected to be passive, dependent, and subordinate, (3) they are expected to have a short time perspective, (4) they are induced to perfect and value the frequent use of a few skin-surface shallow abilities and, (5) they are expected to produce under conditions leading to psychological failure.

All these characteristics are incongruent to the ones *healthy* human beings are postulated to desire (Chapter II). They are much more congruent with the needs of infants in our culture. In effect, therefore, organizations are willing to pay high wages and provide adequate seniority if mature adults will, for eight hours a day, behave in a less than mature manner! *If the analysis is correct, this inevitable incongruency increases as* (1) *the employees are of increasing maturity,* (2) *as the formal structure* (based upon the above principles) *is made more clear-cut and logically tight for maximum formal organizational effectiveness,* (3) *as one goes down the line of command, and* (4) *as the jobs become more and more mechanized* (i.e., take on assembly line characteristics).

As in the case of the personality developmental trends, this picture of formal organization is also a model. Clearly, no company actually uses the formal principles of organization exactly as stated by their creators. There is ample evidence to suggest that they are being modified constantly in actual situations. However, those who expound these principles would probably be willing to defend their position that this is the reason that human relations problems exist; the principles are not followed as they should be.

In the proposed models of the personality and the formal organization, we are assuming the extreme of each in order that the analysis and its results can be highlighted. Speaking in terms of extremes helps us to make the position sharper. In doing this, no assumption is made that all situations in real life are extreme (i.e., that the individuals will always want to be more mature and that the formal organization will always tend to make people more dependent and passive all the time). In fact, much evidence is presented in subsequent chapters to support contrary tendencies.

The model ought to be useful, however, to plot the degree to which each component tends toward extremes and then to predict the problems that will arise. In Chapter VII, for example, numerous illustrations will show how managements are actively trying to decrease the basic incongruency described above.

It is not difficult to see why some students of organization suggest that immature and even mentally retarded individuals would probably make excellent employees. There is little documented experience to support such a hypothesis. One reason for this lack of information is probably the "touchiness" of the subject. Examples of what might be obtained if a systematic study is made may be found in a recent work by Brennan.[48] He cites the Utica Knitting Mill, which made arrangements during 1917 with the Rome Institution for Mentally Defective Girls to employ 24 girls whose mental ages ranged from six to ten years. The girls were such excellent workers that their employment continued after the war emergency ended. In fact the company added forty additional mentally defective girls in another of their plants. The managers praised the subnormal girls highly.

In several important reports, they said that "when business conditions required a reduction of the working staff," the hostel girls were never "laid off" in disproportion to the normal girls; that they were more punctual, more regular in their habits, and did not indulge in as much "gossip and levity." They received the same rate of pay, and they had been employed successfully at almost every process carried out in the workshops.

In another experiment, the Works Manager of the Radio Corporation Ltd. reported that of five young morons:

. . . The three girls compared very favourably with the normal class of employee in that age group. The boy employed in the store performed his work with satisfaction. . . . Although there was some doubt about the fifth child, it was felt that getting the most out of him was just a matter of right placement.

In each of the five cases, the morons were quiet, respectful, well-behaved, and obedient. The Works Manager was especially impressed by their truthfulness, and lack of deceit or suppression of the facts. A year later, the same Works Manager was still able to advise that,

In every case, the girls proved to be exceptionally well-behaved, particularly obedient, and strictly honest and trustworthy. They carried out work required of them to such a degree of efficiency that *we were surprised they were classed as subnormals for their age.*[49] Their attendance was good, and their behavior was, if anything, certainly better than any other employee of the same age.

Let us now turn to the literature to see if there are illustrations of the points made regarding the dependence and subordination created by the nature of formal organization and its impact upon the individuals. Unfortunately, there are not many available studies that focus on the impact of the formal organization on the individuals (holding the leadership variable "constant").

Probably the best available evidence of the impact of formal organization based upon unity of command and task specialization is the experimental work on communication by Bavelas[50] and Leavitt,[51] which is confirmed by Heise and Miller[52] and Shaw and Rothchild.[53] They focus on the question—can the structure of certain patterns of communication result in significantly better performance than others? Their results clearly imply that in a structure where one individual has a "central" position in the communications network and thereby is able to control communications, as would an executive in a plant, he will probably be chosen the leader and have the best morale in the group. The individuals who depend upon him (e.g., supervisors) will tend to have lower morale, feel more frustrated, confused, and irrritated at others along the network. Guetzkow and Simon confirm these results, and through the use of more refined experimental procedure they show strong evidence to support the hypothesis that of all communications structures tried, the "wheel"[54] created initially the *least* organizational problem for the group, thereby permitting the group to organize itself most quickly in order to solve a particular problem.[55]

Further indirect evidence is provided by Arensberg,[56] who "revisited" the famous Hawthorne Studies. He noted that many of the results reported about the relay assembly experiments occurred *after* the girls were placed in a work situation where they were (1) made "subjects" of an "important" experiment, (2) encouraged to participate in decisions affecting their work, (3) given veto power over their supervisors to the point where, as the girls testify, "we have no boss." Clearly these conditions constitute a sweeping shift in the basic relationship of modern industrial work where the employee is subordinate to people above him.

Bakke's study of the unemployed worker includes much evidence that the workers are clearly aware of the differences in the degree of authority and control manifested by themselves and their boss. His evidence suggests that independently of the personality of the boss, the workers perceived their boss as someone with power to achieve his goals; a power which they did not believe they had. For example, one worker defines the boss as someone who, "When he decides to do something, he can carry it through." Another states, "Some birds have got enough (authority) and stand high enough so that what they say goes . . . and anybody who can do that won't be found very often to be what you might call a worker."[58]

Blau,[59] in a study of the departmental structure in a federal enforcement agency, reports that even when deliberate attempts were made to minimize the social distance between leaders and subordinates and where leaders tried to use a "democratic" approach, the supervisors frequently but inadvertently lapsed into behavior more appropriate to the formal authoritarian relationships with the subordinates. Thus, the impact of the formal structure influences leadership behavior toward being more "autocratic" even when there exist informal norms emphasizing a more egalitarian climate and when the leaders consciously try to be more "democratic."

Not only do the supervisors "slip" into more directive leadership, but the subordinates "slip" into dependent, submissive roles even if the supervisor requests their increased participation. As one subordinate states, "Lots of times, I've differed with the supervisor, but I didn't say anything. I just said, 'Yes,' with a smile, *because he gives the efficiency rating.*" Blau continues:

> Bureaucratic authority is *not* based on personal devotion to the supervision or on respect for him as a person but on an adaptation necessitated by his rating power. The *advancement chances of officials and even their chances to keep their civil service jobs depends on the rating they periodically receive from their superior.* . . . The group's insistence that the supervisor discharge his duty of issuing directives—"That's what he gets paid for"—serves to emphasize that their obedience to them does *not* constitute submission to his will but *adherence, on his part as well as theirs, to abstract principles* which they have socially accepted.[60]

In comprehensive reviews of the literature Gibb,[61] Blau[62] and Bierstedt[63] conclude that it is important to differentiate between formal leadership (headship or authority) based upon formal organization and informal leadership (leadership). For example, Gibb states:

> . . . leadership is to be distinguished, by definition, from domination or headship. The principal differentia are these: (i) Domination or headship is maintained through an organized system and not by the spontaneous recognition, by fellow group members, of the individual's contribution to group goals. (ii) The group goal is chosen by the head man

in line with his interests and is not internally determined by the group itself. (iii) In the domination or headship relation there is little or no sense of shared feeling or joint action in the pursuit of the given goal. (iv) There is in the dominance relation a wide social gap between the group members and the head, who strives to maintain this social distance as an aid to his coercion of the group. (v) Most basically, these two forms of influence differ with respect to the *source* of the authority which is exercised. The leader's authority is spontaneously accorded him by his fellow group members, the followers. *The authority of the head derives from some extra-group power which he has over the members of the group, who cannot meaningfully be called his followers. They accept his domination on pain of punishment, rather than follow. The business executive is an excellent example of a head exercising authority derived from his position in an organization through membership in which the workers, his subordinates, satisfy many strong needs. They obey his commands and accept his domination because this is part of their duty as organization members and to reject him would be to discontinue membership, with all the punishments that would involve.*[61]

Carter,[64] in some recent controlled field experiments, points up the importance of the power and status inherent in the formal organizational structure by an interesting study of the behavior of "emergent" vs. "appointed" leaders. He concludes that appointed leaders tend to support their own purposes, defend their proposals from attack, express their own opinions, and argue—all *less* than emergent leaders. Apparently, the data suggests, because the appointed leader feels that he has power and status, he feels less need to defend his position than does an emergent leader.

Fleishman's[65] descriptions of leadership training also point up the degree of dependence and leader-centeredness of a subordinate upon his boss. He reports that subordinates tend to use the same leadership style that their boss tends to use regardless of the training they receive.

Probably no review of the literature would be complete without mentioning the classic work of Max Weber on the study of bureaucracy.[66, 67] It is important to keep in mind that Weber conceived of bureaucracy (formal organization) as "the most efficient form of social organization ever developed."[68] He maintained that bureaucracy was one of the characteristic forms of organization of all modern society, finding wide expression in industry, science, and religion, as well as government.[69] In fact, it may be said that he saw no difference between socialism and capitalism, since the fundamental characteristic of both was (a particular kind of) formal organization. "If Marx said that the workers of the world had nothing to lose but their chains by revolting, Weber contended that they really had nothing to gain."[70] It remained for Merton to try to balance the "rosy" picture that Weber painted about bureaucracy. At the outset of this work, Merton, in clear and concise terms, describes some of the essential conditions of formal organization. Again we note the emphasis made here on the inherent authoritarian power structure of the formal organization which is independent of the leadership pattern of the person holding the power position.

Authority, the power of control which derives from an acknowledged status, inheres in the office and not in the particular person who performs the official role. Official action ordinarily occurs within the framework of preexisting rules of the organization. The system of prescribed relations between the various offices involves a considerable degree of formality and clearly defined social distance between the occupants of these positions. Formality is manifested by means of a more or less complicated social ritual which symbolizes and supports the "pecking order" of the various offices. Such formality, which is integrated with the distribution of authority within the system, serves to minimize friction by largely restricting (official) contact to modes which are previously defined by the rules of the organization . . .[71]

Charles Walker, Robert Guest, and Arthur Turner have been studying the impact of the assembly line (an example of a highly specialized aspect of organizational structure) and of the management upon the workers. Their findings show the degree and kind of impact of the mass production type of organizational structure upon the employee, independent of the personality of the management. Walker and Guest report that about 90 per cent (of 180) workers dislike their actual job because of its mechanical pacing, repetitiveness, minimum skill requirements, minute subdivision of work, and surface mental attention. Their results show that the degree of dislike for the job increased in proportion to the degree to which the job embodies mass production characteristics[72] and to the degree to which the employees are dependent upon management. These results have been confirmed in another study by the same team.[73]

Turner, in an article based upon the second study mentioned above, expands on the impact of the assembly line. The employees especially dislike the mechanical pacing of the assembly line which (1) decreases their control over their own activities, (2) makes them dependent, subordinate, and passive to a machine process, and (3) leads them to forget quality production and aspire to an acceptable minimum quantity output. Turner[74] points out that the men dislike the necessity to work at a job that requires only a minimum skill, and forces them, through repetitiveness, to continue using only a minimum skill. These findings are understandable since these requirements run counter to the needs of relatively mature human beings. Finally, the characteristics of impersonality and anonymity also inveigh against the needs of "ego integrity" and feelings of self worth.

Indirect evidence comes from two studies of organization reported by the writer. In both organizations the employees' degree of morale with the company increased as the degree of directive leadership decreased. Passive leadership (i.e., leadership that seldom contacts the employees) minimized the pressure from above and permitted the employees to feel more "self-responsible" (i.e., they could be their own boss). Over 91 per cent of the respondents (total group sampled about 300) reported that passive leadership (i.e., "we hardly ever talk with the boss") permits them to be their own boss and thereby reduces the potential pressure from above. However, the same number of employees also reported they still feel pressure from the very way the work and the companies are organized. For example, a bank teller states,

I don't know what I would do if Mr. B. supervised us closely. The pressure would be terrific. As it is, I hardly see him. He leaves me alone and that's fine with me. But don't get me wrong. It isn't that I don't feel I haven't got a boss. I have one. *I know I will always have one, if it's Mr. B. or Mr. X.*[75]

Some trade union leaders are aware that the formal organization places the workers in dependent and dissatisfying situations. Many report that the process of management (independent of the personality of the leader) carries with it certain "inevitable" dislikes by the workers, because the workers view management (who represent the formal organization) as the ones who place them in dissatisfying work situations. This may be one reason that many trade union leaders do not aspire to gain political control over the management.

Mr. Green, for example, said, "The line of distinction between the exercise of the rights of labor and of management must be scrupulously observed. The philosophy which some have advanced that labor should join with management in the actual management of the property could not and cannot be accepted."[76] Mr. Murray agrees when he states, "To relieve the boss or the management of proper responsibility for making a success of the enterprise is about the last thing any group of employees would consider workable or even desirable."[77]

The fears implied by these two labor leaders exist as facts in countries like Norway, England, and Holland. The trade union leaders in these countries are partially or indirectly responsible for the economic health of the country (because the party identified with labor has strong political power). It is not uncommon to see trade union leaders "selling" work study, scientific management, and increased productivity to the workers.[78] Many workers feel that their national leaders are closer in outlook with management than with their own members.[79] In short, the American trade union leaders may realize that because of the impact of the nature of formal organization, even if they were perfect administrators, they still would have human problems with the employees.

D. SUMMARY

On the basis of a logical analysis, it is concluded that the formal organizational principles make demands of relatively healthy individuals that are incongruent with their needs. Frustration, conflict, failure, and short time perspective are predicted as resultants of this basic incongruency.

Empirical evidence is presented to illustrate the rational character of the formal organization and to support the proposition that the basic impact of the formal organizational structure is to make the employees feel dependent, submissive, and passive, and to require them to utilize only a few of their less important abilities.

In the next chapter, empirical evidence is amassed to illustrate the existence in the employee of the predicted frustration, conflict, failure, and short time perspective and to show some of the resultants of these factors.

I V

Individual and Group Adaptation

After we defined the basic properties of the human personality and formal organization, we derived the concept that healthy individuals will tend to have their self-actualization blocked or inhibited because of the demands of the formal organization. From this proposition, a further derivation was made to the effect that as a result of this basic incongruency, healthy individuals will tend to experience frustration, conflict, failure, and short time perspective.

In this chapter, we shall provide evidence from the literature that these states of affairs do exist and we shall show the impact they have upon the organization.

The approach is to see if the behavior that results from frustration, conflict, failure, and short time perspective can be observed in actual organizations. The logic behind this approach is to assume that if individuals are *observed* behaving according to the manner expected (on the basis of research) of people experiencing frustration, conflict, failure, and short time perspective, then they may be said to be actually experiencing these four states of affairs. The logic is, if A (frustration) exists, then B (aggression) results. Where B is the case (employees are observed being aggressive), then A also is the case (frustration exists). This is affirming the consequence, but as was pointed out in Chapter I, much progress has been made in the natural and social sciences by using this method of analysis.

One more point by way of introduction. The present analysis

will focus on the employees' adaptation *within* the organization. Other studies have been conducted (and many more are urgently needed) on the firm's adaptation to its environment.[1] Some day, when enough is known about both the "internal" and "external" adaptation, a more complete theory of organization will be available.[2]

A. The Individual Adapts

If the formal organization is defined by the use of such "organization" principles as task specialization, unity of direction, chain of command, and span of control, and if these principles are used *correctly*, the employees will work in situations in which they tend to be dependent, subordinate, and passive toward the leader. They will tend to use few of their abilities (probably none of which are important ones for the individual anyway). The degree of passivity, dependence, and submissiveness tends to increase for those employees as one goes *down* the line of command *and* as the work takes on more of the mass production characteristics. As a result, it is hypothesized that the formal organization creates in a healthy individual feelings of failure and frustration, short time perspective, and conflict.

If this is valid and the employees are affected as hypothesized, it should be possible to turn to the existing research on conflict, frustration, failure, and time perspective to find how people react to these states of affairs and then observe if employees actually behave in this way.

To consider conflict first, the employee will experience it to the extent that the demands made upon him by the formal organization are antagonistic to his needs. As the antagonism increases, the employee increasingly finds himself in the situation where fulfilling his needs frustrates the fulfillment of his formal organizational requirements. Research suggests that there are some possible modes of reaction to this type of conflict.[3, 4, 5]

The employee may leave the conflict situation. He may do this by leaving the organization temporarily or permanently; or by climbing up the organizational ladder, where the conflict is much less; or by transferring to another job along the workflow whose newness may provide temporary opportunity for satisfaction.

The employee may decrease the psychological importance of one set of factors (the organization or the individual). He may decide to say "to hell with the organization," thereby clearing the way, whenever a choice is required between the organization and himself, to fulfill his own needs. This mode of adaptation results in apathy, lack of interest, decreased involvement, and lessened loyalty toward the set of factors rejected.

The employee may choose to remain in conflict. This choice leads to increasing tension. Turning to frustration, the employee may adapt by: (1) Regressing, i.e., becoming less mature and less efficient.[6] (2) Giving up and leaving the situation.[7] (3) Becoming aggressive, hostile, and attacking what is frustrating him. Developing a tendency to blame others. (4) Remaining frustrated by doing nothing. This choice leads to still more tension.[8]

Failure[8a, 9] may cause the employee to: (1) Lose interest in his work. (2) Lose self-confidence. (3) Give up quickly. (4) Lower work standards. (5) Fear new tasks. (6) Expect more failure. (7) Develop a tendency to blame others.

Finally, short time perspective tends to lead the employee to feel: (1) Uncertain. (2) Insecure. (3) If both of these become strong enough, they can increase the tension to the point where the individual regresses further.

All these modes of behavior may be combined. An employee experiencing frustration, failure, conflict, and short time perspective may behave in any one or a combination of the following ways:[10]

a. He may leave the organization. (But where else can he go? Most other companies are organized in the same way.)

b. He may work hard to climb the ladder and become the president. (But how many can become presidents?[11])

c. He may defend his self-concept and adapt through the use of defense mechanisms.

d. He may "pressure" himself to stay and, in spite of the conflict, simultaneously adapt as much as possible by lowering his work standards and becoming apathetic and uninterested.

e. This apathy and disinterest may lead him to place more value on material rewards and to depreciate the value of human or nonmaterial rewards.

f. Although not directly inferable from the above, the employee may teach his children *not* to expect satisfaction on the job; to expect rather to earn good wages and "live" outside the plant (the same lesson the formal organizational experts are teaching him). This hypothesis is based on the known property of human beings of evaluating life in terms of their own self-concept (Chapter II). If the employee's self-concept includes as "good" activities, goldbricking, learning the ropes, and quota restricting, then these will tend to be passed on to his children through the process of acculturation.

Let us turn to the available research to see whether each one of these hypotheses can be illustrated.

Leaving the Organization. Unfortunately, few studies relate turnover to aspects of the *formal* organizational structure. Guest[12] studied 18 assembly line production workers with twelve to fifteen years' seniority. Their wages were equal to, if not slightly higher than, wages in the general industrial area. Most of these workers had held jobs which were mechanically paced and repetitive, which required minimum skill, and which were completely predetermined as to method of performance. When interviewed, they had all left their assembly line jobs. More than half (11 out of 18) now worked full or part time out of doors. None went into repetitive factory work. The majority were getting less pay in their new jobs. All of the employees were rated average or above average by management. None were "transients." All of them had long seniority.

The most frequently mentioned reasons for leaving were the pressure from the machine pacing, the lack of variety, the requirement of minimum skill, and the lack of a challenge from the job. These factors are all aspects of the organizational structure as defined by task specialization. They inhibit the expression of personality needs, such as "control over one's own life," "use many of one's important abilities," "need to be relatively independent," and the need for ego identity and integrity. Two comments representative of the feelings of these men are:

OIL COMPANY PACKER: I look on my new job as a kind of a release. My future is brighter now. I'm relaxed—not nervous any more— no more hustle and bustle. I really am glad I'm out of there. I'd like a job where I can work by myself. That is why I liked one that I had at Plant Y working fast. On the line you knock yourself out.

DELIVERY TRUCK DRIVER: I sometimes see my old friends at Plant Y when I deliver stuff. They say, 'We thought you were on a leave of absence.' I say 'Yes, I am—for good.' All my friends are glad for my sake that I got out. That's the way I used to feel when someone left. You'd be sorry the guy left because you'd miss him, but you'd envy him too for getting out of the place. I used to think that working at Plant Y was a great thing—you know, building automobiles—but then I got so I would dread going into that place in the morning, I hated it so much, and that's no good. On the job I have now I can set my own pace. Now it seems I feel more like doing things in the evening than before.

One might suspect that these employees are atypical. Perhaps they have peculiar personalities that cause them to revolt. Guest reports in another study of 382 workers that the overwhelming majority agreed that if they could quit, it would be for the same reasons as those listed above. In still another article, Guest reports that many more employees would quit if they did not fear meeting difficulties in finding a new job, especially because of their age. Then, too, they would lose the "insurance" value of their substantial seniority and the high wages paid at the plant.[13]

Mann and Baumgartel[14] report that male workers are absent much less often if they are working on jobs that (1) permit them to use the skills they (the workers) feel are important and (2) permit them to have a greater voice in the solution of job problems. Both characteristics are clearly related to the personality characteristics of using one's own important abilities and of having adequate control over one's own world. In another study Metzner and Mann[15] report that absence rate is related significantly, among other factors, to the attitudes employees hold regarding the degree of freedom to discuss problems, the amount of responsibility given to them, and the degree to which they can use skills important to the employees. This relationship, as would be predicted by our analysis, is especially strong with low-skilled (white-collar) workers. The employees in lower-skilled jobs tend to feel the conflict more and, therefore, especially desire an opportunity to express their more important abilities and to have greater control over their work environment.

The extensive studies of Segerstedt and Lundquist[16] confirm the above conclusions. They report that the male workers who quit their jobs tended to do so because they did not feel their abilities were being used properly. "Internal turnover" (i.e., transfers within the organization) is much higher among those who do less skilled work than among those who do skilled work.

Climbing the Organizational Ladder. There do not seem to be any studies that focus on executive upward mobility as an adaptive mechanism. The meager evidence that does exist is obtained indirectly from the studies on executive motivation and behavior observed in various organizations.

Following our framework, we may deduce that mobile executives should be those who manifest needs that are not congruent with being dependent, passive, subordinate, and apathetic, or being confined to the use of a few skin-surface abilities. The upward mobile executive should manifest such needs as activity, directiveness, independence, need for power over others, use of many and important abilities, ego involvement, control over one's own world and recognition of self. If this is the case, studies of executive behavior and motivation should reveal executives as manifesting needs that are similar to the ones mentioned in the second list above.

Turning to the literature, we find that Gordon[17] doubts that money is a primary motivation for executive upward mobility. He believes that financial incentives are "largely a minimum condition for attracting the necessary supply of business leadership in the large corporation." He suggests that power, prestige, security, adventure, creative urge, and identification with the group are more powerful incentives. Copeland[18] agrees that financial incentives are not the most critical ones, and for executives, striving for recognition and prestige are more important. Griffin[19] suggests power, prestige, social approval, competitiveness, creativity, and independence as important factors motivating the executive. Roper, on a basis of several studies, concludes that executives strive for recognition of achievement, dignity of position, autonomy of management, and rewards in the form of leisure.[20] A study by the National Industrial Conference Board concludes that position security is more important than the profit motive as an incentive.[21] Hickman and Kuhn in an exhaustive study of top management motivation for their hard work conclude that although the profit motive is an important motivating factor, there seems to be an increasing tendency for this motive to be translated into something longer run, broader, such as the noneconomic psychosocial rewards.[22] Warner and Abegglen,[23] expanding the picture· of the mobile executive, report that the mobile executives were single-purposed, tense individuals who could never rest. The extreme intensity and sharp focus of their drive left little interest, time, or energy for any activities outside of their career. They were impatient and did not find it easy to get along with other men. Their hard work, single purpose, and immense drive resulted in isolation from their families, their parents, and close friends. Reacting defensively to isolation, they began to mistrust others and to need to work alone. The result is increased isolation. Argyris[24, 25, 26] confirms that upward mobile executives manifest such needs as, activity, power, directiveness, and independence.

The results of research on executive behavior and problems that executives experience also permit us to infer that a mobile executive would be highly frustrated in a situation in which he is forced to be passive, dependent, submissive, and subordinate. Whyte,[27] on the basis of interviews supplemented by questionnaires of 221 management men from a fairly representative industry group describes (and Spencer,[28] on the basis of 950 management respondents, confirms) the hard work and high energy expendability manifested by mobile executives. They report that the average executive has a work week which includes, as a minimum, 45 to 48 hours during the day, one night at the office, two nights at home, and one night entertaining. Moreover, many executives telephone their various units from home in order to spot-check performance. The authors report that the executives are under continual pressure. For example:

"You're always selling," an executive complains, "everything you do is subject to review by all sorts of people. So you have to spend as much time getting allies as you do on your project—you've got to keep making peace with people at all levels. Sometimes I go home worn to a frazzle, just over this."

Newcomer[29] and a study by TIME[30] of 111 top executives reported confirmation of the above results. The latter study reports that the executives work from 67 to 112 hours per week.

It is important to mention one point which will be discussed in detail later on. Because an executive manifests needs that in our model of human growth are found toward the mature end of the continua, it does not follow that he is therefore necessarily mature. It is pointed out in Chapter II that one operational criterion of maturity is not only capability of expressing "mature needs" but simultaneously to be capable of permitting others to do the same. Argyris shows, for example, that one brilliant executive who seemed to manifest relatively mature needs (independence, activity, and the like) was unable to provide the opportunities for his subordinates to express similar needs. He behaved in such a way that the subordinates became dependent, passive and subordinate.[31] An executive may *act* as if he is predisposed toward the mature end of the continua, but a closer examination may suggest that this is not the case. Returning to our main theme, we find that a mobile executive may experience many psychological situations that are potentially disturbing.

Merton describes the hostility and the process of alienation that a mobile executive tends to experience as follows:

What the individual experiences as estrangement from a group of which he is a member tends to be experienced by his associates as repudiation of the group, and this ordinarily evokes a hostile response. As social relations between the individual and the rest of the group deteriorate, the norms of the group become less binding for him. For, since he is progressively seceding from the group and being penalized by it, he is the less likely to experience rewards for adherence to the group's norms.

Once initiated, this process seems to move toward a cumulative detachment from the group, in terms of attitudes and values as well as terms of social relations. And to the degree that he orients himself toward outgroup values, perhaps affirming them verbally and expresing them in action, he only widens the gap and reinforces the hostility between himself and his in-group associates. Through the interplay of dissociation and progressive alienation from the group values, he may become doubly motivated to orient himself toward the values of another group and to affiliate himself with it.[32]

The problems mentioned above of "getting along" with the members of the group to which the mobile executive aspires are also illustrated in a study by Martin and Strauss.[33] They further point out that the psychological problems of relating one's self to a new group having status higher than the one to which the executive belongs can be decreased by being "sponsored" by a member of the new group. However, this can have its dangers if the executive develops difficulties with his sponsor or if the sponsor loses power.[34] Another fear many upward mobile executives experience is that of being "put on ice" and eventually dropped. Examples of this embarrassing experience are "use of seniority to slow up promotion, destruction of mobility drive, forcing of resignation, open demotion, progressive downgrading by merging departments and continual bypassing.[35]

The process of upward mobility is not an easy one. The magnitude of the difficulties becomes apparent when we note that Hollingshead, Ellis, and Kirby,[36] in a recent study of mobile and nonmobile patients find a high correlation between mobility on the one hand and schizophrenia and psychoneurosis on the other. Unfortunately, not much is known about what motivates one individual to be highly mobile and others to be quite content with little or no upward movement.

Warner and Abegglen provide qualitative evidence that the most important causes of upward mobility lie in the relationship the individual has had with his family. Many of them seemed to have unhappy childhoods where they have been dependent and submissive to one or both the parents. As a result they developed a self-concept which makes conditions such as dependency, submissiveness, passivity, and apathy intolerable for the individual. Dynes, Clarke, and Dinitz,[37] in a study of levels of occupational aspiration, also report that high aspirers reported feelings of being dominated and rejected more frequently (from either parent) than the "lower" group. Also the "high" aspirers reported experiencing more parental favoritism toward a brother or sister. Finally, the "high" aspirers more frequently described their childhood as having a higher degree of dissatisfaction than did the "low" aspirers. The authors conclude that their study supports some of the current assumptions in the psychoanalytic literature that "Unsatisfactory interpersonal relationships in the family orientation were significantly related to high aspirational levels and satisfactory relationships were related to lower aspirational levels."[38]

Indirect evidence that upward mobility is related to particular personality needs is obtained by combining Warner and Abegglen's findings of the most and least mobile industries with some results reported by Argyris. Warner and Abegglen report that the electrical machinery, oil, and gas industries have the highest degree of mobility, whereas banking houses, brokerages, and dealerships the least mobility. One might hypothesize that people who are active, independent, and who want to adapt by climbing the ladder will feel the greatest frustration in the banking and brokerage fields, whereas the more passive and dependent people would find such an organization satisfying. Argyris,[39] in a study of three banks, reports that the banks seem to hire a "right type," which on the surface is predisposed to being quiet, passive, obedient, cautious, and careful. Depth interviewing reveals more latent characteristics of (1) strong desire for security, stability, predictability in their lives, (2) strong desire to be left alone and to work in relative isolation, and (3) a strong dislike of aggressiveness and/or hostility in themselves and in others. Argyris further notes that the organization has a number of "control mechanisms" on the management level (the officers doing the hiring), on the informal group level (the work norms of the groups), and on the individual level (the personalities of the majority of the employees), which inhibit a highly aggressive mobile person from entering the system and which help to get rid of him from the bank if somehow he does enter. Thus it seems that there is a social control mechanism that induces the "right type" to go to the bank, and a series of organizational control mechanisms that keep the "right type at the bank." This tends to prevent much frustration that might exist because of the low mobility rate in banking. It also tends to create difficult communications problems between officers and employees, a low standard of production, a negative attitude toward officers, and a norm that "a bank is a good place to work because people let you alone and you don't have to work too hard."

The Use of Defense Mechanisms.[40] The third mode of adaptation, the use of defense mechanisms, is perhaps the least explored. As we have seen in Chapter II, in a defense reaction the individual distorts or denies the "facts" in order that he may live in some sort of equilibrium with himself and his environment. Systematic research is so meager in this area that our illustrations are mostly abstracted anecdotal accounts obtained from field research.[41] We present a few:

a. To *rationalize* the fact that they are not accomplishing what they know the company requires. For example (one operator to another) "Take it easy—don't work too hard; this outfit has plenty of dough. They don't need whatever you give them by breaking your ass." Or, "I know the company doesn't want me to work too fast; I can get all worn out." (typist-secretary). Or (piece rate employee), "Well, they don't need those extra pieces until Monday anyway. Why should I knock myself out?"

b. To *project* their feelings upon others. They may blame them and ignore their own part in the problem.

For example (foreman), "It's those goddamned budgets. If I didn't have those on my neck, I'd have no problem—absolutely none." Or (an order department clerk), "Have you ever tried to keep the sales orders straight with the self-centered thickheads we have for selesmen? All they think of is themselves." Or (a production manager), "The basic problem we have here is that everything we produce is custom-made. We ain't got no long runs like most other plants. We have to be careful of every order." Or (a piece-rate worker), "To hell with it," he said, "let the day man run 'em. He likes 'em. He turned in nine dollars today."

"You've got time to make another dollar yourself," I said.

"To hell with that job!" Gus exclaimed. "I'm not going to bust my neck any more on it! Let the day man run it."[42]

Another example is found in a recent study of a hospital which reports that the nurses partially adapt to their own inability to be what they believe is an effective administrator by projecting their limitations upon the administrative staff of the hospital. As one nurse describes it:

"If you ask me, administration doesn't even know we exist. If they did, they would get busy and solve the many annoying administrative difficulties we have. Just take scheduling. They haven't been able to solve that at O.R. (operating room) or X-ray or the chemical laboratories. If you want to help us nurses, please go upstairs and make administrators out of them."[43]

Finally, workers may defend their resistance to increased mechanization or to the way management is handling the change by blaming increased technology for unemployment.[44] Centers finds that blaming technology for unemployment increases as one goes toward the lower levels of the organization.[45]

c. To be *ambivalent*. "I cannot make up my mind. I like the job—yet I don't. I like the company—yet I'd leave. I don't know what it is, except I know it ain't the boss or the pay" (a clerk-typist). "I run hot and cold about this outfit."

"I can't seem to make up my mind if I should stay or ask for a transfer" (tool and die maker).

RESEARCHER: "What kinds of things do you like and dislike about the company?"

WORKER: "I like the pay; I like the management—I think they're trying to be fair. But I don't like not being my own boss. I want to be my own boss, I guess. Here you've got to be on a schedule. You're always working under pressure for someone else."

d. To *escape from reality*. An increasingly used defense against nonsatisfying work is for the individual to detach himself from his work.[46, 47, 48, 49] For example, a group of adolescent girls learned to use certain semi-automatic bookkeeping equipment.[50] "Without advance notice," as one girl put it, "you suddenly realize you can work and at the same time think of a million other things.

You know what I mean, daydream. You feel free." This phenomenon of daydreaming is true for all girls studied to varying degrees.
Some girls do quite extensive daydreaming while others do a lesser
amount. Although enough cases of the latter are not available,
speculation suggests that these girls (1) are of lower intelligence,
or (2) have personalities which do not require too much emotional
expression, or (3) are apathetic about their work. The mastery
of the machines seems to occur when the girl is able to use the
machine but think of a million other things excepting the
machines.

The reader might immediately wonder if the daydreaming
affects the girls' accuracy. In all the cases the reply "no" may be
given quickly and definitely. All girls except one make it a point
to mention that the most accurate work is done when they are
thinking about activities *other* than their work. The two working
supervisors confirm these results.

The subjects of their daydreams are varied, usually, consisting
of personal occurrences or daydreams of rather long romantic
travels, or daydreams related to romantic jobs. Interestingly enough,
concerning travels, some of the girls take their cue as to what
country they are going to go to "this morning" from the music
which is piped into the bookkeeping department. We may obtain
an indication of sorts of things the girls think about in the quotations presented below.

The mastery of the machine actually means that the person
gains the ability to separate herself from the function. It is as
though she acquires the ability to compartmentalize herself and
keep away from, as one of the girls put it, "a machine that's as cold
as a cucumber and couldn't possibly have a heart."

It wasn't long before I got the hang of it. Then life became bearable.
For one thing, I got onto the knack of daydreaming. (Blushes) You know
you may think I'm loony or something but we all daydream. I come into
the job and think about the things that are worrying me, or I think about
other things. I didn't realize I was posting. This would go on for hours,
the less thinking I do on my job, the less errors I make. As soon as I
concentrate on my job, I make errors.

The music helps, it helps an awful lot.

No, there's no limit to what I think. Mostly, you know, personal things. I dream as long as I'm posting. I'm accurate as long as I'm not thinking about the work.

It was a long time before I felt at home—six months I'd say. But it wasn't long after that when I picked up good speed. Now I can work one of those machines with no trouble. My mind is a million miles away. I guess I'll get fired for this, but honestly, I never concentrate on that machine. Every time I do, I make errors. I find that I can go on for hours being away from my work while working. It's funny, but I do it and I know other girls do it. Once in a while your mind returns to the job and you suddenly realize that you are at work. I think of most anything —my family, my life, any arguments with my husband, my girl friends, oh, just anything.

The Industrial Fatigue Research Board[51] studies in fatigue, boredom, and monotony conclude that individuals' abilities to detach themselves from their work greatly helps their adaptation to boredom and monotony. Daydreaming and mind wandering are prevalent among most of the workers studied.[52]

Fromm,[53] however, questions the implication that daydreaming indicates a healthy state. He states:

It must also be questioned whether the freedom for daydreaming and reverie which mechanized work gives is as positive and healthy a factor as most industrial psychologists assume. Actually, daydreaming is a symptom of lacking relatedness to reality. It is not refreshing or relaxing—it is essentially an escape with all the negative results that go with escape.

e. To develop psychosomatic illnesses. Another type of defensive mechanism which has hardly been studied is the one by which the individual transforms a psychological problem into a physiological one. On the top management level, ulcers is a well-known psychosomatic disease. On the employee level, there is increasing evidence that employees are developing dubious backaches, headaches, and run-down feelings, to adapt to anxieties they tend to experience on the job.[54]

Individual Apathy and Noninvolvement. Apathy, lack of interest, and noninvolvement are types of defense mechanisms that may be becoming so popular that they require special emphasis.

The basis of these defenses, we have pointed out, is the continuous frustration, conflict, and failure an employee experiences.

Let us picture an employee whom we may call Dick. He works on an assembly line and finds that he cannot obtain minimal personality expression on his job. He is frustrated. From the studies of frustration it is hypothesized that Dick will tend to regress to a more childlike state.[55] He will not be as "mature" as he was before he was frustrated. This "primitivation" (regression) of his personality may cause him (1) to leave the situation, (2) to try to change the work situation constructively or destructively, (3) to accept (internalize) the tension and "hang on," i.e., keep working.

If Dick accepts the third possible course,[56] he places himself in a difficult situation. On the one hand, his predisposition for health and maturity puts pressure on him to leave. He feels his *own* pressure to leave. On the other hand, if he decides to stay,[57] *he must create new self-pressures to overcome the ones caused by his own desire to leave and to remain healthy*. Dick is surrounded by his *own* pressures. He may blame management for creating the assembly line world but he also knows they are not *forcing* him to stay. He is forcing himself to stay. If he blames anyone for being where he is, he blames himself. The tension that builds up tends to increase his human ineffectiveness. Recent research suggests quite clearly that such tension leads to a decrease in self-confidence,[58] an increase in aggression,[59] and regression.[60]

One way for Dick to defend himself is to reduce the psychological importance of the work situation. He may say (unconsciously) in effect, "To hell with it; I am not going to permit myself to become involved. Why should I pressure myself to leave and to stay? Why should all this mean so much to me? I'll do just enough to get by. I'll block up my need for self-actualization until I get out of work. Then I will live!"

This is not an easy decision for Dick to make. The existing research suggests that the younger employee may "fight" succumbing to conflict, frustration, and failure in such a manner for at least one to two and as many as three years. A recent comprehensive review of job attitude research concludes that while the young workers generally start out their careers with relatively high morale, the first few years of work for many of them present a serious problem of declining satisfaction. Workers in the age period from the middle twenties through the early thirties usually have lower morale than at any other age.[61] Chinoy,[62] in an analysis of worker aspirations, concludes that once they have become married and middle-aged, workers begin to accept their fate, do not fight the job, and realize that there is no future for them in the traditional sense.

There is ample evidence to show that adaptation by becoming apathetic is increasing on the individual level and spreading to the group level. Focusing on the individual level, a number of studies corroborate the prediction. Dahlstrom,[63] as a result of an intensive study of a large organization, reports the existence of worker apathy. One of his major conclusions, a strong correlation between apathy and the degree to which the job is specialized and standardized, illustrates the hypothesis derived from this analysis. Davis and Josselyn, in their study of how individual employees increase work stoppages, clearly relate the decrease in production to the personal motivation of the employee. They state:

The operator uses the same work methods and continues to work at the same rate of speed whenever the operation is performed, *but introduces more and longer work stoppages as the day progresses.* Since the major part of the work stoppages are personal delays *directly controlled by the operator,* this may explain how productivity is increased under conditions of high motivation. *Accordingly, increases in productivity would result from decreasing personal delays, not from decreasing the effective operation time.*[64]

Davis and Josselyn report that cumulative loss in productive working time is about 30 per cent. Delays and work stoppages increase significantly as the day progresses. During the afternoons there tends to be a significant increase in personal delays, work stoppages, time away from work. These delays and work stoppages cluster about the operation's natural stopping points. Thus we see that operators do find the opportunity to regulate the speed with which they work and that the speed is not only a function of the nature of the job but also the individual's level of aspiration with regard to such criteria as personal satisfaction or sense of achievement.[65]

Argyris suggests that employees cannot completely block up their need for self-actualization while at work. However, he hypothesizes that they may decrease the number of their needs they want to express while at work. It is as if the employee consciously reasons, "O.K., if I am going to work in a situation that prevents need satisfactions, then I will decrease the possibility for, and the degree of, frustration and conflict by decreasing the number of needs that I expect to have fulfilled while working on the job." If the dissatisfaction continues, the employee can take another step. He can reason, "Since decreasing the *number* of needs is not enough, I will also decrease the *psychological importance* these needs have for me, while working in this organization." To use the personality theory presented previously, the employee blocks the expression of *inner* needs and emphasizes the expression of peripheral or skin-surface needs. This leads to work becoming colorless, uninteresting, and non-ego-involving. Fromm suggests:

. . . there are good reasons for the widespread belief in man's innate laziness. The main reason lies in the fact that alienated work is boring and unsatisfactory; that a great deal of tension and hostility is engendered, which leads to an aversion against the work one is doing and everything connected with it.[66]

In a series of three organizational analyses including a total of nearly 400 employees, Argyris reports:

1. Excluding management (anyone above first-line supervision), the total number of different needs (basic *and* skin-surface) expressed by all the employees studied in three different organizations was only 22.

2. With the exception of two needs, not one was ranked by 40 per cent of the employees as being of extremely high importance; the overwhelming majority of the needs fell in the category of "regular importance."

3. The two exceptions occurred in a particular department of one organization where the employees worked under difficult conditions. In this case the two needs that were rated as being of ex-

tremely high importance were a resultant of the employees' attempt to adapt to the abnormal work situation.

These results hold true irrespective of age, sex, and kinds of leadership and are obtained in situations where over 90 per cent of the employees report they do *not* have any close friends within the working force and where almost no need for "group belongingness" is mentioned. It seems safe to infer, therefore, that the critical factors causing the apathy and noninvolvement are related to organizational structure and workflow (i.e., the job).

An analysis of the kinds of needs expressed by employees adds additional evidence. The employees seem to need to be left alone, to be isolated, to be passive. These needs provide excellent motivation for the employee to become apathetic and noninvolved.

a. Self-responsibility—wants to be his own boss, receive minimal supervision, and be willingly his own policeman.

b. Passivity—prefers to receive directions from others.

c. Isolation—wants to work independently from others.

d. Variety—prefers many different kinds of workflow activities.

e. Security—wishes a fairly constant, predictable position as regards his job, his working world, his future.[67]

In a recent study of employees in a large utility, Jackson confirmed these trends. He found that the majority of employees studied preferred jobs that are routine, have relative predictability, and do *not* require initiative and adaptability and the possibility of unpleasant interpersonal relationships with customers.[68]

Dubin,[69] in a study of 491 workers, reported that three out of four employees do not perceive their jobs and work places as central life interests for themselves. These results jibe with those of Argyris, who cites evidence that employees do not tend to see the organizational context as a place to express important needs. Dubin continued by suggesting that the results imply "the factory as a locale for living out a lifetime seems clearly secondary to other areas of central life interests."

In a study conducted by the Survey Research Center 82 per cent of 1000 employees reported they were satisfied, yet only 28 per cent thought they had a fairly good or very good chance to get ahead.[70]

Fromm describes the impact of apathy, lack of interest and isolation upon the employee as follows:

What happens to the industrial worker? He spends his best energy for seven or eight hours a day in producing 'something.' He needs his work in order to make a living, but his role is essentially a passive one. He fulfills a small isolated function in a complicated and highly organized process of production, and is never confronted with 'his' product as a whole, at least not as a producer, but only as a consumer, provided he has the money to buy 'his' product in a store. He is concerned neither with the whole product in its physical aspects nor with its wider economic and social aspects. He is put in a certain place, has to carry out a certain task, but does not participate in the organization of management of the work. He is not interested, nor does he know why one produces this instead of another commodity—what relation it has to the needs of society as a whole. The shoes, the cars, the electric bulbs, are produced by 'the enterprise' using the machines. He is part of the machine, rather than its master as an active agent. The machine, instead of being in his service to do work for him which once had to be performed by sheer physical energy, has become his master. Instead of the machine being the substitute for human energy, man has become a substitute for the machine. *His work can be defined as the performance of acts which cannot yet be performed by machines.*[71]

Experimental evidence suggests that if individuals reduce the number and potency of the needs that they expect a particular group (in this case management) to satisfy, they will also tend to feel less positive toward the group.[72] Thus this mode of adaptation may be one which helps cause the lack of identification that management increasingly implies employees manifest.

One would expect, on the basis of this analysis, that the opposite trend should be found in management. They should express high involvement and require many of their important needs to be fulfilled while at work. This prediction would follow because the fundamental conflict is hypothesized to *decrease* as one goes up the chain of command. The data support the hypothesis. The number and degree of importance of needs that management representatives expect to express and actually do express while at work increases. In a recent study, 10 top managers expressed as many different needs as did the 400 employees. Moreover, 75 per cent of these needs are classified as having "high" or "extremely high" importance.

An analysis of the kind of needs expressed by top management, shows the following to be most frequently expressed:

a. Directive—initiating action for others.

b. Variety—prefers many and different kinds of workflow activities.

c. Challenge-accepting—accepting work which represents a challenge to the intellectual abilities.

d. Problem-solving-minded—continually solving administrative problems and creating new solutions.

e. Success seeking—achieving goals quickly and successfully. There is a tendency to overwork in order to reach the goal.

f. Organizatonally upward mobile—tending to advance in the organizational hierarchy.

B. Group Adaptation

The individual adapts to the impact of the organization[73] by any one or some combination of: (1) leaving the organization, (2) climbing the organizational ladder, (3) using defensive mechanisms, and 4) becoming apathetic and disinterested. These are all adaptive mechanisms and therefore need fulfilling. People will want to maintain these adaptive behaviors.

In order to guarantee their existence, the individual seeks group sanctions. The informal work groups are "organized" to perpetuate these adaptive processes (to reward those employees who follow the informal codes and to penalize those who do not). The individual adaptive acts now become sanctioned by the group, and therefore feed back to reinforce the continuance of the individual need-fulfilling adaptive behavior.

As previously mentioned, one plant manager colorfully described the degree of apathy when he said, "The trouble with the workers today is that 5 per cent work, 10 per cent think they work, and 85 per cent would rather die than work!" Although the research does not confirm these figures, there is clear evidence to suggest such a trend. An increasing number of workers are expressing the attitude, "Take-it-easy; don't-burn-yourself-out; the-company-will-be-here-tomorrow." If this is true, why is it so? It is hypothesized that employees, especially in the lower levels working at repetitive tasks, will tend to experience frustration, conflict, and failure. The conflict tends to arise because the employees want to be creative, active, and independent, but they cannot. One way to reduce the conflict is for the employee to decide not to be creative, active, and independent while at work. This leads to a state of apathy toward the work. Knowing that psychological energy varies with the state of mind of the individual, we may predict low productivity once this psychological state sets in. Thus the conflict is minimized at the expense of organizational and individual productivity.

The frustration, we have seen, can be reduced by aggression. Aggression is harming the object that is perceived as causing the frustration. Thus the employees may become hostile and aggressive toward management or toward anyone perceived to be the cause of their frustration or anyone supporting those who are perceived to be the cause.

Unlike the other two defense mechanisms, it is much more difficult to reduce psychological failure. The best way is to experience psychological success. However, this is not often possible, since by the nature of the formal work situation someone else is defining the production goals, the strength of the barriers to be overcome, and so forth. The adaptive activities, such as aggression and apathy, lead to future failure. The former makes the individual tense, which reduces his capabilities, which in turn increases his chances for failure; the latter induces the individual to reduce his level of aspiration so much that accomplishing a particular goal does not lead to success. As is reported above, people experiencing failure may tend to lose interest in their work; lower their standards of achievement; lose confidence in themselves; give up quickly, lose persistency; fear new tasks and refuse new methods; expect failure; escape by daydreaming; and develop a tendency to blame others.[74, 75]

The resultants of psychological failure, therefore, feed back and reinforce the other two defense mechanisms of aggression and apathy.

Quota Restriction, Goldbricking, and Slowdown on the Group

Level.[76] Restricting production, goldbricking, and slowdown are understandable resultants of apathy, aggression, and failure. They are admirably suited for "getting even" with management while simultaneously reducing one's efforts.[77]

Using the concept of psychological failure, Roy's[78] following findings on group production restriction become explainable. Roy reports:

During over half of his productive time he reduced his effort to much below his own accepted maximum. There were only few occasions that he tried to "make out" (lost interest in work and lower standards of achievement).

Like his fellow operators, he tried out a job for *short* sampling periods and gave up almost immediately if the job was not easy. (Lose persistency and give up quickly.)

Many times trial runs were never attempted if he was forewarned that the job was a "stinker." "Why bust my ass?" is a representative attitude (give up quickly).

However, if Roy's data are representative, the picture may not be as bleak as it sounds. Roy describes a number of occasions where he and others "worked like hell for short periods of time," not necessarily to gain more money, but "to play a game" in order to "overcome boredom."

"Free" time is another occasion when the individual might obtain some psychological success. The free time accumulated by the men as a result of goldbricking is guarded carefully. This is one segment of their work day which *they* control; when they can behave as they desire. Apparently, apathy, lack of interest, and a low level of aspiration have become so much a part of the employees and their culture that when given an opportunity they use their leisure time in creating nonconstructive, passive, non-ego-involving activities. This behavior is quite common for people experiencing psychological failure. Dalton and Roy[79] report that most employees may be observed "shooting the breeze," or "reading newspapers in the toilets." The only creative work observed was "government work," which consisted of making illegal devices and pictures to short-cut production or to repair parts damaged by men in other departments so that repair tickets might be avoided, and making equipment for their autos and homes.

The frequency of occurrence of quota restriction, goldbricking, and slowdowns is documented by several studies. Beginning with Roy, we note that waste time in his plant lasted from 3 to 6 hours a working day. Roy himself hit his peak when he worked 3½ hours out of 8.

The representative attitude of the worker seemed to be "They're not going to get much work out of me for this pay." If the piece rates continued to be low and if the jobs came often and were long, the employees continued to systematically slow down their production by "dogging it along."

Roy summarizes some of his conclusions on the influence of the group to induce him to slowdown and goldbrick as follows:

I was able to speculate with some objective evidence on the degree of slowdown goldbricking practiced on non-make-out piecework. It was pointed out that four drill operators had been restricting production at a rate of 3.5 waste hours out of 8, as indicated by the output achieved by one of the four men when he ceased goldbricking. Efficiency had been 56 per cent, with immediate possibilities for a 78 per cent production increase. Renunciation of goldbricking did not, in this particular case, mean fulfillment of possibilities, however; for the conversion was to quota restriction with stabilization at 75 per cent efficiency.

In addition, I essayed an estimate on daywork goldbricking, first cousin to piece work goldbricking and easily mistaken for the latter. This estimate was obtained by comparing output on a job before and after it was timed. The 'before' efficiency was determined to be at least as low as 40 per cent, possibly 35 per cent, with 150 per cent improvement in production a 'cinch' and 186 per cent improvement an immediate possibility. But like the case of piecework goldbricking just cited, the switch was to quota restriction; so possibilities were never realized.

Roy[80] also indicates the possible severity of rate setting and slowdown as follows:

I have indicated that the 'wasted' on my own quota restriction for a six-month period was 1.39 hours out of every 8. I was 83 per cent 'efficient' for the 469.6 quota piecework hours put in, by my own standards of performance, and thus could have increased production by 21 per cent by abandoning quota limitations. If my wastage of 2 hours a day on quota restriction during the last two months of employment is accepted as characteristic of the behavior of more seasoned operators, efficiency would be 75 per cent, with immediate possibilities for a 33.3 per cent increase in production on quota jobs. Also, by experimenting with twenty jobs which represented 58 per cent of the total piecework hours put in during a ten-month period, and which offered earning possibilities beyond quota limits, I derived an estimate of "potential quota restriction" of 2.9 hours a day. This restriction represented an efficiency of 64 per cent, with possibilities for a 57 per cent increase in production.

Moore,[81] summarizing ten years of attitude measurement by the Industrial Relations Center at the University of Chicago, concludes that worker enthusiasm and motivation are not high. One-third of the American workers are apathetic and indifferent about their work and their relations with the company. Production workers typically show a lack of interest in the company as a whole.[82]

Renck, reporting on research involving 4,345 semiskilled production workers in 14 companies states,[83]

"The feelings and attitudes of production workers toward their work situation are at best lukewarm. They do not have strong feelings of involvement and integration with the company as it is true of Executives and First-Line Supervisors."

Brown[84] believes that worker apathy, disinterest, and resistance to change are so great that they are key factors in preventing England from increasing her national income (without additional capital). He suggests that if the employee apathy decreased England could increase her national income by one-half within a five-year period. Brown also cites research in America and England which shows that employee attitudes of apathy and indifference were key factors in production. Controlling for technology, type of product, availability of raw material, number of employees and management, the production time for a particular boat varied in shipyards from 60 to 200 days.

Turning to the employees' own reports, in a poll conducted by the Opinion Research Corporation in 1945, 49 per cent of all the manual workers interviewed answered that a man should produce as much as he can but 41 per cent answered he should *not* do his best, but only "turn out the average amount."[85]

Drucker[86] confirms the existence of output restriction among workers. Mathewson[87] presents evidence for its existence among office employees and even among executives. He concludes that "restriction is a widespread institution, deeply entrenched in the working habits of American labouring people," and that "underwork and restriction are greater problems than overspeeding and overwork," and finally, "the efforts of managers to speed up working people have been offset by the ingenuity of the workers in developing restrictive practices."[88]

One important consequence of apathy is to *decrease* the possible conflict and failure that an employee might feel if he deviates from the codes and policies defined by management. As long as these codes have little potency for the employee, he will tend not to feel hesitant or guilty about breaking them. Recent research by Rosmussen and Zander[89] and Stotland, Thorley, and Zander[90, 91] illustrate this result. They find that feelings of failure for deviating from group norms are decreased if strength of attraction to group is low and if the particular issue is not important to the group members.

Another interesting consequence of apathy, lack of interest, and aggression in the employee culture is that it may act to influence the type of individuals who ultimately become shop stewards and foremen.

Lieberman[92] found that employees who were selected to be foremen and stewards did not hold positive pro-management or pro-union attitudes, respectively. If anything, they were anti-management and anti-union, respectively. Lieberman explains their selection on demographic grounds (i.e., the men were more able, more upward mobile and more stable). However, another possibility may be that the men selected mirrored the apathy, noninvolvement, and aggression "in" the employee culture toward management and toward their union in such a way that the employees had confidence enough to select them (in case of the stewards) or to accept them (in the case of the foremen). There is ample research to suggest that "natural" leaders tend to be perceived by their group as being aware of their needs and capable of fulfilling them.

CONTINUING EDUC.
CONFERENCE LIBRARY

According to our analysis, this apathy, noninvolvement, and aggression "in" the employee culture are due to the dependence, subordination, and so forth that the employees (or union members) experience. It also follows from the framework that the dependence and subordination should decrease as one goes up the chain of command. Thus, one would expect as the employees became foremen or stewards their opportunity for self-actualization would increase. The increase in self-actualization, in turn would tend to decrease the necessity for apathy, noninvolvement, and aggression. If this occurs, the negative feelings toward management and/or the union leaders should decrease. Lieberman reports that as soon as the employees accept and play the role of the foremen or stewards, they do acquire pro-management and pro-union attitudes, respectively.

The logics of formal organization seem lost when one immerses himself in these data. As Whyte suggests, the majority of the employees do not tend to follow the values set by management that:

a. Workers will make an all-out response to incentives.
b. Workers will work at a normal pace when they are being time-studied. When proper study methods are used, there will be no intergroup problem because
c. There will be no tight and no loose rates, and
d. The nonincentive worker will accept the extra money received by incentive workers as compensation for extra effort.[93]

There are, however, a few employees who do tend to behave according to the management logic. They are called rate-busters in the literature and all sorts of profane names in real life. Workers dislike rate-busters, and rate-busters apparently have little love for the workers.

Homans[94] points out that employees hold strong feelings toward rate-busters and rate-busting. In the groups studied, there existed clearly defined upper and lower limits of work. Anyone who exceeded the upper limits (and thereby worked in accordance with the incentive engineer's design) was a rate-buster. Rate-busters were definitely disliked and pressure was brought upon them by the use of physical force, sarcasm, the use of invectives, and group ostracism.

Some of the informal group norms that arose were:

You should not turn out too much work. If you do, you are a 'rate-buster.'

You should not turn out too little work. If you do, you are a 'chiseler.'

You should not tell a supervisor anything that will react to the detriment of an associate. If you do, you are a 'squealer.'

You should not attempt to maintain social distance or act officious. If you are an inspector, for example, you should not act like one.

Rate-busters tend to follow management's assumptions and "make all-out responses to incentives." Interestingly, the research of Dalton and Roy[95] suggests that rate-busters tend to (1) behave aggressively and with hostility towards others; (2) be rigid, narrow-minded, and prejudiced; (3) mistrust most of the employees with whom they work; and (4) behave in an asocial manner.

The employees reciprocate with intense dislike of the rate-buster. He is ostracized and kept in almost complete isolation. One employee describes a rate-buster as follows:

He can't get along with men. He's so damned overbearing and domineering that he couldn't get along with Jesus Christ himself. He treated his men like dogs, and tried to treat his superiors the same way. There's nothing he can't do on a lathe, though. We couldn't replace him.

Two others are described by two of their fellow workers in the following manner:

Look at Richter over there! He's so damned worried about how much bonus he's going to get that he can't act like a human being. I wouldn't be in the shape he is for an extra thousand a year.

Pat is killing himself. He said during the war that he was working hard because of his two sons in the service. That's a damn lie. Look at him now —still working like hell! And did you ever see the kind of work he turns out? He can't do a decent job. I wouldn't be guilty of finishing work the way he does.

Thus the men whose behavior is *closest* to the assumptions made by the formal organization tend to be disliked, asocial, prejudiced, and rigid.

Formalizing Small Groups (Trade Unions). Up to now we note that the individual adapts on the psychological level and on the small informal group level. The latter are initially created to sanction and therefore perpetuate those activities that the work group on any level of the organization finds need-fulfilling.

However, if the company decides to disband the informal activities, in the final analysis they could be defended by the employees only by threatening to do harm to the productive process (e.g., strike, slow down). Such measures are not easily used and the psychological and financial costs on both sides are high.

Management's formal power is basically derived by making the employees dependent on management for their rewards, directions, positions, and so forth.[96] It follows logically from the above that one way for the employees to reduce their dependence is to take away some of the management's formal authority and place it within their own control. According to Coleman[97] this is an important basis for the rise of trade unions. As McGregor[98] states, "And to the extent to which unions have attempted to place restrictions upon management's authority reflects not only a desire for power, but a conscious attempt to reduce the dependence of the workers upon their bosses." McGregor cites Brooks[99] and a Twentieth Century Fund study[100] as supporting evidence.[101] Bakke[102] reports that workers join unions when they are frustrated in and anxious about their fulfillment of such basic needs as the desire to have independence in and control over their own affairs, understanding and predicting the forces at work in their world, a feeling of integrity, and a minimal degree of creature comforts.

In order to create trade unions, the employees must reach *outside* the organization into the political world, where their power and managements (due to our political system) is, man for man, equal. Once trade unions come to existence, the employees can sanction many of their informal activities through the formal power residing in the union as an organization.

The employees now live between two sets of dependencies. They depend upon both management and the trade union leaders. Theoretically, the critical difference is that the former dependence is mandatory while the latter is voluntary. In actual practice, however, it is common knowledge that trade unions are becoming increasingly formalized and routinized. Many have already reached the stage where a primary objective is to maintain themselves internally and adapt to their external environment.

In order to do this, the unions tend to organize themselves by creating a formal organization whose structure is based upon the principles of chain of command, unity of direction, task specialization and span of control. The moment this occurs, they become, in administrative make-up (not necessarily in philosophy) similar to other industrial organizations. The members become dependent, passive, and subordinate to their trade union officers. To the extent that they desire to actualize themselves in the trade union organization, they will be frustrated and experience conflict and failure. Once this occurs, the adaptive behavior predicted above in relation to the formal industrial structure can be predicted to manifest itself in the union.

Evidence that these adaptive behaviors may be found in trade union locals is increasingly becoming available. Rosen and Rosen[103] in a recent study of trade union organization point up the fact that trade union members are increasingly finding the initiation of decisions and enforcement of policy to be turned over to the new full-time paid union leaders. Neufeld goes as far as to describe these leaders as a new managerial class. To be sure, the degree of control exercised by the trade union leadership varies with locals and may even vary within the same local.[104] Not all unions are bureaucratically bound. Some do have a high degree of democracy.[105, 106] Nevertheless, the trend seems to be definitely toward greater bureaucratization.[107, 108] Lipset,[109] Kopald,[110] Howe and Widick,[111] Hardman,[112] Taft,[113, 114, 115] and Shister[116] are other researchers who conclude that slowly but surely the trade unions are becoming more bureaucratic (i.e., organizing themselves according to the principles of formal organization) so that decision-making and decision-implementing are increasingly centralized in and controlled by the officers. Coleman provides evidence that trade union leaders are becoming bureaucratically oriented when he concludes that the most frequent ideal held by leaders related to why members should attend the meetings is that, "The meeting will produce an attentive audience, receptive to reports from the leadership and active only when activity can be directed elsewhere than against the leadership."[117]

As is hypothesized above, as bureaucratization increases, the trade unions should be faced with the same human problems as is management. For example, one should find apathy, lack of interest, goldbricking, and lack of ego-involvement.

In a study of six locals in the Cleveland, Ohio area, Miller and Young[118] conclude that the most prevalent attitude toward the union was uninterested allegiance and acceptance.

But this acceptance or allegiance usually does not carry with it a willingness to give of time and effort which would contribute to a better understanding of the problems and result in a more effective member role in the functioning of the group in its efforts to solve its problem.

"Let George do it" seems to typify the attitude of most union members when the expenditure of effort for the union comes before them; such members are quite willing to accept benefits resulting from the efforts of others.[119]

Miller and Rosen[119A] in a study of attitudes toward shop stewards confirm these results.

There are some who suggest that member apathy and uninterest in local union meetings (when contract negotiations are not imminent) are signs of confidence in the trade union leadership and not, as is suggested above, resultants of the impact of the organizational structure.[120] This may be the case, but it may also be the case that:

a. The members have confidence in the union leaders to handle justly relatively less important routine activities. However, when it comes to something very important, like contract negotiations or grievances, attendance increases.

b. The members do *not* have confidence in the trade union

leaders, but *do* have confidence in management *not* to take any unjust or underhanded actions.

c. The members have confidence in *both* management and trade union leaders.

Unfortunately, there are few empirical studies to test these hypotheses. Rosen and Rosen, however, report indirect evidence to illustrate the first hypothesis. "Union members seem to want unionism to be primarily job oriented as indicated both by their apparent lack of enthusiasm for union political action and by their concern with discussion of shop problems.[121]

Recently, in studies conducted by Purcell, Stagner, and Kerr, support for the third hypothesis has been found. Purcell,[122] in a three-year study where 385 packinghouse workers, foremen, and union leaders were interviewed, reported:

... The rank and file workers want *both* their company and union to coexist.

The desire for a union is so great that "Even while opposing their leaders, they (workers) would not think of being without their union. Seventy-five per cent tenaciously hold on to their union allegiance. Nor do Swift's advanced personnel policies woo them away from it.

Stagner, after extensive research in eight establishments reported: "We were at once impressed with the fact that those establishments ranking high in percentage of responses favorable to the company also ranked high in responses favorable to the union."[123]

Finally, Kerr states:

Mutual emotional acceptance and cooperation between management and union had tended to structure employees' satisfaction attitudes along integrated rather than divisive lines. Evidence for this is a positive Pearsonian coefficient of correlation between the total scores on the management-oriented ballot and the union-oriented ballot of .74. Connected for attenuation, this value increases to unity, suggesting that personnel no longer carry "either-or" exclusive allegiance attitudes.[124]

In short, there is evidence that the apathy of trade union members can be caused by the organizational structure of the union.

Summarizing to this point:

1) There is a fundamental incongruence between the demands of the organization and the needs of healthy individuals.

2) Employees may adapt to the conflict by a number of measures, one of which is to create informal groups to reduce the degree of dependency upon management.

3) Once informal groups prove useful, the employees will want to perpetuate them by formalizing them, thus giving rise to trade unionism.

4) Trade unionism, in order to maintain itself, must organize. Basically, it organizes itself in the same way as does management.

5) To the extent that formal organizational principles are used,[125] the trade union leaders will experience with its members the same problems management is experiencing with its employees (e.g., apathy and lack of interest).

6) It is important for an adminstrator to be aware that, according to this scheme, trade unions are adaptive mechanisms. They exist because workers are trying to achieve the organization's goals in spite of the dependence, passivity, and submissiveness that they experience.[126]

Emphasis on Monetary and Other Material Rewards. Implicit in the above material is a causal trend from the conflict of the individual and organization to increased feelings of apathy, lack of interest, goldbricking, and rate-setting. These resultants are all predictable ways of adaptation based upon psychological research. There is a definite trend, therefore, that dissatisfied workers will tend to decrease the psychological importance of their work and emphasize the material aspects.

This leads to the proposition that increasingly the employees will not "use" work as an area from which to get satisfaction. They will tend to feel, as one employee put it, "Let's get our $1.92 an hour and live *outside*" of the work situation. Thus money becomes important not only because it provides the necessities of life but because it is a symbol (unconscious) of being paid off by management for being required to work under unsatisfactory conditions.

Blum[127] gives evidence of the desire to get away from work and "live" outside. He finds that workers are anxious to leave their work. They rush out of the plants making certain they do not lose a minute when "quitting time" comes. Most employees report that they work in the plant in order to make money "to live" outside.

An unusual experimental study that taps factors in "depth" with a relatively large sample (219 women in seven factories in Sweden) provides more evidence for the increasing importance of money. Smith and Lund report that employees are not necessarily aware of their own inner needs. Money is a factor used by many to rationalize their lack of self-satisfaction on the job. Thus the women studied *overemphasized* the importance of money for them, whereas they deemphasized their need for satisfying human relationships, which is exactly what we predict. Because of the conditions described previously, the workers will tend to deemphasize the importance of human relationships and for them substitute and put emphasis on money.

... While most female workers tended to overemphasize the importance of "payment" and similar factors they often were not conscious of the problem of personal relationship, and dissatisfaction with the latter was partly projected into accepted scapegoats of complaint.[128]

Ling, Wilson, and Briggs[129] provide further evidence. A sample of 139 male and female workers was studied to determine the degree of readjustment to work after medical psychiatric rehabilitation. They report that of the workers who were not able to obtain need satisfactions from their present jobs (21 per cent of the total sample) but who were working full time (most of them to the satisfaction of their employers), all felt most strongly the lack of job security and dissatisfaction with the pay. The researchers conclude, "The sub-group (of dissatisfied workers) emphasize more the material aspects of work like the pay, the conditions of work, and the welfare amenities, and less the social and emotional factors." These results confirm previous conclusions that workers who are not satisfied tend to pin their hopes on the material aspects of work.[130] Chinoy[131] concludes that automobile workers by the time they reach middle age realize that their jobs are not and never will be satisfying, and that advancement for them will be difficult. They adapt, he reports, by placing an even greater emphasis on employment, security, constant increases in wages, and the increased consumption of material goods. Moreover, he confirms the Ling-Wilson-Briggs studies when he reports that workers who could have left their jobs for new ones which would increase their sense of independence and control did not. They rationalized their weaknesses and lack of motivation by blaming management, "the times," and many other institutions that govern the pursuit of wealth.

Friedman and Havighurst,[132] in a study of over 600 steel workers, miners, sales persons, skilled workers, and doctors, conclude that, "Workers at the lower skill and socio-economic levels regard their work more frequently as merely a way to earn a living and in general recognize fewer extra-financial meanings in their work than do workers of high skill and socio-economic levels." It is important to note that it was primarily the unskilled workers who saw money as the primary reason for work. This is consistent with our hypothesis that this phenomenon occurs primarily in employees at the lower end of the chain working at unskilled jobs. One retired worker describes the situation bluntly in his answer to the following question:

Q: Was there anything you liked about the job?
A: No, I can't think of anything. It was hard, hard work and I wouldn't go through it again.
WIFE: Come, now, honey, you couldn't have worked there all those years and not found something you liked.
A: There is nothing I can think of—only the money—I couldn't think of anything else.[133]

Reigel,[134] in a study of employee interest in company success in eight corporations, notes that half of the respondents report economic incentive as the best means to increase their interest in the company, while less than one-third report human incentives.

Viteles[135] presents evidence that management reinforces the employee behavior in emphasizing money because they believe that the worker is primarily motivated by money.

Moreover, others suggest that industry fosters the importance of more money through advertising, offering easy credit, and other techniques to increase the employees' needs to buy more material goods. Thus we have a vicious cycle composed of the following components: (1) the industrial work situation frustrates the employee; (2) the employee partially responds by placing great emphasis on material rewards; (3) the unions fight to obtain these material rewards; (4) management not only gives the rewards, but (5) reinforces the importance of them through advertising campaigns, which (6) reinforces the employees' desire for still more material rewards, and we are right back where we began.

In short, there may be a new norm arising. Apathy, lack of interest, goldbricking, and lack of identification may become part of what a worker learns and expects. The workers themselves deemphasize the human aspects and overemphasize the material ones. If so, management and trade unions may be partially responsible.

In numerous cases, instead of trying to do something about the fundamental causes of apathy, management has responded by providing more material benefits, such as playgrounds, baseball teams, cafeterias, bonuses, company papers, and suggestion schemes. None of these attack the fundamental problems. On the contrary, they may help to maintain and reinforce the conflict because they "tell" the workers, "Okay, we'll do our best to make your life a happy one *outside of the immediate job environment that you experience.* In other words, we will give you all sorts of material rewards if you will please continue to produce in spite of the human difficulties that you will experience while at work."

The limitations of such a policy are illustrated by Jaques in a new report continuing depth analysis of the Glacier Metal Company. As a result of numerous observations, interviews, and group discussions (many of them on a clinical level), Jaques[136] reported that outside-the-work-situation-benefits do not substitute for frustrations caused while on the job. If a realistic attack is to be made on the human problems it must be directed at the cause, namely, the total work situation in which the employee is embedded.

If the analysis is valid, we are entering an era where the employee will be paid for his *dissatisfaction* on the job and where he will have his tendencies to become more materialistic and less human (unknowingly) reinforced by management's action. We will enter an era where, as Fromm points out:

. . . There is no frame of reference left which is manageable, observable, which is adapted to *human dimensions*. While our eyes and ears receive impressions only in humanly manageable proportions, our concept of the world has lost just that quality; it does not any longer correspond to our human dimensions. . . .[137]

Dissatisfaction, apathy, boredom, lack of joy and happiness, a sense of futility and vague feeling that life is meaningless, are the unavoidable results of this situation. *This socially patterned syndrome of pathology may not be in the awareness of people; it may be covered by a frantic flight* into escape activities, or by a craving for more money, power, prestige.[138] But the weight of the latter motivations is so great only because the alienated person cannot help seeking for such compensations for his inner vacuity, not because these desires are the "natural" or most important incentives for work.[139]

Drucker makes the same observation when he states:

For the great majority of automobile workers, the only meaning of the job is in the pay check, not in anything connected with the work or the product. Work appears as something unnatural, a disagreeable, meaningless and stultifying condition of getting the pay check, devoid of dignity as well as of importance. No wonder that this puts a premium on slovenly work, on slowdowns, and on other tricks to get the same pay check with less work.[140]

The workers seem to accept the new material goals. In fact, research shows that they are continually pressuring the union to ask for more wages and benefits and greater job security.[141] This is *not* to say that workers will not accept and appreciate such benefits. They will. It *is* suggested that such benefits will tend to maintain the fundamental conflicts and reinforce, in the employees' minds, the importance of wages and the like.

Reynolds finds that, fundamentally, wages and security are very important for the employees, especially at the lower levels[142] (where presumably the insecurity is the highest *and* where the loyalty to the company is probably the lowest).[143] These findings are confirmed by several studies covering 11,000 workers where the workers report that job security and wages are most important to them.[144] Studies conducted by the life insurance industry find that wages are most important in the eyes of the respondents.[145] A recent survey of 1,000 employees concluded that wages are the greatest cause of dissatisfaction.[146]

The analysis sheds some light on the economist's assumption that the employees' emphasis on monetary rewards is primarily economic; the early human relations students unknowingly accepted the validity of this thinking by trying to prove that money was not the most important factor in the eyes of the employees. *It is now clear that an emphasis on monetary rewards may well be a more crucial human problem than no emphasis or a minimal emphasis.* Human relations research does not need to have as one of its reasons for existence "proof" that so-called human factors are more important than material ones.

Develop Youth to Be Apathetic in, and Not Expect Happiness From, Their Work. Employees may adapt to the organization through individual defenses, small group sanctions, and trade unions. Goldbricking, apathy, lack of interest in the formal aspects of the company, decrease in production, increase in the emphasis upon money and other material benefits, and a decrease in the employees' ranking of human satisfactions are all expected (i.e., predicted) ways of adaptation.

Let us assume that the employees have children. What happens then? One may recall in the discussion of personality research that the greatest impact upon a child's development occurs in the family during his early years of life (i.e., first twelve years). Kahl, in a careful depth study of 24 youths drawn from a larger sample of 3971 boys on whom questionnaire data were available, states:

> The interviews indicated that the boys learned to an extraordinary degree to view the occupational system from their parents' perspective. They took over their parents' views of the opportunities available, the desirability and possibility of change of status, the techniques to be used if change was desired. . . .[147]

Since the child acquires his basic aspects of his self-conception from his parents, and since the parents behave toward their child in terms of their own self-conception, it follows that the child will tend to make part of his self concept those modes of adaptation found useful by the parents. Thus the child may be taught any one of a combination of the following modes of adaptation.

a. *Don't expect "happiness" on the job.* He ought to expect frustration and tension. As one parent said, "I've told him not to knock himself out. He's young, full of piss and vinegar. He thinks he's going out and find a job that he likes. I have to laugh at the kid. He told me the other day, 'not me,' he said, 'I'm not going to work at anything I don't like.' I told him, he's got a rude shock awaiting him. As I told him, you think your old man is tough, wait till you meet up with your boss!"

Teaching a child not to expect happiness decreases the degree of frustration he will probably experience when he enters the factory. If one expects dissatisfaction, then when the dissatisfaction does occur it will not have as much of an impact.

b. *Leave if you don't like it.*

c. *"Take" the frustration and work hard to become a member of management.*

d. *Play it smart, join the union, gain seniority, don't work too hard, don't work too little. Keep in the middle.*

e. *Once you have seniority, take it easy. Listen to the old timers. They'll show you the ropes.*

f. *Make as much money as you can.*

g. *Make enough money to buy your own business.*

It is impossible to say ahead of time exactly what mode of adaptation any given individual will take. It depends upon his family life, his schooling, his playmates, his social class, his work, and the climate. Moreover, the same individual can change his modes of adaptation at different times.

This is to be expected. Science can predict only under specific conditions. To be able to predict what Mr. A. will do five years from now, without knowing the conditions in which Mr. A. will be living, is *not* science. It is prophesying. For example, a physicist can predict that if one passes electricity through wire, one will get heat. Similarly, a social scientist can say that if a man is frustrated, he will regress. The physicist cannot say *how much* heat will result until he knows the type of battery used, the wire, the external conditions, and so on. Similarly, a social scientist cannot predict how much a person will regress under frustration until he knows the individual's personality and the conditions under which he lives.

There is some evidence, however, that helps us predict (within relatively wide tolerances) the possible behavior of groups of individuals.

Bakke's[148] results based upon intensive interviews of workers clearly related the decrease in the level of aspiration of the employee to the type of work situation. He noted, "Many a working-class family was integrated around the effort to provide children with educational and training equipment which would make possible for them a non-working-class life. This desire was shared also by the children *until they took their first job*. Very few ambitions to get out of the working class apparently survived the actual experience of having made a start as a worker."[149]

In a later volume Bakke summarized the problem of "getting ahead" as follows:

Workers have not succumbed to the American success philosophy. More unrealistic assumptions have been made in this matter than in the discussion of almost any other set of workers' motives. We would have to assume millions of people living under the circumstances we have described, observing the experience of those about them, listening to the conversation of fathers and grandfathers whose lives had been spent on the comparatively dead level of work for wages, knowing the sort of meager opportunities for advancement offered their mates, and still, in spite of the wisdom of experience, believing that the success stories held the clue to their own possibilities. That is an evaluation of working-class common sense that has little basis in fact. A few individuals with ambitions to be world beaters and the superb audacity to hope that they could overcome the almost impossible obstacles? Yes. But the working masses motivated by the same hope? No.

Research by Davis,[150] and Guest,[151] suggests that the lower-working-class youngsters do not tend to have aspirations that administrators might expect their employees to have.

For example, Guest reports on a sample of 202 hourly production workers (representing a carefully chosen sample of 14 per cent of the 1435 total sample). He concludes, "Workers do not look for, nor do they expect, jobs which will give them a higher economic and social status within the existing organization. Instead, they hope for the break which will relieve them of the anonymity and impersonality of the line."[152]

Two examples:

I live close to the plant and make good pay—what else do I want? I don't want to make a pile of dough. All I want is to have my bills paid and keep my house.

It's hard to make plans working in that place. You never know what you are going to be doing next, and with today's prices you can't get ahead at all. I just gave up hopes . . . I'll be on the line fifteen years in July, and I think I can last another fifteen, if I take care of myself. Then I'll get a job off the line—maybe a sweeper's job. It's not a tough job, it's easy. Wouldn't that be something, to end my years at Plant F in a blaze of glory as a sweeper!

Hyman,[153] after a careful analysis of some 300 cases, concludes, "Thus far the data presented show clearly that there is reduced striving for success among the lower classes, an awareness of lack of opportunity and a lack of valuation of education, normalcy, the major avenue to achievement of high status."

Chinoy provides further evidence when he states, "By and large the (automobile workers) confine their aims to those limited alternatives which seem possible for men with their skills and resources."[154]

The statistical data in support of this conclusion are that: only 8 out of his 62 subjects felt they had a promising future outside the factory; only 5 felt they had any real hope of becoming foremen within the factory; only 3 of the semiskilled group felt it might be possible to move up to skilled levels. The remaining 46 subjects could see little in the way of opportunity, and hence reduced their goals. Hollingshead,[155] Galler,[156] Centers,[157] and Archibald[158] confirm the above findings.

Erich Fromm states that the desire to be dependent and submissive, can be learned by all classes of people.[159] It is first learned in the early family life and reinforced by the experiences one has in industry. David Riesman goes as far as to suggest that America is beginning to experience a mass insecurity where *passive* conformity is found in an increasing number of "suburbanites."

Such a person tends to be shallow, free with his money, friendly, uncertain of himself and his values, and showy with his tangible possessions (his car, his house, his wife's fur coat). Socially he belongs to the "new" middle class; in business, he is the bureaucrat and the salaried employee. *Passive conformity*[160] is his mode. Approval from others is his big goal. Nothing in his character, no possession he owns, no inheritance of name or talent, no work he has done has value for itself; its only worth is its effect on others. He is afraid to be 'different.'[161]

Do People Adapt Through Outside Activities? The answer is yes—and no.

There has been some sound research on the effects of frustration and tension in one activity upon another activity. Perhaps the most detailed studies available are those by Barker, Dembo, and Lewin.[162] These researchers definitely show that the tensions created in one situation can have effects in another situation. The rule seems to be, if the tension is greater than what the individual can tolerate, then it will have negative effects on other activities. If it is not greater than his "frustration tolerance," it will not tend to have effects in other activities. Moreover, if the tension from frustration while at work is so great that it leads a person to feel he is (psychologically) failing, then the chances for constructive adaptive activities outside of work are decreased.

Recent data obtained in four different organizations suggest that the more satisfied workers inside the plant are also the ones who are more active in community activities, church activities, and fraternal organizations.[163] This trend is independent of age and sex.

Clarke's[164] study supports these findings. He reports that a statistically significant number of people on the management levels spend their free time participating in such activities as "community service," "attending conventions," "attending fraternal organizations." No statistically significant frequency is reported for the skilled, semiskilled, and unskilled employees on the above activities. From answers to the question, "What would you do with an extra two hours in your day?" Clarke concludes "that a substantially greater proportion of the higher prestige groups would use this hypothetical increase in leisure time largely to implement their business and professional interests."[165] Komarovsky[166] reports that male urban dwellers' participation in voluntary associations increases regularly from the occupation of lowest status and income to those of the highest. Goldhamer[167] reports similar results. Scott,[168] in a 5 percent random sample of family dwelling units in Bennington, Vermont, reports that the average participation (for men and women) in voluntary associations increases regularly from the low to the higher classes.

According to research, frustration produces personality primitivation (regression) and feelings of failure. Two possible ways for a "primitivized" (i.e., less mature) personality to adapt are by "blowing his top," "working himself to death," or "by becoming apathetic about his free time." Argyris reports that most of the bank employees who felt failure and frustration took the latter mode of adaptation. Blum,[169] however, reports that pro-production workers are capable of taking both modes of adaptation. They can work hard during week ends and/or they can become apathetic and listless. The workers are neither "boomin' with enthusiasm" nor completely "dead." Another possible mode of adaptation is suggested by Frumkin,[170] who after studying 1192 male and 347 female cases of first admissions with major mental disorders, concludes that the lower-class occupational groups manifest those mental disorders that are oriented against society and its mores (e.g., alcoholism and syphilitic psychosis). The upper classes, on the other hand, manifest those mental disorders that are oriented mainly against the self (e.g., manic-depressive and involutional psychoses). He finds this aggression against society on the part of the lower-class individuals predictable, since they perceive society as depriving them of important ego-satisfactions.

Some people may point to the increase in do-it-yourself activities as signs that the workers do obtain satisfactions outside the job. An analysis of these activities suggests that most of them place the individual in a situation in which his abilities (i.e., primarily the doing abilities) find expression *but* in a situation in which he is isolated, alone, passive, and quiet; the same characteristics we saw that the job and the organization tend to induce in the individual.

It would be interesting to conduct research on the exact relationship between the tendency for increased political apathy that has been reported[171, 172] and the apathy reported in the plant. The research would focus not so much on which causes which (that would be like the old chicken or egg conflict) but on the way that each feeds back and mutually reinforces the other (i.e., how industrial apathy influences political apathy and vice versa). Rosenberg, in a depth interview study of 70 respondents, suggests that the three most important areas for political apathy are (1) the threatening consequences of political activity, (2) the futility of political activity, and (3) the absence of spurs to interest and participation.[173] Rosenberg points out that people often lack a personal thrust to action. The comments of respondents below are similar to the one management usually hears when it inquires why the employees are not more spontaneous in their suggestions.

"No, I wasn't asked to do anything . . ."

"Well, I might have helped if they'd really wanted me to and if it didn't take too much time. . . . Besides, no one asked me to help out, so I didn't volunteer."

"You can probably class me as apathetic, except when it's brought right to my attention, but I think most people are the same way."[174]

Summary and Concluding Comments.

1. The available research on the human personality suggests that, in our culture, psychologically healthy individuals tend to develop along certain lines (i.e., toward independence, and activity). The hypothesis is derived that the individual will need to find expression for his own particular growth trends (i.e., need for self-actualization).

2. The available research on formal organizations suggests that

if it is to obtain ideal expression, the formal organization will tend to place employees in work situations where they are dependent, subordinate, and submissive. This trend increases as one goes down the chain of command, as the individual increases in degree of maturity, and as jobs become more and more of the mass production type.

3. To the extent that the requirements of the individual and of the formal organization are not congruent, the individual will tend to feel frustration, conflict, and feelings of failure.[175] The individuals may adapt by leaving, working their way up the ladder, distorting their world through defense mechanisms, becoming apathetic and uninterested, reducing production, goldbricking, rate-setting, creating informal groups to counteract the cause of the conflict (i.e., the inherent formal power of management and the task specialization of their work). They may also *increase* in their minds the importance of money and job security and *decrease* the importance of the human factors.[176] Needless to say, the modes of adaptation are highly interdependent and can easily influence one another. For example, Mayo and Lombard[177] have shown that low turnover is related to cohesive informal employee groups. Presumably once employees create their informal groups, they may be induced by the desire for group belongingness to attend the plant more frequently than employees who do not belong to informal groups.

4. Since these activities are adaptive, the employees will want to perpetuate them. They create informal sanctions (codes) and formalize the groups (trade unions). Thus the behavior (in 3. above) becomes accepted behavior. It is behavior that every "loyal" worker is expected to learn.

5. The parents may decrease the possible conflict and frustration of their children by lowering their standards as to how much happiness they should expect from their work and/or by teaching them the ropes on "how not to burn themselves out."

6. It is possible to conclude that to the extent the employees become ego-involved in the informal activities, they may have their need structure changed. The basic growth trends outlined in Chapter II may be modified so that neither the needs for de-

pendence and passivity nor the needs for relative independence and activity are completely accurate. For them may be substituted apathy, lack of interest, and lack of ego-involvement. These needs in turn may be inculcated into the youth by the parents. If this trend is strong enough, a new feedback process may be begun which will permanently modify the basic growth trends.

Turning to the impact of the organization upon the individual, we may begin to wonder what kind of an individual would tend to feel adapted and adjusted on the job. In a preliminary analysis by Argyris of interviews of 10 assembly line workers who were judged to be *adapted and adjusted,* it was found that they tended to have the following personal characteristics:

a. They value money as most important. Seniority is second most important.

b. They all perceive themselves as having poor education.

c. They are unable to perform several different things at the same time. "I can use a screwdriver, but I can't talk at the same time."

d. They aspire to doing the minimum quantity of work. They do not tend to aspire for quality work. They do not feel badly about doing work that is of poor quality.

e. They tend to desire to be isolated and alone. They express no desire for group cohesiveness or "we-feeling."

f. They are not loyal to their company and would leave to go to another if they could be guaranteed a few cents more and their present seniority.

g. They feel *satisfied* with the foreman because they hardly see him and he hardly contacts them.

h. They tend to be *satisfied* with the working conditions.

i. They are *hardly ever late or absent* from work.

j. They tend to dislike changes and are very rigid in their attitudes. They place a great deal of emphasis on predictability and surety in life. Change tends to threaten them.

These results, although preliminary, have interesting implications. For example, they suggest that the apathetic, uninterested worker on the assembly line is also the one most satisfied with his foreman and his working conditions, and is seldom late or absent from work. If these results are found to hold generally, they raise important questions about the "measures" of "healthy organization" so frequently used by some industrial psychologists. It is assumed for example, that absenteeism, dislike of working conditions and management, and lateness to work are negative signs of human difficulties. It may be equally valid to look upon these indices as *positive signs of the employees trying to maintain minimum personality satisfaction and production* under difficult psychological conditions.

These conclusions also have important implications for influencing productivity. For example, Morse finds that productivity is a function of:

1. The strength of needs for which productivity is a path.
2. The probability that productivity will yield some degree of tension reduction of these needs.
3. The amount of productivity required for a given unit of tension reduction of these needs.
4. The likelihood that the individual will spend time in activities other than producing. (This is a function of the strength of the needs which cannot be satisfied through the behavior of producing and the probability of tension reduction of these needs.)
5. The likelihood that the individual will use other behavior to satisfy the needs which can also be satisfied through productivity. (This is a function of the relative energy expenditure cost of getting satisfaction through the productivity path as compared to other paths.)[178]

If Morse's hypotheses are valid, then an administrator will find it difficult to raise productivity. For example, if we take condition 1., then the administrator will have a better chance of increasing productivity if the employees have many and important needs which are satisfied through productivity. As we have seen, the opposite seems to be the case. The employees, for the most part, have few and relatively unimportant needs that are related to productivity. This means that "the probability that productivity will yield some degree of tension reduction" to these needs is decreased. Moreover, "the amount of productivity required for a given unit of tension reduction of these needs" may not be great, since the needs are peripheral and not central. The exception to this trend is, of course, the need for material rewards. Thus we may predict that if the trend continues, the administrator will find that only material needs are related to productivity. This leads us to the already mentioned results that, as a result, a circular process is set in motion where higher wages (and other material rewards) for *dissatisfaction* not only becomes a goal, but the very basis of the employee's life.

Lewis Way, in his book *Man's Quest for Significance,* describes how the worker whose job had been relieved of all social and psychological meaning finally began to adapt by no longer perceiving work as a pleasure and a challenge, the accomplishment of which resulted in personal pride. The worker soon became indifferent to the quality of his work. So long as he was paid he was indifferent to the type of work he was supposed to do. But, behind this apathy and indifference the worker felt humiliated and hostile, "Given no responsibility, he showed none; treated as an automaton, he behaved as such." Soon he became passively hostile by cutting his production, and making deliberate errors. It was not long before he felt a deep and wide gulf between himself and those who were in control.

V

Management's Reaction and Its Impact Upon the Employees

We have been primarily concerned with the employees' adaptation to the formal organizational structure, such as decreases in production and identification with the organization; increases in waste, errors, absenteeism, sickness, apathy, disinterest in work, and increase in importance of material (financial) aspects of work. These are all understandable and predictable ways for relatively healthy employees to adapt to the conflict, frustration, and failure they experience as a result of the formal organization.

A. MANAGEMENT'S DOMINANT ASSUMPTIONS

The top administrators, however, tend to diagnose the problems in another way. They observe their employees while at work and they conclude: (1) *The employees* are lazy. (2) *The employees* are uninterested and apathetic. (3) *The employees* are money crazy. (4) *The employees* create errors and waste.

Management blames the employees and "sees" the disloyalty, disinterest, and goldbricking as being "in" and caused by the employees. It follows logically for management, that if any changes are to occur the *employees* must be changed. Thus management initiates programs to "change peoples' attitudes," to "sell them free enterprise," to "make people more interested in the company."

Williams and Peterfreund[1] conclude that a substantial number of businessmen are looking for "Means of changing employee attitudes and behavior in a favorable direction." Two attitudes illustrative of this group are:

We must get information to people in order to keep them from going socialistic if a depression should set in, and we must educate them to support monetary and fiscal policies that would prevent depressions.

The lack of understanding of the economic system and its advantages today creates the tendency for people to think of unions and (gives rise to) other problems which greater education would make unnecessary.

Many managers believe that their employees, because of their *human nature,* want to work as little as possible, to be unconcerned over errors and waste, to ask always for more wages and benefits, to resist change, and to show decreasing loyalty toward the company and the free enterprise system and increasing loyalty to trade unions. But our analysis suggests that people are *not* necessarily the basic cause of their "negative behavior." Apparently, few managers see that the formal organization (and later on we shall see that leadership and management controls) can be the cause of these "negative characteristics."

It is interesting to compare and note the similarity of this diagnosis with one made by a representative group of British managements. They blame low productivity on (1) management's lack of power to dismiss or to threaten dismissal, (2) apathy and indifference of the employees, (3) worker resistance to change, (4) worker desire for more money with less effort—in fact, laziness, (5) workers' emphasis on security and guaranteed employment, and (6) worker informal setting of production levels.

Both sets of diagnoses place the "blame" for many of the productivity problems on the employees (and some upon the trade unions and government).

The basic action policy that management tends to define to solve the above "problems" actually stems from the logics of the formal organization and formal leadership already discussed in Chapter III.

For example, the logics of the formal organization tend to influence management to assume that: (1) The only relations that matter between people in organizations are those defined by organization charts and manuals.[2] (2) The behavior of people in organizations is governed by explicit logical thinking.[3] (3) The subordinates will do what the purpose and circumstances of the organization require only under logical incentives and clear communications.[4] (4) The administrator is responsible to solve the problem. He knows best what should be done.[5] (5) The way to get things done is through authority of the leader's position. He can apply persuasion and compulsion if necessary.[6] (6) The employees at the bottom would behave differently if they understood the economic problems of the business.[7]

There are three fundamental policy decisions running through these six policy assumptions. The first is the importance of strong, "dynamic," loyal leadership. Second, is the importance of a logical and systematic control over the employees' behavior. Finally, is the importance of communicating to the employees management's thinking related to their organization and its economic problems. Let us examine each of these to see what action management takes to implement these policy decisions and then to analyze the impact of management's actions on the employees and the organization.

B. STRONGER "DYNAMIC" LEADERSHIP AND ITS IMPACT UPON THE EMPLOYEES

An important pillar of most management policy is to develop competent executives who among other things: (1) are able to "needle," "drive," "sell," "push," "pressure," "persuade," "urge," "coerce," "win" employees to increase productivity, loyalty, and interest for the organization and for their job; (2) are able to get all the facts, weigh them correctly, and make effective decisions; (3) know clearly management's objectives, policies, and practices; (4) communicate these policies and practices clearly to the employees; and (5) evaluate the performance of the employee strictly and honestly according to these policies and practices.

There is ample evidence to illustrate management's use of pressure-oriented leadership. Youmann,[8] Moore,[9] Argyris and Miller,[10] are a few examples. The latter report on a study of four organizations in which the majority of the managers interviewed feel that employees are basically lazy, have no desire to work, and need to be pressured and needled.

For example:

1. I think there is a need for more pressure. People need to be needled a bit. I think man is inherently lazy and if we could only increase the pressure, I think things would be more effective.
2. There are lots of workers in the plant, hundreds of them, who don't have any more capacity to do things other than what they're doing. And they're *lazy*. They might be able to develop some capacities, and I think there's a lot of them in their desire to do so couldn't do it, even if they want to. But, they *don't even have the desire*.
3. Nine-tenths of the employees have no goals, and they don't give a damn, and they're glad not to have a goal. It's the same all over, in our plant or anywhere. People got to be pressured—needled. I don't mean you have to hit them over the head with a hammer . . . just keep needling them.[11]

The same attitudes are described in a dramatic fashion by one executive who says, "The majority of workers are good-natured slobs who want to be left alone in routine jobs. . . ." "Thousands resist promotion because they do not want to be lifted out of a rut."[12]

The spontaneous conversations of a top management group trying to understand effective leadership in industry conclude: "The chief executive in a company like our own is responsible for the team and the way the team plays." (Another executive adds), "Our past president was a master at reconciling opinions and guiding a group to sound decisions. However, there was never any question as to where the head of the table was."[13] Still another states that the president cannot afford to concern himself with smoothing out the relations "because he would then be just a mopper-upper" and would not fulfill his duty of staying out of current operations and concerning himself with future plans.[14] Even when the top executive asks questions, his impact should be "needling," "stimulating."

Ask him the things that will help him—or scare him: or stimulate him —to do his job right. You have to ask questions that will cause him not to be complacent, but to consider his whole activities broadly. By less checking and more asking you show confidence in the operating manager. He'll like it a lot better and he'll work a lot harder.[15]

In these top management conversations discussing conception of effective leadership it is the executive who plans, who is responsible, who is at the head of the table, who guides and reconciles points of view, who makes decisions, and who asks in a way to stimulate, scare, motivate the subordinate to work harder, and who gives confidence, gives information, arouses interest.

An insightful top executive (in the competitive and pressure-laden world of department stores) summarizes the reasons why it is easy for the executive to fall into a directive leadership pattern:

As an executive, you don't realize until you look at yourself how much you take for granted the fact that when someone comes into your office to make a complaint or express himself, sooner or later you are dominating the conversation.

You are in your position because you have an ability to dominate conversation. You've been chosen for your managerial place because you may be a little more skillful in winning out in verbal fisticuffs with your associates, the people who are below you or on the same level with you. If that is true, unconsciously then, you are going to impose what you think is the right approach to a problem upon the person. And he or she is going to leave the office completely dissatisfied with the result of the conversation, but you're going to say, 'We keep an open door in this plant, and anybody can come in and talk to me.' In my own viewpoint— I hope none of you will think that I'm completely irreverent on this—I think the myth of the open door, so far as industrial and commercial management is concerned, is one of the worst plagues with which we've cursed ourselves. We think that simply because we say to people, 'You can always come and talk to us,' that they will. They're not going to come in and talk to us, because of our symbols of authority. Again, as all of us know, the higher you get up the ladder, the less likely you are to get real expressions of what individuals are thinking.[16]

McMurry[17] concludes as a result of an intensive study of top executives that the autocratic-bureaucratic philosophy of leadership is dominant in industry today, despite the protestations of many leaders to the contrary.

Further evidence of the importance of pressure for management has to do with a top executive who, when studied in depth, emphasized that a good manager is one who is not afraid to "push," "sell," "be strong," and "hit hard." For example:

I think the average supervisor does not face up to his responsibilities. He's afraid to tell the employees what to do and what not to do. Don't get me wrong. I'm not suggesting the supervisor should be a fighter. I simply mean that a supervisor, when he comes to work, should work hard. The people under him should come to realize that when he says something he really means it.

Most of our supervisors haven't developed the leadership strength-push they should have. And mind you, I think the employees want a leader who is strong![18]

From another depth study of ten executives it is concluded that eight believe that a "good" leader is a strong leader who works hard, pushes, pressures, and needles employees to work hard.[19] As one company vice president describes it:

You know, I used to be a son-of-a-gun. I was the one who got out the hatchet and really got tough when we held a meeting to talk about reducing costs or increasing sales. My subordinates didn't like it very well when I shocked their complacency. I would point out that while they had been fairly successful in their management of a particular phase of our business, some one of the other executives was doing an even better job in his division. I don't find myself doing that very much anymore and it disturbs me. I believe that some of these department heads are getting to be a bit too complacent. Don't you think that every organization should have someone with a needle to jab these complacent guys in the right place at the right time?[20]

Turning from the executives' description of "dynamic" leadership to the researchers' definition of the same phenomenon, we find that the latter define "dynamic leadership" as "autocratic" or "directive" leadership. Lippitt and White, define an "authoritarian" leader as anyone who creates a situation for his subordinates in which:

1. All policy is determined by the leader.
2. The leader dictates techniques and activities so that future steps are always uncertain to a large degree.

3. The leader directs people in what to do, how to do it, and with whom to work.

4. The leader tends to be 'personal' in his criticism of the work of each member. However, the leader remains aloof from active group participation except when actually working with the group.[21] [22]

What is the impact of directive leadership upon the employees? Will it tend to solve the problems of dependence, submissiveness, and the resultant apathy, disinterest, that management dislikes?

White and Lippitt,[23] whose results are confirmed by Adams,[24] Mowrer,[25] and Robbins[26] find that the subordinates tend to adapt to authoritarian leadership by: (1) leaving, (2) becoming submissive and dependent, (3) releasing their pent-up feelings when the leader is away, (4) demanding increasing attention from the leader, (5) fighting and competing among each other (inter-departmental conflict) especially for the leader's favor, (6) releasing some of their pent-up feelings by creating a scapegoat, and (7) increasing their emphasis on material aspects of their relationships.

These adaptive reactions are confirmed by the work of Bavelas[27] in a field experiment and Preston and Heintz[28] in a controlled laboratory situation. Also, the Survey Research Center under the direction of Likert in a summary report of studies of a large insurance company, maintenance of way-section gangs on a railroad, an electric utility, an automotive manufacturer, a tractor company, an appliance manufacturer, and two agencies of the federal government report that directive, pushing production-oriented leadership tends to create a situation of low morale where the workers feel they are dependent, submissive, subordinate, and passive to the leader.[29]

Worthy,[30] summarizing twelve years of research in Sears Roebuck and Company, is in agreement with Fleishman, Harris, and Burtt, who show quite clearly that:

1. Subordinates dislike pressure from directive leadership.

2. Subordinates who had directive leaders also tended to have higher absentee records and greater number of grievances filed.[31]

Campbell,[32] summarizing the results of the "autocratic" leadership studies reports that this type of leadership creates among the group members (1) more hostility and rivalry, (2) identification with the leader rather than the group, (3) anxiety about the future, (4) aggression toward others, (5) the creation of scapegoats, (6) over-dependence on and submission toward the leader, and (7) rigidity of behavior. At the same time autocratic, directive leadership decreased (1) group cohesion, (2) individual morale, (3) group productivity.

Summarizing the characteristics found in most of the research, one may conclude that the autocratic, directive leader places the followers in a situation where they tend to be (1) passive, dependent, subordinate, and submissive; (2) centered toward the organization's and the leader's needs rather than the needs of all the followers; (3) competing with each other for the leader's favor; (4) confronted with a short time perspective; and (5) experiencing psychological failure.

We must conclude that the impact of directive leadership upon the subordinates is similar to that which the formal organization has upon the subordinate. Pressure-oriented directive leadership "compounds the felony" that the formal organization commits every minute every hour of the day and every day of the year. Authoritarian leadership reinforces and perpetuates the "damage" created by the organizational structure. The adaptive activities reported in Chapter IV are also caused by directive leadership. Directive leadership helps to reinforce, in the employees' minds, the necessity for the same adaptive activities that this leadership is originally designed to decrease.

C. Tighter Management Controls and Their Impact Upon the Employees

The second policy decision made by many managers to combat reduced productivity is careful definition, inspection, and evaluaton of the quality and quantity of every employee's performance. This leads us to the field of management controls.

Management controls are becoming increasingly important in the eyes of top management. Management control is seen as a fundamental process in all organization.[33] The field has grown so large and so deep that one can find entire books written on any one or a combination of the following:

1. Control over organization policies.
2. Control over rate of production.
3. Control over inventory.
4. Control over job specifications.
5. Control over planning.
6. Control over quality of production.
7. Control over product specifications.
8. Control over wages and salaries.
9. Control over costs.
10. Control over manpower.
11. Control over production methods.
12. Control over expenditures.
13. Control over sales.
14. Control over executive time.
15. Control over public relations.

Management controls are not only necessary and inevitable if the traditional formal organizational structure is to be maintained, but they also become increasingly important as the formal organization becomes larger and more decentralized. Management decision making would suffer if management controls were abandoned.

What is the impact of management controls upon the employees? In order to answer this, it is necessary that we know the basic properties of "good" management controls.

The beginnings of modern scientific management control probably originated with Taylor. Villers, correctly points out that Taylor emphasized the following principles basic to management control:

1. *Separation of planning from performance principle.* Management should take over from the workers the responsibility for planning the work and making the performance physically possible. Planning should be based on time studies and other data related to production, scientifically determined and systematically classified; it should be facilitated by standardization of tools, implements, and methods.
2. *Scientific methods of work principle.* Management should take over from the workers the responsibility for their methods of work, determine scientifically the best methods and train the workers accordingly.

3. *Managerial control principles.* Managers should be trained and taught to apply scientific principles of management and control (such as management by exception and comparison with valid standards).[34]

Hodges,[35] basing his comments on Rathe's analysis of management controls defines the basic control activities as follows. First, management should determine the over-all plan. Included in this activity are such subactivities as "the design of the specific program" (including the policies and plans), and "the development of tools" such as "organization," "system," "procedures," "methods," and "standards." Second, management must control and determine what actually takes place. Are the plans followed according to definition and are the tools used as suggested? In order to answer questions like these, data must be obtained for management to evaluate. Martin[36] makes the same point when he states, "the operator must not only be told 'what to do,' but also 'how to do it,' and 'what equipment' to use. This means planning a job in *detail* and issuing comprehensive instructions so that the operator may perform the job in accordance with the plan."

What impact will such controls tend to have upon the employees? First, the principle takes away from the workers the planning for the work (and all its aspects) and leaves them primarily with the responsibility to perform. But, as we have already seen, the employees tend to be assigned highly fractionized and specialized jobs whose performance leads to little satisfaction. Moreover, taking away the planning deprives the employees of an opportunity to participate in important decisions affecting their working life. They feel a loss of control over their work world; and these conditions tend to be disliked by mature individuals. Finally, the lack of participation in defining the goals will tend to cause the employee to feel psychological failure.

Psychological failure is compounded by turning the responsibility for work methods to management. The employee is told not only *how much* he shall produce but also *how* this should be produced. The psychological failure, in turn, is doubly compounded by the "managerial control principles" which make *management* responsible for the evaluation of the employees' work.

The impact of psychological failure can be observed in the employees' behavior towards such management controls as time and motion study, quality control, and incentive systems. The conclusions by Whyte[37] based on detailed studies of several incentive systems can be understood in terms of the concept of psychological failure. The first deals with conditions which will lead to successful piecework systems and the second those which will cause failure.

Piecework has a chance to succeed:[38]

1. When outcome is reasonably possible, but not completely certain.

Piecework will tend to fail:

2. If quota earnings seem clearly unattainable . . . the worker abandons the goal.
3. If quota is completely predictable and certain, the work becomes monotonous and meaningless.
4. If achievement depends upon factors outside worker's control.

Conclusions of researchers on psychological success:[39]

1. Barrier to the goal must be strong enough to require effort but not so strong as to prevent achievement.
2. Same as above
3. The barrier is so weak that no sense of success is achieved by overcoming it.
4. Barrier must be overcome and goal achieved through individual's own effort. Help or hindrance from outside leads to failure.

In the second set of results Whyte concludes:

Workers' behavior caused by incentive systems:[40]

1. Workers will resist output to a point well below their capacity.[41]
2. Workers will develop many incentives which they will tend to keep secret from management.

3. When they are being observed for rate-setting purposes, they will use all their ingenuity in working slowly yet giving the impression of working fast.

Conclusions of researchers on psychological failure:

1. People experiencing failure may lower their work aspiration much below their capability. This will lead to increased failure.
2. Create behavior that assures lower work aspiration. Also tending to express aggression toward object seen as responsible for the failure.
3. Same as above.

The third finding in the column above, although relatable to psychological failure, apathy, and aggression, is also influenced by another characteristic of the employees' world, namely the short time perspective. Since the employees have little knowledge of and even less control over their future, they will tend to fear the unknown.[42] As a result they may reason it is to their advantage to restrict output. It will help prevent reduction in work force and an increase in production standards without a comparable increase in wages.

Abruzzi confirms the conclusion that the employees "cheat," "distort," their production records in order to make the record look the way they believe is in their interest. He notes that this behavior acts to question the validity of the resultant production standards.

Production standards may seem 'accurate,' but only because they are made to look that way when this is in the workers' interest. This kind of verification is verification with a strong condition; the condition is worker acceptance. The result is that 'accuracy' is a conditional function of many behavioral variables, which are sometimes complementary, more often conflicting, and always interacting and varying in weight.[43]

Jasinski[44] in an analysis of the impact of accounting controls presents evidence that workers "fudge" the records for their own interests. He also concludes that as a result of budgets, interdepartmental conflicts arise (supervisors blaming each other for waste and errors), production and maintenance costs are increased (bleeding the line—that is stopping operations near the start of the cycle and shifting labor to final operations in order to complete more units by the deadline), which in turn results in impairment of quality and irregular output. All of these lead to much waste of the executive's time.

Dalton[45] reports that not only do management controls lead to interdepartmental strife and politics, but in order to resolve these strifes, new control systems may be created which may solve some of the problems but also create new ones. In the process, those who identified with the old system tend to dislike the new one and do their best to disrupt it.

Bakke presents evidence that the management control engineers (e.g., job analysis, time and motion and piece rate setting) are perceived by foremen and workers as not being able to understand and respect their capacity to contribute in the productive process. Bakke notes:

> Workers feel that the production engineers, with general management's approval, look upon them as bundles of human energy (or as machines), to be analyzed, rated, and applied to the production progress. This is particularly true in relation to job analysis, time and motion study, and piece rate setting. The engineers, therefore, as the workers see the matter, conceive of themselves as calculators of the capacities of and manipulators of human energy. The reciprocal to this conception is that of the workers as a pliable and manipulable bundle of energies and skills. This mechanical picture of the worker conflicts sharply with his conception of himself as a whole person.[46]

Segerstedt and Lundquist[47] report that employees not only tend to express negative feelings about time and motion studies but those employees who participated in time and motion studies also want to change work more often than those who have not.

In another study of three medium-large and one large manufacturing plant evidence is presented that management controls, such as budgets, are definitely disliked by the supervisors and foremen and the workers. For example:

> I'm violently against the figures. I keep away from showing them to the workers. I *know my boys* are doing a good job. They're trying to do their best. If I give them the heat with this stuff they'll blow their top.

Another supervisor states:

> You can't use budgets with people. Just can't do anything like that. People have to be handled carefully and in our plant, carefully doesn't mean with budgets. Besides, I don't think my people are lazy.[48]

The data suggest that the supervisors dislike budgets of all types because (1) they tend to report only results, not reasons; (2) they emphasize the past and not the present; (3) they are rigid; (4) they apply pressure for an ever-changing goal; (5) they tend to create failure for the supervisor.

Budgets, being based on the "logics" of formal organization, tend to make the foremen more department-centered rather than organization-centered. In Chapter III, it is pointed out that as a result of the principles of task specialization, chain of command, and unity of direction, the foreman or supervisor is rated as being effective if he is able to achieve the goal of his department. He is asked to focus upon, feel responsible for *his* department's record and not the record of the over-all organization. The latter is the responsibility of the top management. Since budgets are one type of management control that evaluate the performance of the department, the foreman or supervisor soon learns to worry about *his* and *primarily* his department. In short, the individual is placed in a situation in which he is rewarded for effective performance independently of how the other members of the organization perform. Berkowitz and Levy,[48A] in some controlled experiments, report that these conditions tend to lead individuals to feel a relatively low interest and pride in group performance. They note that high group task motivation is related to high pride in group performance when the individuals perceive they are highly interdependent upon one another with respect to the attainment of reward.

Returning to the interviews with the factory supervisors there is little doubt that they were department-centered in outlook rather than plant-centered. Typical comments were:

> The other day I received an order to do a job, but no requisition. I called up production control and asked what was going on. I said to them, 'Why didn't I get the requisition on that order?' They started to give

excuses. Sure, they didn't worry. *This was my job, just like I don't have to worry when the other departments stand still.*

Each one of us gets *his* own picture when we get the budget results. Even if we got the total picture, it wouldn't mean much to us. We go right for our sheet. As I said, we might get the whole plant picture, *but we're primarily interested in our own department.*

I don't get a picture of the other people's budgets in this place, and I don't think I need one or even want one. My main responsibility is in this here outfit of mine. *Nowhere else.* So, let them worry about their problem and I'll worry about mine.

As a result of the pressure, tension, and general mistrust of management controls, employees tend to unite *against* management. Psychological research shows that people can stand only a certain amount of pressure and tension, after which it becomes intolerable. One method people use to reduce the effect of the pressure (assuming that the employees cannot reduce the pressure itself) is to join groups, which help absorb much of the pressure and thus relieve the individual personally. Gradually, therefore, the individuals become a group because in so doing they are able to satisfy their need to (1) reduce the pressure on each individual; (2) get rid of tension; (3) feel more secure by belonging to a group which can counteract the pressure. In short, new cohesive groups developed to *combat* management pressure. In a sense, the people had learned that they could be happier if they combined against it. This result is predicted in Chapter IV as a "natural" consequence of the employees' adapting to the dependence and submissiveness that they experience.

To summarize up to this point, management controls like budgets tend to make the employees feel dependent, passive, and subordinate to management. As a result of budgets, they experience pressure, interdepartmental strife, psychological failure, lack of control over their work environment, barriers to communication between the budget people and the line pople, pressure to be department-centered rather than organization-centered.

Why are management controls used if their impact tends to create human problems? As long as the traditional formal organizational structure is used, some controls will always be needed. Management controls are in agreement with many of management's assumptions about how to motivate employees. Whyte suggests that management controls such as motion study, quality control incentive systems are based upon four erroneous assumptions. They are:

1. Man is a rational animal striving to maximize his economic gains. It follows that the employee ought to be paid according to how much he produces.
2. Man is an isolated individual when it comes to computing his salary. He is not affected (or at least should not be affected) by work group norms and pressures.
3. Man, like a machine, can be treated in a standardized fashion. While individual differences are recognized, it is assumed that there is "one best way" to do the job so that variations in method of work can and should be eliminated.
4. Man, like machines, needs to be stimulated by management to work. Machines are stimulated by electricity; man, by money.[49]

There is a fundamental similarity between this list of assumptions and those listed in the discussion of formal organization (Chapter III) and dynamic directive leadership (in the previous section). All three lists place great importance on rational behavior. All three treat the employee as if he were isolated, not affected by group standards, and loyal to the company needs. All three assume it is good to reward those employees who behave as the company wants and to penalize those who do not. All three assume that "good" behavior is doing one's own job best and not impinging on the work of others. All three assume that material rewards are the most effective.

The impact of management controls is similar to that which the formal organization and directive leadership have upon the subordinates. Management controls feed back upon and give support to directive leadership as both "compound the felony" committed by the formal organization every hour of the day and every day of the year. Again we find that a management action designed to decrease the informal activities described in Chapter

IV actually tends to reinforce their necessity in the minds of the employees.[49A]

D. THE "HUMAN RELATIONS FAD" AND ITS IMPACT UPON THE EMPLOYEES

The third response by management to the problems of inadequate productivity and employee apathy is the let's-be-human approach. If directive leadership and tight management controls do not succeed, perhaps helping the workers to identify with their jobs and the company might succeed.[50]

How did the human relations fad begin? The growth of trade unionism brought to light much of the discontent the employees had been feeling for years, and placed much of the blame on poor management. A second important stimulus was the research by Mayo,[51] Roethlisberger and Dickson,[52] who presented concrete evidence showing that productivity and human relations were intimately tied up. Poor human relations, wrote the authors, creates low production (e.g., rate-setting and goldbricking which leads to worse human relations which in turn leads to lower production). A key to the solution, Mayo suggests, is to help the employees feel that they belong to a small primary work group. If people could be helped to feel they belong, he suggested, human relations would be better. Both of these events had a strong impact upon management, many of whom still did not fully accept trade unionism. Third, many executives were beginning to develop a sense of social responsibility.

A difficulty with Mayo and other "human realtors" is that they observed employees goldbricking, rate-setting, expressing low feelings of identification, apathy, and disinterest and they conclude, like management, that this is "bad."[53] It may be bad from management's point of view, but as our analysis suggests, it may also be adaptive as long as relatively mature workers are working in a difficult work situation.

Management picked up the message and for the next fifteen to twenty years there existed a great interest in human relations. Every conference, if it was to succeed, had at least one presentation on human relations. Human relations soon became the panacea for most industrial ills. Literally hundreds of articles were written by top managers on their human relations programs.

An interesting and authentic story which indirectly indicates the impact of human relations in the United States has to do with the technical assistance program of the United States (originally called the Marshall Plan), under which thousands of European top managers have visited America in small teams to observe how the American "know-how" in manufacturing works to give high productivity. A reading of their reports impresses one with the fact that no matter how technical the report, almost always (over 95 per cent of several hundred cases) the managers concluded by saying in effect, "The true secret of American success is human relations!" Where do they get this information? One look at their crammed schedule and it became obvious that there was little time for interviewing employees. Usually they obtained this message from management.

As a result, the human relations bug is spreading all over Europe like wildfire. But once bitten, the European is lost. The most frequent questions that over two thousand top representatives of management, trade union leaders, government officials, and even human relations researchers asked of a visiting American team on which the writer served were: (1) What *is* human relations? (2) What *isn't* human relations? (3) How human relations conscious *ought* we be? (4) How happy should workers be? (5) Can't we think of the interests of the organization?

Hundreds of Europeans *feel strongly* that they must have good human relations, yet they do not seem to have any idea what is good human relations. An analysis of the comments of over two hundred top managers in an industrially advanced country in Europe leads one to conclude: (1) The majority of the top administrators feel strongly about the importance of good human relations. (2) The majority are unable to give a definition of "good" human relations that satisfies even them! (3) Over 75 per cent of the managers interviewed expressed antagonistic opinions about good human relations within the same discussion period.[54]

These results are *not* atypical. Quite the contrary, they are the pattern found in eight different European countries. For example:

a. We've never used the word 'human relations,' but I'm *certain* we have *always* had such programs. When you get right down to it, human relations is being fair—as fair as we can be—to everyone.

b. We *are* running a decent show. Wouldn't you say that, John? Now, you know our plants. I don't think I'm off if I say that our chaps feel we have pretty good human relations in our plants.

John: There's no question about it in my mind.

Original Speaker: The same can be said for your firm, I'm sure.

John: I think so, but I'm glad you point it out.

c. Everyone . . . no matter what grade, should feel content in their grade. They should feel that this is where they belong. *Any* bloke wants to feel that his job is important. We *all* do. It is up to management to point out how important that job is in the plant.

d. We want our people to feel our firm is worth working for. They should feel they have a fair chance. We want a happy company. People are happy when they know they can get a fair hearing.

e. Damn it all, I don't know how to give definitions, but I *know* I *feel* it, when we have good human relations. I'd say that's a characteristic of a top manager. He can sense when things are wrong.

f. I don't know a definition of human relations, but I'm certain that our human relations are good.[55]

Returning to the United States, research suggests that the situation is not much different. Some of the best evidence is to be found in the surveys that *Fortune* magazine has conducted concerning programs for employee participation and communication. William H. Whyte presents a cogent evaluation of these "fads." He describes vividly top management's anxiety over the gap in communication and the apparent lack, on the part of the workers, of enthusiasm for free enterprise system.

Never before have businessmen appeared to be gripped with a single idea; there is scarcely a convention that is not exhorted with it, and of all the general speeches made by businessmen, by far the greatest single category is that in which the audience is warned to spread the gospel before it is too late. And so it goes, this message, We must cure misinformation with information; we must tell the business story; above all, we must *sell* Free Enterprise.

And sell we have. . . .

Within industry itself, many of the country's largest firms have started extensive programs to indoctrinate employees. Swift and Co., for example, is conducting in-plant conferences; General Motors has produced a full-length Hollywood movie on the profit system (to be shown in the theaters and clubs as well as in plants); G.E., Proctor and Gamble, Republic Steel, are among other things, making wide distribution of Free Enterprise comic books.

And it is not worth a damn.[56, 57]

It has been estimated that $140,000,000 is being spent on such communication programs[58] even though recent research clearly suggests that there seems to be no correlation between job satisfaction and reading company communication programs.[59]

Katz and Kahn,[60] summarizing the Survey Research Center's experience with many of these programs, conclude that the typical "morale programs," "slick magazines," "canned talks," "coordinators of human relations" have not much positive value, in fact are capable of causing more harm than good.

Lystad and Stone[61] present evidence that organizational communication schemes do not communicate what the employees wish they would. Moreover, a content analysis suggests that the messages from above tend to emphasize the importance of formal procedures and the importance of *impersonality* in social relationships. Both of these messages are completely congruent with the logics of formal organization described in Chapter III.

This selling approach pervades the human relations programs to such an extent that in a unit of one of the largest utility companies, the supervisors have been instructed to induct employees as follows:[62]

"*Give* the employee confidence in himself and a feeling of belonging.

"*Instill* in him confidence in his department and his company.

"*Give* him complete information about the company, its employee relations, policies and procedures.

"*Give* the employee a proper understanding of his job.

"*Arouse* his interest in the company and create pride in being associated with it."

Where does management obtain these ideas for "better" human relations? These programs are primarily related to management's dominant assumptions that the *employees* are lazy and apathetic.

It follows, for management, that the employees must be "rejuvenated," "motivated," "fired with enthusiasm," and "inspired."

Why does this particular action follow? Perhaps it is because management thinks the fault lies *in* the employees (not in the company, management's leadership, management controls, and human relations programs). It is the *employee* who must be changed. But where does management obtain the idea that the way to "change" employees is to fire them with enthusiasm? The first possible answer comes from the proposition that an individual behaves according to his self-concept. An individual A (management) will tend to act toward individual B (employee) the way A would act toward himself. A can act toward B only in terms of his own self-concept. One reason management assumes these programs are "good" is because the messages these programs communicate inspire *management*.

A second reason is that those responsible for these programs have derived their "principles for action" from principles of selling, marketing, production, engineering, and other long established staff services which in turn are based on the logics of formal organization and management controls discussed previously. They *assume* that people can be handled in the same way as other problems are handled by staff employees.

Unfortunately there do not seem to be available any systematic studies evaluating the actual impact of these communications programs. Some insight can be obtained and hypotheses formulated by drawing on the research in the field of racial prejudice and mass communication. Marrow reports that even if the information communicated is valid and well presented, "those who find it antagonistic to their own viewpoint evade it by not paying attention."[63] In some cases the communications programs designed to decrease prejudice in individuals actually made them even more defensive and increased the degree of tenacity with which they held their prejudiced viewpoints. One may hypothesize that if the employees feel a basic conflict of interest between management and themselves, if they feel, for any reason, that they cannot trust management, then it is possible that the communication programs used by management may serve to increase these feelings rather than to decrease them. Hovland, Janis, and Kelley[64] support this conclusion when they report that "communications attributed to low credibility sources tended to be considered more biased and unfair in presentation than identical ones attributed to high credibility sources."

These three researchers also describe some interesting conclusions regarding the impact of communications whose objective is to change attitudes that are based upon the individual's membership in certain "salient" groups. They report that, "persons who are most strongly motivated to retain their membership in a group will be most resistant to communication contrary to the standards of that group" and to change their own opinions related to the group.[65] Smith, Bruner, White[66] report that information does not tend to change attitudes held by individuals to fulfill needs of group security. It may be that as management communicates information designed to win the employees to the management side, the employees will tend to resist this communication, if union membership is important to them. Employees feel strongly about their union membership even though they do not take active participation in the internal activities of the union. One may even go further in raising questions about the impact of communications programs. Let us assume that they did change people's attitudes. Is this necessarily good from the viewpoint of the manager? Perhaps not. What kind of employees would he tend to have if their basic attitudes could be changed easily through written or oral communications? Hovland, Janis, and Kelley suggest that in their research the individual most easily influenced by others' persuasion was an individual with low self-esteem, who tended to perceive himself as socially inadequate.[67] The studies by Crutchfield[68] and by Rogers[69] indirectly support these conclusions. Rogers points out that the person who is most easily "managed" by the communication of others is the person who tends to be passive, rigid, insecure, and authoritarian.

Moreover, the works of Merton,[70A] Katz and Lazarsfeld,[70B] Berelson, Lazarsfeld and McPhee,[70C] and Coleman, Katz and Menzel[70D] shows important evidence that mass attitudes are not changed by mass media as much as by personal, individual influence of what they call "opinion leaders." Administrators might profit greatly by noting the lessons learned by opinion pollsters.[70E]

Leaving the field of communication and turning to the fad of participation, some similar searching questions may be asked on the basis of existing research. Researchers report, as a result of depth interviews with thirty managers, that many of the managers are "for" human relations and that "participation," "democracy" are definitely a part of what they *say* is good management. However, there appears to be a discrepancy between what they *say* and what they *do*. They found[70] that all the managers emphasized the need for participation of all key people in instituting any changes. The insistence on participation sounded good to the research staff. But after a few minutes of discussion, they began to wonder if the word "participation" had the same meaning for the researcher and administrator. One thing happened in every interview which led the researcher to believe that the word was being used differently. After the executive had told them that he insisted on participation, he would then continue by describing the difficulty he had in getting the supervisors to speak freely. "We bring them in, we *tell* them that we want their frank opinion, but most of them just sit there and nod their heads. We know they're not coming out with exactly how they feel."

Such statements seem to indicate "pseudo-participation." That is, participation which looks like, but is not, real participation. True participation means that the people can be observed to be spontaneous and free in their discussion. Participation, in the real sense of the word, also involves a group decision which leads the group to accept or reject some course of action. Of course, organizations need to have their supervisors accept the new goals, not reject them, but if the supervisors do not really accept the new changes, but say they do, then trouble will exist. Such an acceptance is characterized by the necessity of the person who induced the change to be always on the "look out," to request signatures of the "accepted" change should the subordinates later complain, and to constantly apply pressure (through informal talks, meetings, and "educational discussions of accounting") upon the "acceptors."

In other words, if top management executives are going to use participation, it should be used in the real sense of the word. A dilution of the real stuff will taste funny and people may not like it.

A few examples from the more mature and research grounded management literature may help to make the point more concretely.

To get a better idea of how consultative management works, consider what happened in the production department of the mythical Whiteside Manufacturing Company.

Jake Morgan, foreman, leaned back in his swivel chair. He was thinking hard. One drill press had to be moved and he had to decide where it should go. After examining the possibilities, he decided that the best place was on the other side of the electric switches. Jake picked up the phone and ordered the machine moved that night. Then he went to Tony, the operator.

'Tony,' he said, 'Your machine has to be moved. We're putting it over there on the other side of the switches. When you report to work tomorrow your machine will be there ready for you. You understand?'

'Okay, boss, I got it,' said Tony. But the more Tony thought about this, the madder he got. 'How come they gotta move my machine? Why not somebody else? I got plenty seniority around here. Over by the switch is not good. The boss says move, I move but by God, I don't have to like it.' Tony went back to work with a chip on his shoulder and with lead in his feet and heart.

Six months later Jake was up against the same problem. Tony's drill press had to be moved back near where it had been before. But this time Jake handled it differently. He had just completed a company course on how to be a better supervisor.

'Tony,' he said, 'I have to move your machine back near where it was before. Do you see any objections to that?'

'No boss, I think you got it doped out about right.'

'All right, Tony, but don't forget we want your ideas.'

The more Tony thought about this the madder he got. His reaction could be summed up in one word, Nuts! 'Who,' he asked his pal, 'does this guy think he's kidding? Why ask me what I think? He already decided. Nothing I'd say would change anything. I'd be crazy to say anything but Yes, Yes, Yes. Human relations—Ha! These guys make me sick with their cute tricks.' Tony went back to work with a chip on his shoulder and with lead in his feet and heart.

A year later Jake Morgan had to talk to Tony again about the machine. Jake had learned a lot in this year. And this time he started by explaining to Tony why the machine had to be moved. 'But before I decide where your machine ought to go, Tony,' Jake continued, 'I need your ideas on where the best place might be. Can you help me?'

Tony did have some ideas. And together they talked over the advantages and disadvantages of three locations. During the discussion Tony brought up a point that Jake had not considered. The result was that the third location, which neither Tony nor Jake had favored at first, now seemed the best place to put the machine. Then, and only then, did Jake decide.

That day Tony ate his lunch without danger of indigestion as he reflected on the fact that he had had the chance to have his say when it really counted. His boss had made the decision, sure, but that's what bosses are for. And even if Jake had not decided on what Tony wanted, Tony would still have felt the same glow of pride because he knew that he had had a part in the decision.[71]

There are a number of questions that may be asked about this story. First, is the writer trying to imply that *all* employees like Tony will become angry if they are led autocratically? Evidence has already been presented that an apathetic, disinterested worker may enjoy Jake's original attempt.

In the second attempt Jake still starts out by saying that the machine must be moved. Then he asks if Tony has any objections. This is not being participative. Turning to the third attempt, however, the "correct" one, there still is evidence of directive leadership, although somewhat sugar-coated to be sure. First, Tony is still not permitted any participation as to whether or not his machine should be moved. In fact, in some way the "correct" way may add more pressure in that it starts out with a "barrage" of reasons why the machine must be moved. It's like softening up the enemy before an attack. Then Jake says to Tony, "Before *I* (not we) decide what to do and '*I*' (not we) need your (not our) ideas and can you help *me* (not how can *we* help)." Is there any doubt as to who really is the leader?

Jake is still the boss. He has the power. He is *not* really going to turn over any of his responsibility and authority to Tony. As the writer states:

> Nothing could be further from fact. In any position, responsibility and authority must be commensurate. The authority to make any decision and the responsibility for it must be delegated to a single individual. Thus the manager may count noses to find out how many members of the team favor this and how many favor that, but it is the *manager, and no one else*,[72] who is accountable for what is done. And his final decision, after weighing all the available facts and ideas of his team, may be quite different from the views expressed by any or even all members of the group.
>
> When this occurs, it is unlikely that those who disagree with the final decision will suddenly change their minds. But as team members, their ideas have been asked for, they understand the problems involved and the reasons for the decision.

This is not the kind of leadership used in the several research works on democratic leadership so often quoted. Lewin and his students, for example, always faced the possibility that the group members might *not* want to drink more orange juice, eat more wheat bread, produce better pajamas. The leaders in those experimental groups had a faith that if the group, after careful consideration, freely decided against orange juice, against high production, this decision was *their* responsibility. They did not use the principle of one leader, one authority, one responsibility. To be sure, their participative experiments seem to work in the direction favored by the government (in the case of orange juice) or management (in the case of pajamas). But the important point is that all these groups felt free to choose as they wished and to change leadership if necessary.

Jake's kind of leadership emphasizes directive leadership plus the inherent autocracy of organization. The writer of Jake's case admits this when he states that Jake is still the leader *and* when he (inadvertently?) notes that the group is *Jake's* team . . . and *his* final decision, after weighing all of the available facts and ideas of *his* team. In true participative management, the team belongs to *no one* individual. It belongs to itself.

The criticism of this type of participative management should not be interpreted as implying that organization based upon such principles as chain of command and unity of direction should or even can have truly participative management. Some of the research demonstrates the superiority of participative management in terms of higher morale and possibly higher productivity.[73] These results, however, are achieved through experimental procedure, where participative management is *temporarily substituted* for the basically inherent authoritarian structure of the organization and role of the management. If this cannot be done in the regular everyday activity, we ought then to be careful in applying the results of these experiments lest we fall into the trap of manipulative management in the negative sense of the word. There is no guarantee that increased group cohesiveness (brought upon by increased participation) will tend to increase productivity. Increased cohesiveness serves to heighten the susceptibility of group members to influence from other members. Thus if the predominant influences are to restrict production, the cohesiveness will lead to lower production.[74]

Let us take another example. In one of the more carefully thought out programs of supervisory-worker communication,[75] the supervisor is told that he must communicate *down* to the line so that the employee will know what is expected of him, how to proceed with his job, and to what extent he has succeeded with his job. One reads that under good communication conditions, the supervisor asks the employee to feel free to give him his response to his instruction and to report the progress on the work at hand. But most important, the manual continues, "good communication is essential so that the employee, through an exchange of opinions and understanding and a chance to freely express himself will *feel* that his job and status are secure, that his judgment and ideas are important, that he's part of the team, and so forth."

What is happening here? Someone read the many leadership studies on "democratic" leadership and noted that as a result of "free" communication the group members tend to feel that their opinions are respected, that they are part of the team. Thus they include in the manual advice to the supervisor to make

certain the employee feels free to communicate. Note they emphasize that it is the supervisor's responsibility to make the employee
feel free.

If we examine carefully the research upon which the above
is probably based we will find that the subordinates feel part of
the team and respected *not* because of the leader but because
fundamentally they preserve for themselves the final authority
on any question in their group.[76] *They* are in control, not the
leader whom they have appointed. Thus in the research situation
the democratic leader does not tell the members what is expected
of them, how to proceed, how successful they are. These are the
functions of directive leadership. In other words, if the research
is valid, people cannot be made to feel they are part of the team
if the supervisor does what he is told to do from above. Actually,
the expert who wrote the material quoted above may be making
it difficult for the supervisor because he is in effect asking the
supervisor to be directive but to achieve the results of a democratic leadership. This is not possible.

If we examine the leader's guide to this "communications conference" we find that it is full of suggestions (from the training
expert) for the leader "to point out at this point such and such,"
"to introduce such and such picture," "to ask the group about
their experiences," "to begin a discussion on." If the individual
using this guide followed these instructions, he (not the group)
would be defining the goals, and the paths to the goals. The
manual is actually telling the leader how to teach "democratic"
leadership in a rather directive autocratic manner.

To summarize, research shows that under democratic conditions people do tend to feel that they are part of a team and
respected. However, this does not mean this will tend to be the
case if a supervisor tries to be pseudo democratic or democratic
under autocratic conditions. We must not forget that the formal
structure of most organizations and the management controls are
fundamentally autocratic. The small groups experiments from
which the use of "democratic leadership" seems to have arisen
never coped with these two factors.

Gordon[77] provides an example of participation truly based

on the democratic leadership studies. He describes how his colleagues and he attempted to create a workshop training experience for a selected number of delegates that would be group-centered or democratic in orientation. During planning stages even the experts who were planning the institute on group-centered leadership expressed conflicts of becoming "too much" group-centered and not meeting the responsibility the delegates expected the planners to have. Types of questions asked by the planners were: "How am I going to get across my point of view if I am group-centered? Will the delegates think that I don't know my stuff? Maybe they'll feel that we didn't plan a damn thing? After all, aren't *we* the experts; won't they expect us to at least begin by telling them something about group-centered leadership?" A conflict arose because the group-centered approach implies maximum freedom and every bit of pre-planning about what to tell the delegates seemed to decrease the freedom the delegates would have. Gordon suggests that the experts' anxieties about giving "too much" freedom is related to their own unresolved anxieties about leadership. This topic became an important subject for discussion in the planning stages. Thus planning became involved in *preparing the experts* rather than the subject matter. For example:

One of the first conclusions reached by the staff was that group-centered leadership requires a kind of preparation that is quite different from the preparation for traditional leadership. Committed to an approach that left responsibility with the group, we soon discovered, and with some relief, that we need not concern ourselves with organizational plans. How the group was to be split up, who was to be in charge of each group, how lectures would be scheduled—these were among the many organizational matters for which the staff did not need to plan . . . Thus preparing lecture notes, outlining topics, working up lesson plans, and developing visual aids consumed no part of our planning time.

It is more difficult to describe what the staff's preparation *did* consist of. As indicated . . . earlier . . . much of our time was spent in earnestly examining our own basic attitudes and beliefs and in constantly checking them against the philosophical and theoretical foundations of group-centered leadership . . . Preparation for the Workshop required us to face up to many basic attitudes which we held in varying degrees—our own insecurities, our lack of faith in people, our tendencies to use others for our own ends, our needs for prestige and status, our lack of tolerance of ambiguity, our fear of hostility expressed toward us, and the inconsistencies that often appeared in our systems of values.

Ordinarily leaders devote much time and thought to developing skills and techniques of influencing their group members to select certain goals or achieve particular objectives. This aspect of planning goes hand in hand with the traditional conception of the leader as the influencer, the persuader, and the inspirer. In the Workshop experiment, however, the leaders' preparation could be characterized *as an effort to plan how we could avoid influencing the group.* Here is an entirely different orientation toward a group, one in which the leader tries to prepare himself to *guard against* the tendency to manipulate the group. It is a preparation for removing the leader's influence rather than improving it, for enlarging the group's area of freedom rather than restricting it, for transferring the leader's power to the group rather than holding on to it.[78]

Can an industrial organization, a union, or any other type of on-going formal organization utilize such a philosophy of leadership? Gordon thinks it is not necessarily possible. He notes that the degree of freedom to use group-centered leadership in an industrial organization will be perhaps a little more than the military type of organization. But as the degree of freedom that is given to the group is decreased, and the power given to the leader is increased, one leaves the concept of group-centered leadership and enters the area of the more traditional directive leadership.

The same problem if not a bit more extreme exists in Europe. In many countries the idea of worker participation caught on so quickly and so intensely that it became law! The companies have what may be freely translated as "production committees." An analysis of the top management basic attitudes suggests that in over 75 per cent of the cases these production committees are seen as (1) an excellent device to bypass many layers of line authority and communicate directly with the workers, and (2) a tool for the manipulation of the workers. In the latter case, one hears many managers speaking of production committees (formal or informal) in terms of what top management is going to do *to* and *for* the employees and what it expects in return. Little if anything is said about what the employees will do for and to management. Two typical statements are:

a. I'm very much in favor of production committees. It is important that the employees get to understand us. So many have the wrong idea about us. I hold meetings with my people. They are informal. We have some food and a little to drink. This I believe is good. It softens them up. We sit down together, as one family, and I get them to talking about the important problems of the plant.

b. Production committees can be quite useful. I find that I can get much more done through them. People get together and talk with management. They get to know us. We can lessen their resistance to change this way. Officially, I am not a member of this committee. Of course, I can get my questions in. I go and tell them, why do you fellows not do something really important. (Instead of arguing about screens, paint, etc.)

Dahlstrom[79] confirms these results in a study of a large Swedish factory. He finds, for example, that management's information-giving dominated the works council's meeting.

Returning to research in America, Whyte describes similar results in his study of American management's conception of participation:

Now participation, of course, is a very good work and everybody is for it. Unfortunately, however, too few have stuck to the idea in its basic sense—that of giving the individual more responsibility and autonomy. In far too many instances, 'participation' has meant putting people together in a hall, and the results have been little more than well-meant fictions designed to give the worker a 'feeling' of belonging and very little else.[80]

Communications programs, benefits, suggestion programs, better working conditions, cafeterias, clean locker rooms, uniforms become part of "good" human relations. In an analysis of thirty communication programs, for example, management "communicates" frequently the following topics: (1) "Make the worker feel he's part of the company." (2) "Tell him how important his job is to the whole picture." (3) "Show him that management is truly interested in the employees." (4) "Keep him informed of costs, errors, and the financial progress of the company." (5) "Sell him on the importance of free enterprise system." (6) "Emphasize the possibilities of opportunity for advancement."

With the possible exception of aspects of 4 and 6, topics like these represent management's worries more than they do employees' needs. Communication programs have become an excellent medium for management to express and try to do something about its own worries.

Research suggests that telling a worker he is an important part of the company, when through *actual experience* he sees he is a very minor part (thanks to task specialization) with little responsibility (thanks to chain of command, directive leadership, and management controls) may only *increase* the employees' dissatisfaction with management. As one worker concluded, "Who are they kidding, us or themselves?" To emphasize to an assembly line worker that he should feel proud of the four bolts that he puts into the right rear end of a car may be viewed as an insult by the worker who is a "whole" human being (although it allays management's anxieties about employee apathy). As one employee remarked, "It's ironic—damn. It *hurts* to know that four bolts are important. What a hell of a life."

Another impact of communication programs is that many managers are spending some time every day talking with their employees. They do this because they believe the employee will produce more and feel better if they have more information about the company and the management. Although there is evidence that there is no relationship between how much a person knows and his morale or productivity,[82] management places much emphasis on this personal communication.

Another example is the case of the twenty executives who "knew their workers by their first names and who always made it a practice to visit a certain number each day to ask them about their problems, admitted that never during these thousands of 'quickie' interviews did the *employees* ask the executives about *their* problems." People who truly feel on an equal level would presumably have the interest and desire to ask about the executive's family problems if he has the graciousness to ask them about theirs. Does the reader know of any "friends" with whom he feels on an equal level yet does not feel free to ask them the same questions that they ask him?

These "fads" assume it is possible to make human relations better, *not* by attacking the causes (formal organization, directive leadership, and management controls) but in effect by making the activities outside the actual work situation more pleasant for the worker (e.g., new toilets, new cafeterias, sports, picnics, newspapers,) or by sugar-coating the work situation. In the case of the former, management is in effect paying the worker to live in the tension-producing life of the plant. Thus employees find their predisposition for more materialistic things reinforced by management's own behavior. In the case of the latter, they are simply ignoring the problem and maybe teaching the employees, *by their behavior,* that it is acceptable to sugar-coat problems.

Katz and Kahn, on the basis of morale studies of thousands of workers, correctly emphasize that such programs will tend to defeat their purpose because they assume workers will react favorably to a system of rewards linked to good working conditions, vacations with pay, bowling alleys, and baseball teams. *This assumption breaks down, however, because it depends upon an over-simplified application of a reward formula to a complex industrial setting.*[83]

Another result of the "let's be human" approach is the idea that human relations means being nice to people. Never get people upset. Feelings should not be expressed. Keep your personality to yourself. It's wrong to be emotional. This idea has become so much of a "norm" that managers may tend not to communicate directly and honestly to their subordinates, especially when they have something negative to say to them. As a result, the executive's view of why he is leaving may differ sharply from the view of his superior. For example:

1. Executive: I need broader experience than I could ever get in engineering.
Superior: He just can't get things organized. He does little planning and gets into a lot of picayune details. He has cost us a lot of money in his engineering job.
2. Executive: There was a cut-back in the size of the organization and I was one of the unfortunates laid off.
Superior: He was technically incompetent. His training and aptitude just did not qualify him for the job of screening applicants and coping with

our labor relations problems. Everything of any consequence came right upstairs to me for settlement.

3. Project Engineer: In this outfit you have to have a college degree or you don't get anywhere. I know more and can do a better job than these younger fellows, but they won't give me a chance.

Superior: He has a belligerent attitude toward anyone with a college degree. Sure, he has ability, but he won't even listen to anyone who gained his knowledge from books instead of on the job. We can't afford to promote him.

4. Vice President (resigned): You can't compete with the fair-haired boys. The boss wouldn't talk with me or accept any of my ideas. But some of those others, including his son who got his degree at M.I.T. two years ago—man, they get away with murder.

President: I just couldn't understand Walt. Sometimes it sounded as though we weren't talking the same language. He'd get mad when I didn't agree with him right away and I'd have to assign somebody else to a job to handle it.[84]

To summarize, an increase in certain types of human relations programs may place the employee in the position where he increasingly feels dependent, subordinate; that his management is trying to placate him with benefits and other material rewards. This jibes with his increasing interest in material rewards.

As a result of the tremendous need by management for good human relations without knowing what this is, hundreds of "experts" have "sprung up" overnight. They guarantee results! I have received advertisements of a new human relations program which includes a guarantee of satisfaction or one can cancel his subscription with a full refund. Another advertisement by a leading management group guarantees to teach, through its publications, among other things, "The 30 rules for getting things done through people." Still other materials claim that basically, "All workers like to be treated fairly, they need to belong, they all like a good scrap." Still others highly recommended to management the qualities of "being a man among men," "facing the facts squarely," "laying it on the line—diplomatically of course," and "being Christian," as examples of rules for "good" human relations. Then there is a book that gives you the exact steps to making a gloomy apathetic worker happy. It guarantees to help you help the employee "snap out of it."

If we analyze all these solutions we find: (1) They represent what management wishes it could do (e.g., make apathetic workers happy). (2) They assume what makes management unhappy is bad for the company. (3) They assume what is bad for management is also bad for the worker. (4) Most important, they "take management for a ride" because they are selling the invalid notion that management, with the help of certain gimmicks, can make the employee happy. The door to happiness for every individual is locked from the inside. Only he can unlock it.

There are more problems. Our analysis in Chapter IV states that employees are adapting to their work-a-day world by such ways as apathy, disinterest, goldbricking, and rate-setting. Management dislikes this and tries to solve or alleviate the problems. One important method is to increase communication. They communicate to the worker that he should feel "important," "loyal," "part of the company," "interested." But this is *not* necessarily how the employees actually feel. It follows, therefore, that *to the extent the employees behave in a way they know is antagonistic to management's values, and to the extent that they want to remain in the organization with a minimum of employee-management friction, the employees must not communicate to management these antagonistic activities.* Thus, the program management originally defined to increase communication may have the opposite effect in the area where the employees know they are doing something "illegal." This is precisely the area management would want to know of and to correct! It is not long before the manager becomes isolated from the realities that exist "down in the shop," "out on the floor" along the flow of work.

This leads to what is commonly known as *executive isolation.* As he goes up the line, the executive, slowly, surely, and increasingly, *becomes* isolated from the people below. He is increasingly alone, wondering who is and who is not telling him the facts. Those people that do *not* tell him all the facts are not necessarily to be solely evaluated as liars. They are lying, to be sure. However, they may be doing it out of respect to the norms of the company's communication program. After all, it states that, "We're all one happy family." "Our workers are loyal workers."

It is not only the human relations programs that lead to executive isolation. The formal organization, directive leadership, and management controls will also tend to increase executive isolation. This conclusion follows logically from what we have presented to date. The logic is as follows:

1. Mature individuals are predisposed to be in situations where they feel in varying degree independent, active, and equal.

2. Ideal expression of the formal organization, directive leadership, and management controls places individuals in a situation where they are coerced to be dependent, passive, subordinate. This tendency increases as we go down the line and as the job becomes more specialized.

3. Individuals adapt by such activities as leaving, being mobile, goldbricking, rate-setting, causing waste, errors, and becoming apathetic.

4. Such activities are antagonistic to management values especially as communicated in "human relations and communication" programs.

5. To the extent that the subordinates want to remain in the organization with minimal employee management conflict, they will be predisposed not to communicate activities they view as being antagonistic to management's values, objectives, and attitudes.[85]

6. There is *always an inherent tendency in the organization toward a barrier of secrecy created, at the outset, by formal organization and/or directive leadership and/or management controls. This tendency is reinforced by pseudo human relations and communication programs.*

The tendency for secrecy can exist on any level where the subordinates feel dependent upon their leader. Thus a directive leader could create barriers to communication within his own management. Argyris[81] cites examples of this possibility in a study of the impact of a directive leader upon nearly twenty middle management supervisors.

For example: Communications must somehow be "cleared"

through the leader. The supervisors talk directly to each other; but in the presence of their leader they are careful to communicate only that which they know is approved by the leader. Thus we can infer a barrier to spontaneous communication even when all supervisors and the leader are seated together in a group.

The leadership pattern affects the communication process in other ways. First, the leader has disbanded most bulletin boards and dismissed office boys excepting a mail clerk. The loudspeaker system and the telephone have taken the office boy's place. Today the supervisors know that when the leader communicates, or when they communicate to each other, it must be done quickly. The emphasis is on speed and conciseness of messages. Every message the leader demands must be clear, concise, and to the point.

The characteristics of this leadership pattern pervade the entire communication system. The supervisors try to speak fast in front of him. Some, who are not good at speaking quickly, actually rehearse what they are going to say before going into the office of the Leader.

The written word is always used when possible on important matters. The supervisors revert to writing memos lest one of their fellow supervisors blame them unfairly for something. Written memos with the leader help them "defend themselves" if they need to, without shouting or becoming aggressive. They can politely and quietly show the memo to the leader and thus make their point. Communicating in this manner permits them to correct the leader in a "submissive sort of way."

Furthermore, due to the fact that the supervisors are leader-dependent and leader-centered, they consistently tend to be less spontaneous in their communication. The leader, on the other hand, has little difficulty in saying what he wants to say and how he wants to say it.

The supervisors' dependence upon the leader for rewards and authority even influences the content of communications with the leader. Thus the supervisors: (1) Try always to show that everything "is going along fine." (2) Try to show that they are all one happy, hard-working team. (3) Try to keep any communication with the leader that might be perceived as pressure on or dominance of him at a minimum. (4) Try to keep the expression of their own frustrations and conflicts at a minimum. (5) Try to communicate information that may be detrimental to others and favorable to themselves, thereby furthering their competitive "cause" for the leader's reward.

On the other hand, the leader: (1) Communicates his energetic, pugnacious, prodding characteristics. (2) Communicates his frustrations and gripes "caused" by the employees or others. (3) Communicates that things are not as they could be. There is always room for improvement. (4) Communicates his praise of the company as a whole.

In a controlled field experiment Mellinger[86] confirms the above results. He states that in any given situation if B (in this case the subordinates) lacks trust in A (the leader), he will tend to conceal his attitudes and feelings when communicating with A. Concealment, aggression, and evasiveness arise. Moreover, A's perception of the "realities" is impaired causing him to overestimate agreement in some cases or to underestimate it in others.

The analysis on pseudo human relations policies leads us to some inherent difficulties faced by most top administrators. They are responsible for the "human relations climate" in their organization. To act responsibly they must have accurate facts. But because of the barrier to communication, the chances are high that they will *not* obtain all the information they need. Thus the top managers are charged with the responsibility of accurate diagnosis of human relations problems; yet (1) They occupy a position that prevents free upward communication, (2) The communication upward is distorted to fit what subordinates feel are their expectancies, (3) Because of their own personality, they tend to have different values about work and loyalty. Thus they will have certain built-in "blind spots" even before they begin their diagnosis. (4) Any frustration and tension resulting from feelings of isolation will tend to make them even less effective in their diagnosis. (5) Many managers react negatively to isolation. They may feel defensive about the union being closer to the employees than management. As a result, many increase their efforts in terms of personal visits, communication, and "human relations" programs. All of these may tend to make the situation even worse.

One result of this frustration is for management to tend to diagnose their internal human problems as being the fault of social trends ("workers aren't what they used to be") trade unions ("they're always undercutting us"), and technology ("what can you expect of a guy who has to use that machine?").

Such diagnoses have the advantage of placing the blame on factors *outside* management's immediate control. This may be, therefore, a defense mechanism (projection) whereby management projects the "blame" they may feel is theirs onto such phenomena as social trends, unions, and technology. This is not to imply that the three factors are not at all relevant. However, to the extent that it is possible to find within the same industrial area two plants with comparable technology, economic position, and unions and yet one has far better human relations than the other, to that extent our hypothesis of the diagnoses being a defense mechanism is supported.[87]

Clearly the basic assumptions of formal organization, directive leadership, and management controls that "management is responsible," that "they know best," and that "people are inherently lazy and must be pushed," must be revamped. Hower provides a few for consideration.

1. That the administrator does not necessarily know what should be done. His subordinates may have better ideas. It follows that he should enlist the aid of his subordinates.

2. People, unless discouraged from doing so, will do their best to achieve what the purposes and the circumstances of the organization require. Consequently, they need to be informed about the situation but do not require driving to meet it.

3. Unless they are discouraged from doing so, people will regard their jobs as ends in themselves and as part of their daily lives. It follows that if the jobs are reasonably interesting and responsible, people will try to do them well.

4. That the behavior of people in organizations is related only slightly to logical thinking. Hence, to explain, reason, or argue is of little value by itself in changing behavior.

5. That people tend to have many nonlogical feelings, sentiments, and

beliefs which are of paramount importance to them and hence to the administrator. In consequence, the administrator must be aware of these nonlogical elements and must have some means of coping with them other than logical argumentation.[88]

To summarize, management diagnoses the employees to be at fault for high turnover; high absence rates; low productivity, apathy, disinterest, and low identifications with the free enterprise system. Following their diagnosis and using their assumptions about effective formal organization leadership control they make basic decisions on basic policy to remedy the situation. They conclude that stronger, dynamic leadership, management controls, and "human relations" are the answer. Our analysis suggests that instead of ameliorating the basic causes, these three practices tend to reinforce the problems caused by the organization, thus increasing the very behavior these practices were supposed to decrease. Evidence that turnover and in some cases accidents can be viewed as the employee's attempt to withdraw from a frustrating work situation is presented by two studies of Hill and Trist[89, 90] and studies by Castle[91] and by Noland.[92] These studies relate turnover or accidents to more than one aspect of the work situation, not simply to the formal organizational structure. For example, Noland's work related turnover to the directive leadership of the supervisor and to organizational structure.

VI

The First-line Supervisor

The formal organization, directive leadership, and management controls tend to create a situation in which the employees adapt by behaving in ways antagonistic to the desires of management. Management in turn tends to react in a way that increases the antagonism, which in turn leads to a barrier toward upward communication of these antagonistic activities by the employees who are aware of and centered toward management's needs. As a result there begins to exist a feeling of two worlds; the employee and the management. The barrier of secrecy serves an important function for the employees because it prevents their informal behavior from being discovered, and decreases the possible embarrassment and conflict with management. As long as each side remains in its own world neither is (psychologically) hurt.

A. MEN IN THE MIDDLE

This logic may work for the employee and top management. It does not work so well for the first-line supervisor (foreman) because he is the link between the two worlds. It is his job to gain the respect of the employees and of management. But how can he do this when each has different values? The foreman replies:

I'll tell you one thing that you can put down in your little black book, and I want you to remember this, and that is that the supervisor is a 'bumping post.' That's something you can remember, he's a 'bumping post' because he's in the middle; he has to take it from both ends; and those running the place don't give him any credit for it.[1]

Another foreman describes the problem as follows:

When you get right down to it, the supervisor really doesn't have very much to say. He just tries to keep everybody happy down here, but he can't say anything to management, if it's doing something that's not going to work out for the best interest of everybody concerned.

Gardner[2] summarizes and Wray[3] is in agreement about the existing research regarding the problems and position of the foreman as follows:

In many cases he is expected to collect data and prepare reports which his supervisors then use to put pressure on him. He is impatient, therefore, of elaborate reports of paper controls, since they mean extra work and may mean more pressure from above. Also, he knows the inadequacies (his workers change reports) of such records and is critical of decisions based upon them.

Gardner elaborates this in the following words:

There are cases where the foreman is in sympathy with the workers. In such cases there is usually a very friendly and informal relationship between the foreman and his group. Generally, in this situation, there seems to be a small barrier between them because of the difference in rank, and the foreman maintains little social distance between himself and the group. Many of these situations are characterized by a much greater distinction between foreman and his department chief and there is a very strong barrier between these two levels.

There is, of course, the opposite. In this type of situation the workers feel forced to be on their guard against their foreman and think of him as someone who is against them rather than for them. They develop various defenses; they watch their behavior whenever he is in sight— they may restrict output without his knowledge.

Lieberman confirms the existence of the same conflict in a study of 300 foremen when he states that where the management-employee relationships are compatible foremen who have been shop stewards . . . "are no more prone to feel they are in a conflict situation than foremen who have not been stewards. However, where the employee-management relationships are not compatible, foremen who have been stewards will tend to feel (more) conflict than those who have not been stewards."[4] Thus the conflict exists but it is less where the management-employee relationships are compatible.

In a survey of foremen and their problems Guy B. Arthur reports that "54 per cent of the foremen are still plagued with the absence of definite lines of authority and 70 per cent have more than one boss." Moreover, nearly three-fourths of the foremen report that they perceive themselves as being between the "devil and the deep blue sea."[5]

Moore[6] confirms these results. He notes that the foreman is caught between representing the needs of management and the needs of the employee. The fact that he has a formal management title tends to increase his difficulty to really integrate himself with the employees.

Renck concludes on the basis of a study of 791 production foremen and assistant foremen in fourteen companies:

The fact that the foremen have membership in two different and sometimes conflicting groups is not only a source of pressure for the foremen—but it is also often a source of emotional conflict. It is a source of conflict which neither the executive nor the production worker meets. The conflict stems from this source: The foreman recognizes that he doesn't have all the facts, that he is not in a position to make clear-cut judgments on the actions of his superiors. But he is in a position—a better position than anyone else—to judge the impact of these actions on himself and his work group. Because this impact is often a negative one—one of change—he is frequently frustrated in attempting to implement it with his employees. Frequently, and from time to time, he may identify more strongly with his employees than he does with management. Unlike the executive he cannot be analytical because he is not informed; more like the production worker, he can be critical in spite of the fact that he is usually willing to give management the benefit of the doubt over the long haul. And in addition, he, too, is dealing with problems of the organization; problems which he more often sees as "mistakes" of management rather than as the inevitable result of maintaining and expanding the company.[7]

One result of the conflicting values between management and the worker is that the foreman who is the communicating link between them becomes a "marginal man; a man caught between two worlds." Argyris[8] suggests that the foreman will tend to work in a world in which:

1. The foreman is aware that there is a difference between the employees' world and the management world.
2. The foreman may feel that:
   a. He belongs to neither world.
   b. He belongs to one, but not the other.
   c. He belongs to both.
3. Although he is responsible for the employees' world, the employees may not inform him of all their activities (e.g., rate-setting, loafing in the washrooms, and goldbricking on the job).
4. Although he is a member of the management world, the management may not keep him informed about all their activities involving him (e.g., their evaluation of him, a possible raise, and possible long-run technological changes.)
5. The foreman is not only a marginal man; he also tends to be in the dark about certain activities which may be crucial in the effective administration of his unit.
6. The foreman may be aware of certain employee and/or management activities and he may wish he could participate in them. The employees and management respectively can prevent him from participation. To the extent these activities are highly important to him, the foreman will experience frustration.
7. The foreman may be permitted, and at times be asked by the employees, to sanction certain informal activities that they know are antagonistic to management. To the extent that the foreman is loyal to the management, he will tend to be in a conflict situation.
8. The foreman may be permitted, and at times be requested by the management, to support certain activities that they know are antagonistic to the employees. To the extent that the foreman is loyal to the employees, he will tend to be in a conflict situation.
9. The foreman can experience conflict when the employees and/or management fluctuate about their decisions. (E.g., the foreman may complain, "I wish management would make up its mind as to what is the policy on the union," or "Those damn employees,

one day they want something, the next day they change their minds.")

10. The foreman will tend to experience conflict if he is coerced by management:

    a. To cooperate in an employee activity which the employees like (e.g., cooperate with shop steward).

    b. Not to participate in an activity the employees like.

    c. To coerce the employees to participate in an activity that they do not like.

    d. To coerce the employees not to participate in an activity they like.[9]

On the basis of many large studies of supervision by the Survey Research Center, Kahn confirms the above analysis and enlarges upon it by making the following prediction as to factors that can influence the foreman's conflict.

1. When the foreman perceives the expectations of the men as being the same as those of management, he will see his role as congruent with those expectations.

2. When the foreman perceives a conflict between the expectations of the men and those of management, his perceptions of his own role will depend upon:

    a. His sensitivity to the attitudes of the workers.

    b. His concern for the problems of persons under his supervision.

    c. His awareness of what factors are responsible for worker motivation.

    d. His perception of the job of foreman as defined by management.

    e. His perceptions of the demands of his own supervisors, and

    f. His perception of the degree of consensus among the men in their demands of him.[10]

Recent results by Mann and Dent[11] suggest that 47% of the supervisors report the conflict discussed above. A large proportion of the remaining 53% do not report the conflict. They apparently are able to relate themselves to both management and the workers. It is interesting to note, however, that this "double membership" succeeds if management does *not* try to make the foreman exclusively a member of management *or* if the employees do *not* try to capture the foreman's complete loyalty.[12]

B. The Trade Union Enters

Another important problem faced by the foreman is related to his power when the trade union enters the plant. According to the principles of chain of command and task specialization, employees are welded into an organization by being made dependent upon their leader, especially for their directions, rewards, and penalties and perpetuation. Their leader leads because he has this formal power to support him. As we have shown previously (Chapter IV) the net effect of unionization is that the foreman loses substantial amounts of this power. Thus the foreman not only works in a situation loaded with conflict and frustration but he has his power taken away from him.

Selekman,[13] Roethlisberger,[14] Gross,[15] Gardiner and Whyte[16] describe the plight of the foreman when the union enters. Before the union entered, the foreman was the sole formal leader. His initial reactions to unionization are inevitably related to the emotions and feelings that cluster about his original leadership position. He fears his position has deteriorated although his formal title remains the same and his responsibilities have increased tremendously. Before, he could fire and hire; he could set production standards; he could maintain his own quality control. With the entrance of the union and the emergence of the union contract as a potent policy statement, the foreman finds himself hedged in on all sides with cost standards, production standards, quality standards, specifications, regulations, rules, laws, and agreements. Most of these are formulated without his participation.

Perhaps even more threatening in the eyes of the foreman is the new human relationship between the employees and himself created by the union. He no longer feels that all the employee loyalties are centered toward the company and toward him. The union and the union officials are receiving a substantial part of the employees' loyalties. Moreover, his management, still a bit dazed, tends to react to uionization with a get-tough-tighten-the-screws policy. Naturally the foreman is expected to pass this pressure down to the employees. It is not uncommon for the foreman to find himself the recipient of an unexplained order to raise production which, if he tried to put into action, could lead the "other side" to open up with a barrage of defensive reactions. The employees, under their new-found protection may thumb their noses at any speed-up. If the foreman decides to push hard he may find his pressure boomeranged into a grievance which, because of the grievance machinery, may eventually be communicated to top management. It is not difficult to see why the foreman may easily become an anxious individual. The union looks after the employees. The employer is able to take care of himself. Who will look after the foreman?

Gardiner[17] is in substantial agreement with the above and with the following advice given to foremen by the Department of Labor.

1. Do not try to discover whether or not any of your employees are members of a union.
2. Do not discuss union matters with your employees, nor express an opinion for or against a union or unionism. This goes while you are off duty as well as on duty.
3. In making any decision regarding an employee such as promotion, discipline, merit rating, transfer or reclassification disregard completely the fact of his union membership or activity.[18]

Newton, reporting on a series of studies involving over 1000 foremen confirms the above results. The majority of foremen are dissatisfied with the limitations imposed upon them. Fifty-two per cent view their job as being one of passing on routine information while 57% report they get top-level news first through the grapevine. The majority of the foremen feel that they have little control over decisions affecting their men, that they are inadequately informed on company policies and plans, that they were held accountable for matters beyond their control, and that their pay is by no means adequate to their responsibilities.[19]

The foreman is faced with the dilemma of being "in the middle" and losing much of his authority and status to the union. He is also greatly influenced by the impact of increased rationalization of equipment and organization. Mills[20] points out that with the coming of big industry, the foreman's function has been diminished by the new technical dictates of modern mechanization. The increasing use of semi-automatic machinery run by trained technicians diminishes the foreman's sphere of technical competence, and his skills become those of the personnel agent "human whip" rather than of the master craftsman and work guide.

Fundamentally, these researchers all agree that before the entrance of the trade union into the plant, the foreman:

1) Made his own decisions.
2) Changed situations as he felt necessary.
3) Defined his own goals and paths to achieve these goals.
4) Worked in a world with few people (other than management) who could give him orders.

However, after unionization, the foreman:

1) Cannot make his own decisions in many critical areas such as production rate, hiring and firing, and discipline.
2) Cannot make changes without consulting management and the trade union.
3) Cannot define unilaterally many of his goals and paths to achieve these goals.
4) Works in a world where the workers shop steward, shop committee, local president, business agent, and even the international representative can modify or prevent many of his actions.

The foreman's freedom of action, his "space of free movement" is greatly restricted. Available personality research suggests that a decrease in an individual's psychological space of free movement usually:

1) Produces high internal tension.
2) The high tension, in turn, we have already seen, leads to a primitivation of the individual's personality. The foreman, in effect, operates at a lower level of maturity.
3) As a result, the tension may increase as failure and frustration also increase.
4) If primitivation continues long enough and becomes strong enough, the foreman may become aggressive and hostile.[21]
5) If the tension continues "being a foreman" itself becomes a negative role for the foreman. As a result, the foreman may:

a. Leave the management work and become a worker.

b. Become a management man completely.

c. Vacillate between the two worlds.[22]

d. Psychologically leave the present and negative situation and dream, speak of the "good old days."[23]

e. Try to join a union.

f. Place a great emphasis on material rewards to make up for his tension.

g. Become apathetic and do just enough not to be rejected by either management or the employees.

Pelz[24] has presented evidence that a restriction of the supervisor's space of free movement and of his power leads to a decrease in the degree of influence he is able to exercise over his department. This in turn will lead to a decrease in the supervisor's effectiveness. Pelz suggests that a noninfluential supervisor who attempts to help employees achieve their goals will tend to fail, not necessarily because of "poor" leadership style, but because of lack of organizational influence.[25] A supervisor soon finds himself in the difficult position of being unable to make desired changes even if he were personally capable.

In short, the foreman's life is not pleasant. It is understandable why management is finding it increasingly difficult to obtain new candidates for the foreman's position.

C. MANAGEMENT REACTS TO THE FOREMAN PROBLEM

How do some managements react to these problems? An analysis of twenty supervisory programs (mostly in large organizations) suggests that management reacts to the "foreman problem" by:

1) "Making" the foreman a part of management through the use of inspiring speeches, bonuses,[26] extra pay,[27] moving pictures, and magazines.

2) Foremen banquets.

3) Foremen discussions of all types to arouse interest.

4) Increasing emphasis on "alert," "dynamic," "forceful," leadership that keeps closer control over the employees.

5) Greater emphasis on:

    a) Company policy, rules, regulations.

b) Company's cost system, payment system, and manufacturing methods.

c) Theories of production control, cost control, quality control, and time and motion study.

d) Labor laws of the U.S.

e) Labor laws of the state within which his company operates.

f) Specific labor contract.

g) How to induct, instruct, and train new workers.

h) How to handle and prevent grievances.

i) How to improve conditions of safety.

6) Greater emphasis on training to "make" the foremen better leaders:

a) How to correct workers and maintain discipline.

b) How never to lose his temper, always be "fair."

c) How to get cooperation from the wide assortment of people with whom he has to deal.

d) How to get along with the shop steward.

e) And in some companies he must know how to do the jobs he supervises better than the employees themselves.

Postponing discussion on training, we find that the first five actions do little to solve the basic problems. Actions 1., 2., and 3. are attempts at "paying for" (not eliminating) the foreman's dissatisfaction. Actions 4. and 5. fundamentally pressure the foreman to learn more about "foremanship" to be able to cope with (not eliminate) his frustrations. Under these conditions, it is understandable why foremen may perceive speeches, magazines, banquets, small discussions, and training in safety and laws as "not very helpful," and creating feelings of pressure.[28]

There is a similarity between management's approach to the foreman problem and their approach with the employees. In both cases, they take a "selling," "pressuring," "educating," approach where the basic assumption is that the foreman and the employee lack something. As in the case of the employees, the management action tends to make the problem more difficult.

Turning to training, recent research suggests quite clearly that typical foremanship training in human relations and leadership is not viewed by foremen as realistic and useful.[29] There is good evidence that it has little impact upon the actual behavior of the foreman.[30] Moreover, there is evidence to suggest that the foreman may view training as management's lack of respect for the foreman.[31] The foreman's logic seems to be as follows:

1) Management wants to train me in leadership.

2) This means they must feel I lack something as a leader.

3) I cannot see what I lack. Moreover, it is my feeling that the *organization* (or the boss or the employees) is what really needs changing.

4) Management thinks that whatever I lack can be taught to me by a training expert who is not a line supervisor.

5) It follows that management doesn't have much respect for me.

Some preliminary research by the writer on the basis of an analysis of three training sessions in human relations suggests that foremen may react by:

1) Taking courses lightly, not seriously.

2) Listening but not learning. They build up pride among themselves by seeing how quickly and how much they can forget.

3) Arguing with instructor, trying to "nail" him about the validity and practicality of what he is teaching.

4) Criticizing the training expert for not knowing the true plant situation and for being staff and not on the firing line.

5) Feeling hostile toward management because, by sending them to this class, they imply a training expert can know more than they do.

6) Blaming top management, budgets, and sales for their problems. *They* are the ones who need the training.

Guest[32] presents evidence that even if the principles learned during training were valid and useful, many foremen are so busy handling production problems that they do not have time to think of them, much less use them. Jasinski[33] presents evidence that even if the foremen did find time to use the principles most of them do not because their superiors do not tend to accept the change in their behavior implied by the "new" principles of leadership learned in the course. For example, the superiors of the foremen rated as "good" foremen those men who kept tight control over their employees while the training director taught the foremen to decrease their control if they are to be effective leaders.

In summary, much of management's reaction to the foreman problem does not attack the basic causes and therefore may lead to increased tension for foremen. It has been shown on the basis of careful experimental research and field research, that such tension can lead to:

1. Further tension.
2. Increased frustration and failure.
3. Interdepartmental strife.
4. Staff versus factory strife.
5. "Internalizing" pressure.
    a. Aggressively
    b. Passively[34]

This acts to make the foreman's position a negative activity. To the extent the foremen feel the pressure and negativeness, they will want (assuming they are relatively healthy) to leave the situation.[35] However, since they need a job and have learned (through the actions of management) to emphasize the importance of and necessity for material rewards, especially, money, they will probably tend to stay as long as the rewards are adequate. In other words, their need for satisfaction being frustrated, they are impelled to leave. However, their need for a job, for money and other material rewards effectively pressures them to remain. Thus as long as they remain, they are actually pressuring themselves to remain.

As a result of the formal organizational structure, directive leadership, and management controls the self-pressured and/or apathetic, disinterested employees must be led by self-pressured, increasingly frustrated foremen.

The foreman's life is not easy. Before closing, it is important to emphasize that we are *not* saying *all* foremen experience all these frustrations, conflicts, and tensions to the same degree. They may, but there is not enough research to permit us to make this conclusion with certainty. The analysis above presents the possible range of factors causing difficulties for the foremen.

The time has now arrived to consider some "action" approaches that an administrator may take based upon the existing research.

VII

Decreasing the Degree of Incongruence Between the Formal Organization and the Healthy Individual

Up to this point the emphasis has been on creating a framework for analysis to begin to understand *why* people behave the way they do in on-going organizations. Although the framework and the understanding it provides are far from complete, a first step has been taken towards a theory of organizational behavior.

The framework begins with the assumption that organizational behavior develops from the interaction of the individual and the formal organization. An analysis of the basic properties of relatively mature[1] human beings and formal organization leads to the conclusion that there is an inherent incongruency between the self-actualization of the two. This basic incongruency creates a situation of conflict, frustration, and failure for the participants. The conflict, frustration, and failure is hypothesized to increase as the individual increases in degree of maturity and/or as he becomes increasingly subordinate along the chain of command and/or as his immediate work environment becomes increasingly specialized. The individual may adapt to the conflict, frustration, and failure by leaving, climbing the organizational ladder, be-

175

coming apathetic, disinterested, and noninvolved, by creating informal groups which develop into formal trade unions, by accepting dissatisfaction as inevitable, and consequently increasing his desire for money and decreasing his desire for human rewards, and finally by acculturating his childern with these adaptive informal activities.

Management, as agents of the formal organization, react to these adaptive informal activities by increasing the degree of directive technically competent leadership, clarifying, redefining, and unintentionally rigidifying the formal structure, increasing and tightening management controls, and finally developing "information," "education," "communication" and "human relations" programs. These management reactions tend to "compound the felony" of the formal organizational structure. Instead of reducing the basic cause of the human problems, they tend to perpetuate the original ones and create new ones.

A systematic framework, if it is to be useful, must help us to understand human behavior in organizations. One sign of understanding is to be able to state the conditions under which specific events are predicted. A more rigorous criterion is to actually *create* these conditions and then to demonstrate that they do lead to the events predicted by the framework. In medicine, for example, a milestone in cancer research is achieved when the scientist actually creates cancer.

It is beyond the present scope to achieve the second criterion of understanding. It would require years of research with a "real live" organization as a laboratory whose parts could be varied systematically as desired. However, the analysis has provided evidence in terms of the first criterion, namely, stating the conditions under which certain behavior is presumed to be caused.

If this analysis is valid, then knowing the condition under which behavior occurs, it should be possible to make predictions as to how this behavior may be changed or modified by stating how the conditions under which this specific behavior can be modified.[2] For example, if management desires to change the apathy or goldbricking or disinterest, what specific action ought they to take? In using this example, employee informal behavior is not viewed by the scientist as a social problem. He does not label apathy as "bad" or high productivity as "good." He simply acts as an advisor to those interested in understanding the causes of this behavior. If any decisions for modification are made they are made by the employees, management, and trade unions, but not by the scientist.

Returning to the question of how to modify the informal employee behavior, we already have seen that apathy, goldbricking, disinterest are resultants of the basic conflict between the needs of healthy individuals and formal organizations, directive leadership, management controls, and pseudo human relations programs. Assuming that the healthy individuals are not to be changed, one way to reduce the "negative" (from management's point of view) informal behavior is to change the formal organizational structure so that the employee experiences more activity than passivity; greater relative independence than dependence; uses more, rather than less, of his important, rather than skin-surface abilities; has a longer rather than a shorter time perspective; and finally, is in an equal if not higher position than his peers.

According to our analysis, in addition to the formal organizational structure, directive leadership, management controls, and pseudo human relations programs are also viewed as causes of the basic conflict, it follows that these particular activities also require changing. Let us consider the first two at this time. What research is available which suggests the type of changes that are necessary in the formal organizational structure in order to make people feel less dependent and submissive thereby decreasing in apathy, disinterest, low involvement in the firm, and low productivity?

A. JOB ENLARGEMENT

One of the predictions derivable from the framework presented up to this point is that the informal activities disliked by management will tend to decrease as the individual employee is given a greater opportunity to use *more* of his *important* abilities. This leads to *job enlargement*. Job enlargement is the increase of the number of tasks performed by the employee along the flow of work. It is the lengthening of the time cycle required to complete one unit of operation.

Walker,[3] and Walker and Guest[4] report that one way to increase employee satisfaction or self-actualization is to increase the number of formal tasks assigned to an employee along the flow of work. The employee will consequently use more of his abilities, and therefore will feel more satisfied.

Job enlargement is the second recommendation that emerged in our study of repetitiveness. It is a concept and a practice that has proved successful in decreasing monotony without impairing efficiency in certain sectors of other industries. We here suggest that it be introduced experimentally into auto assembly work. Job enlargement is simply the recombining of two or more separate jobs into one. Certain plant managers in other industries have been finding that a law of diminishing returns applies to the subdivision of jobs and that a recombination of certain fractured parts has increased efficiency. This means a lengthening of time cycles. Job enlargement in the sense in which we suggest it does not mean turning automobiles back into the hands of master mechanics with one worker assigned to the assembly of one car. It does mean that greater attention be paid to psychological and social variables in the determination of time cycles, and by the same token, more attention be paid to the *content* of individual jobs.

To one unfamiliar with assembly line work experience, the difference between a job with five operations and a job with ten, or between a job taking two minutes to perform and a job taking four might seem a matter far too trivial to concern anyone. Our data have shown that this is not true. Management has a vital interest in such matters: the proper assignment of time cycles throughout an assembly plant will make an important difference in the efficiency of the plant. As for the worker, one of the most striking findings of this study is the psychological importance of even minute changes in his immediate job experience. The point may be given an oversimplified summary by saying: other things being equal, the difference between a satisfied and a dissatisfied worker *may* rest on whether he has a five-operation or a ten-operation job.[5]

Schwab[6] confirms these findings when he reports increased feelings of satisfaction on the part of the employees through job enlargement. Katz and Kahn,[7] Hoppock,[8] Super,[9] and Marks[10] state that one of the most frequent agreements found in research of employee satisfaction is that satisfaction increases as work becomes more complex and skilled. Worthy,[11] reporting studies during the past twelve years that have been conducted at Sears Roebuck and Company covering several hundred different company units and over 100,000 employees,[12] concludes that job enlargement has been found to be effective in increasing morale.[13] He suggests that through job enlargement they have been able to reduce the "negative" impact of specialization by decreasing the concentration of employees on lower job levels that tends to occur with overspecialization, by increasing the degree of variety and interest in the work, and by providing the employee with an increased opportunity to participate in larger chunks of the production process thereby increasing the psychological meaning work has for the employee.

In a study of 355 experienced girls employed in four factories, Wyatt and Langdon conclude: "A significant feature of the results obtained in this inquiry was the notable change in attitude produced in the same operator by slight differences in the type of work. Even the packing of articles in boxes of different size gave rise to marked differences in satisfaction and pleasure in work."[14, 15]

Mann and Hoffman[16] report a study of job enlargement where, as a result of automation, different skills have been combined to make more complex and challenging jobs. Because the technology permits, management decided to train as many of the employees to perform all of the different functions in the department. In order to accomplish this objective, they instituted job rotation so that each employee works at a particular family of operations for a few weeks and then shifts to another set. Job enlargement and rotation, report the authors, "have resulted in greater job interest and satisfaction, but also in a higher tension level on the job."[17] The higher tension is related to the employees' feeling of inadequate training and from the greater mutual dependence upon one another to achieve the work goals.

Bibby reports a number of interesting examples of job enlargement at International Business Machines Corporation. For example:

Here's how one milling machine job was enlarged. Formerly, the operator inserted a metal part, pushed a level to start the cut, and removed the part when the machine stopped automatically after completing the cut. This was his job all day long. When a new job came along, he waited for the set-up man to put in a new fixture and adjust the speeds and feeds. Then he waited while the first samples from the new set-up were checked for accuracy by a process inspector. After this, he could then proceed again with the simple, repetitive task of putting in and taking out parts and pushing a start lever.

Today, when a new job comes along, he checks the blueprints and specifications and set-ups his own machine. He now makes his own dimensional checks of the sample parts from the set-up and makes whatever adjustments are needed in the set-up. During the run, he makes his periodic quality checks and also has the responsibility of watching the condition of his cutting tools.

Based upon our experience in the Endicott plant, we began to apply the principle of job enlargement to the other operating plants in the company. Here is an example of job enlargement in the assembly of the frame for the IBM electric typewriter. Prior to our job enlargement program, a typical sub-assembler might have had the job of simply fastening some parts to a typewriter frame. On down the line the parts would be aligned by a higher paid final assembly man and later on the operation would be checked for accuracy by a process inspector. In the new program, this same typical assembler now aligns as well as fits his parts and checks the accuracy of his alignment. He is now completely responsible for all the operations along his two-yard stretch of the assembly line. To do this, he has had to learn how to read a blue-print showing the electrical wiring and other mechanical insides of the typewriter frame. At the same time he has become a more skilled assembler and he has a job which has become more varied and interesting.[18]

Bibby concludes that job enlargement resulted in marked improvement in morale, an increase in productivity, and a decrease in apathy, disinterest, and goldbricking, although it is not clear how these results are obtained. Krugman agrees that job enlargement may be of value but presents evidence of its failing especially when it was not supported by the managerial personnel.[18A]

Argyris,[19] on the other hand, does not find satisfaction to increase as the tasks along the work flow become more complex and/or numerous. One possible explanation is that in the situations studied by him, the employees already obtained high satisfactions from the formal organizational context and thus might require "more" before satisfaction would incerase significantly through job enlargement.

What "more" can the employees require? In the examples cited above, the fundamental nature of job enlargement is to increase the number of already specialized tasks along the flow of work. These tasks primarily utilize the doing abilities of the individuals. These abilities, we have seen in Chapter II, are not the psychologically important ones for the mature individual. The abilities that involve more of the whole human personality are the knowing and feeling abilities. Few of these abilities can be expressed in the highly atomized jobs usually assigned to employees. In order for the individual to express more of his knowing and feeling abilities, he requires a work environment over which he has greater control, where he can make decisions concerning goals, policies, and practices. This type of job enlargement cannot be restricted to the tasks found along the flow of work. The employee must be provided more "power" over his own work environment and therefore he must be given responsibility, authority, and increased control over the decision-making that affects his immediate work environment. He must become self-responsible.[20]

This suggestion is supported by the writer's findings. The degree of self-actualization increases sharply for individuals as their dependence, subordination, and submissiveness are decreased and as their control over their work is increased and as the time perspective is enlarged.

There are very few systematic studies reported on this second type of enlargement. It may be that joint management-labor committees,[21] "multiple management,"[22, 23] "bottom-up management,"[24] and "reaching-out management,"[25] have the attribute of enlarging the individual's job to include tasks from more than the work-flow process. This should permit the individual to use more of his personality. Moreover, these schemes may have the advantage of making this job enlargement a *formal* characteristic of the organization and not one the employees had to create in spite of the top administrators.[26]

McCormick and Given both state that ultimately these plans are useful and bring good results.[27] Unfortunately, no systematic studies have been made of these pioneering attempts. Along with an evaluation of the impact of these programs, it would be interesting to know what resistance was encountered, the difficulties that arose in instituting these programs, and the action taken by management; as well as the problems that arose from competition and from the desire to be or remain on the board.

Perhaps the best known plan of this second type of job enlargement is the Scanlon Plan.[28, 29, 30] The basic foundations of this plan are participation and reward for results of participation. The employees are not only asked to join groups to help solve particular cost, production, waste, and other problems, but these groups are provided with the necessary staff help and authority to make recommendations. If their recommendations result in lower costs and/or higher production, the employees share a proportion of the increased profits. In all cases reported in the literature, the plan results in the employees' using many of their more important abilities, in being less dependent, passive, and subordinate toward management, in having increased control over their own immediate work environment. The results seem to point to increased profits, employee bonuses, employee and management morale. Part of the increase in morale is due to the employees' perceiving a decrease of favoritism. For example:

> What does this (Scanlon Plan) mean to him? It means that you have a willing worker who does any job, good or bad, as it comes to him. He now feels that there is no favoritism in giving out the good jobs and his mind is free to give all his attention to the particular job at hand. Under the old system, if he was working on a 'gravy' job, he would be wondering if the next job would be a tough one and wipe out all the earnings he was making on the 'gravy' job he was then doing. Under this new setup it gives him peace of mind, which always makes a better worker.[31]

Gilson and Lefcowitz[32] report a case where the Scanlon plan failed. They attribute the failure to lack of mutual trust between the employees and management, an unwillingness of either party to accept the responsibilities inherent in the plan, and a lack of a colorful evangelist type of leader.

Gillespie cites an interesting example from his experience of the "enlarged" job enlargement:

The example I wish to quote is from a study of a quite ordinary group of craftsmen working in a factory. These craftsmen, twelve in number, were engaged on complex metal work requiring a high degree of skill and they worked in a small shop by themselves in the midst of a large factory. I was assisting the management to organize the various departments in the factory and after considerable economies in six departments, I came to this particular craft shop. To my surprise and righteous horror (sic) I found this group was allowed to:

a. supply estimates for material and labor costs for inclusion in sales quotation.

b. say what particular methods should be adopted in the doing of any particular job, and

c. suggest what times and money rates should be allowed for each job.

The foreman of this shop was also foreman of a larger shop and, in fact, he was not a skilled craftsman. When a new job was to be quoted, the job description was sent to the shop and the men got together and worked out methods, times and prices; the result went back via the foreman to the sales department in order that a quotation could be sent. I was, as said above, surprised and horrified at this unplanned, non-specialized and dishonesty-provoking procedure and set about to improve organization and method. As I went deeper into the study of department economies, I found:

a. The group's estimates were intelligent.

b. The estimates were honest and enabled the men, working consistently at a good speed, to earn a figure *LESS THAN THAT COMMON TO SIMILAR SHOPS ON ORGANIZED PIECEWORK.*

c. The overhead costs were lower than they would have been if the shop was run on modern lines.

d. There was no group leader in the dominant sense of leadership. One skilled person received the job data and undertook to collect and coordinate the data supplied by members of the group, i.e., the leader was a secretary leader rather than a dominant in group thinking and activity.

e. Leadership shifted from one person to another as the situation required.

f. The group psychic texture I would describe as a mild *WE* one.

g. Inquiry among the group members showed no evidence of the group having or exhibiting aggressive feelings about other groups in the large factory. Some pity for the other groups engaged on the less skilled varieties of work organized on modern lines was expressed.

h. The foreman who was nominally in charge of this group dubbed it the best group in the factory and the least greedy.

i. The manager of this and many other groups took this group's honesty for granted. 'They never trouble me, they do good work, costs are low and profits good, why should I worry?' summed up his expressed attitude.[33]

Thelen's[34] suggestions for job enlargement are of this variety rather than those discussed above. He not only enlarges the job by increasing the number and variety of tasks but he also suggests that the employees should be given the responsibility to organize themselves within the limits set by the engineers. Thus, if a group must include twenty employees and if a group must be broken into teams the choice of grouping should be in the hands of the employees. They could form their teams in any way they desire. Rotation between teams and reconstruction of teams would be possible. Clearly, Thelen is asking for the employee to be given some increased decision-making power over problems influencing his own world.

The work of Coch and French[35] may be viewed in terms of job enlargement because the groups which were permitted "total participation" in making decisions about the impending change, during the time of the experiment, had their jobs enlarged to provide them more control over their activities than they ever had enjoyed (e.g., the employees decided to remove the frills and fancy from the garments, discussed and helped set their piece rates, helped train other employees, and helped to design new jobs[36]). During the experiment Coch and French were not using the traditional formal structure of the organization but instead created one which greatly enlarged the jobs of all employees and vastly increased their degree of control over their jobs.

The same dynamics seem to hold in the feedback research conducted by Mann. During the feedback sessions members of each group were shown the relevant data of their own operations and comparative data from the rest of the organization. Instead of

Mann telling, interpreting, advising the members regarding the meaning of the results, he asked the members to interpret the results and to formulate any policies that they desired for constructive administrative action. The groups were led by the members of the organization with Mann acting primarily as a resource person.

Such meetings enlarge the job of an employee who participates. They require that he use his knowing and feeling abilities instead of the few doing abilities commonly assigned to him. Moreover, he is given power to plan and to suggest constructive action which is taken seriously by the management. Mann reports that four departments decided to feed back the data with varying degrees of employee participation. Two departments were used as controls with no feedback through group meetings. No significant change was found in the employee morale of the control groups. In the experimental groups, however, the results clearly suggest that "favorable change in employee morale is proportional to feedback."[37]

Richardson and Walker[38] report that enlarging the job of supervisors at IBM by giving back to the foremen much of the control over personnel activities that they had lost, *and simultaneously* decreasing the number of levels in the hierarchy had a definite effect in increasing the number of satisfying contacts; foremen, in increasing the job satisfaction and the feelings of dependability, cooperation, and regularity. Woodhead[39] reports substantial savings in time on standard maintenance jobs when a team of workers participated in deciding the content of the various jobs by the members of the work group.

How can job enlargement of this sort be introduced in an organization? A concrete plan for job enlargement of the foreman's and supervisor's jobs has been suggested by Thelen. He suggests that when decisions from above are transmitted downward, the following might be useful:

Thelen's suggestions[40]	*Probable impact on supervisors in terms of our framework*
1. Demands from above made on each group and its leader together.	1. Increases supervisor's control over the way goals are to be

Thelen's suggestions[40]	Probable impact on supervisors in terms of our framework
The leader and his group together then face the problem of meeting the demands. This means that the leader, in all his working with his group, never is placed in the position of the demander or 'enemy.'	achieved. Increases group's time perspective because they will have more knowledge of the future. These two conditions will tend to lead to a decrease in feeling of dependency and subordination.
2. The demand is made by someone superior to the leader in a meeting with the group. This superior stays around long enough to be sure that the demands are clearly understood. The leader is likely to mediate between the group and the superior; his job is to help the group ask the questions necessary for clarification.	2. Increase group's feelings of self-competence in the problem area. Increases the use of their knowing and feeling abilities. (Note that basic authoritarian structure still exists, since there is no discussion on whether or not the group wants the demand.)
3. Since all demands originate from outside the group, they can be translated objectively into problems for the group as a whole to solve. The existence of problems to be solved (or changes to be made) provides the necessary focus and discipline for group discussion, and the group has sufficient autonomy to deal with the problem.	3. Translating demands in the group's language increases the chances for psychological success.
4. Since the demand is made by a superior, he is also the person responsible for evaluation of results. It is up to him to decide (preferably with the group's help) just how the evaluation is to be done. He may delegate some of the procedures to the group or to the leader, but he must keep the responsibility.	4. Goes against self-actualization. Would tend to lead toward dependence and submissiveness, toward the superior.

Thelen's suggestions	*Probable impact on supervisors in terms of our framework*
5. Because the group's leader now has a clearly cooperative role in his group, he is able more accurately to carry the group's thinking 'upstairs,' and thus is able to help his group exert an influence toward a more realistic formulation of the demands which it receives.	5. Decreases feelings of dependence and submissiveness toward group leader. Chances for psychological success are increased since group makes its own formulation.
6. Because each man has contact not only with his immediate superior but also with higher-ups, he has less feeling of isolation, better understanding of the total operation, and an opportunity to assess the implications of his relation to his leader.	6. Increases feelings of control over one's working environment and tends to decrease feelings of dependence and submissiveness.

The practitioner may question the advisability of such a plan on the grounds that it would lead to numerous conferences. But, as Thelen points out, the proper division between "working" and "conferencing" is that division which leads to satisfactory productivity. An extra hour spent in a conference that leads to increased productivity may be considered worthwhile by the administrator. Second, the need for conferences decreases as increased cooperation between the superior and the men leads to more initiative and less interpersonal and interdepartmental hostility. Sometimes conferences may consume time because of the lack of ability of the leader or because the management "team" isn't really a team.

B. Participative or Employee-Centered Leadership

In Chapter V, it is shown that a directive leader compounds the felony of the formal organization, management controls, and pseudo human relations programs. Another basic action, therefore, to decrease the employees' feelings of dependence and submissiveness (which in turn leads to apathy and indifference) is to change the directive authoritarian leadership into a more "democratic," "participative," "collaborative," "employee-centered" one. Modifying the organizational structure through the leadership patterns of the superiors is not as drastic as it may sound. As was mentioned in Chapter III Stogdill and Koehler,[41] and Arensberg and McGregor[42] present evidence to show that executive behavior frequently modifies the organizational structure.

There are numerous examples of the impact of participative or "democratic" leadership.

Beginning with the experimental literature, we find that the experiments of Preston and Heintz,[43] Laurence and Smith,[44] and Lippitt and White[45] show that a "democratic" leader permits much more self-actualization. Lippitt's and White's operational definitions of a "democratic" leader clearly suggest that he is one who increases the subordinates' control over their work environment, encourages them to use their knowing and feeling abilities, decreases the feelings of dependence upon the leader, and increases the subordinates' time perspective. They write that a democratic leader:

1. Permits all members to discuss policy formation. He encourages the group to make necessary decisions.
2. Permits discussions on future as well as present activity. Does not try to keep members 'in the dark' about future plans.
3. Permits members to define their own job situation as much as possible. For example, the defining of the way to accomplish the tasks and the division of tasks is left up to the group.
4. Focuses on obtaining 'objective' facts on 'human problems.' Tries to base any necessary 'praise' or 'discipline' upon these objective facts and not upon his personal needs.[46]

Gordon[47] emphasizes the same results. Leadership is a set of functions which are the property of the group. Ideally they are distributed within the group according to the abilities of the members. Thus the (formal) leader does not always lead. The subordinates are not always followers. The group will tend to maximize its adjustive behavior if each member is free to take on some leadership functions. Group-centered leadership, continues Gordon, differs from formal organizational leadership in that subordinates are not viewed as persons to be influenced or directed to accomplish the leader's aims. They are not people to be "led" by someone who has "superior" qualities. A primary force in group-centered leadership is the group's fundamental right to self-direction and to self-actualization on its own terms.

Whyte,[48] Mann and Dent,[49] Zaleznik,[50] and Baumgartel[51] are in agreement with Katz,[52] who summarizes some of the crucial findings of the Michigan Survey Research Center on Group Leadership. He reports that the more effective supervisors tend (1) to pay more attention to the long-range direction of their group, (2) to spend more time on motivational problems, (3) to increase the employees' feeling of freedom and self-responsibility by not supervising too closely and by increasing the degree of participation of employees in decisions related to problems affecting their own immediate world.

Campbell,[53] reviewing the literature on democratic leadership, concludes that it tends to create within a group (1) greater feelings of cohesiveness, (2) greater group productivity whether the leader is present or not, (3) increased job satisfaction and morale, (4) relatively broader time perspective, and (5) greater flexibility in behavior. Simultaneously, democratic leadership decreases (1) the amount of interpersonal hostility, frustration and aggression, (2) the number of gripes, (3) the degree of dependence and submissiveness toward the leader, and (4) the necessity for scapegoats.

McGregor[54] in a penetrating analysis of leadership states that the outstanding characteristic of the relationship between the subordinate and his superiors is his dependence upon them for the satisfaction of his needs. In a fundamental and persuasive sense, the subordinate is dependent upon his superiors for his job, for the continuity of his employment, for promotion, increased pay, responsibility, and prestige. McGregor concludes that it is a fundamental task of management to decrease this dependence.

Turner,[55] Bavelas,[56] Nelson,[57] Kahn and Katz,[58] Mann and Dent,[59] Likert,[60, 61] Halpin,[62] and Laurence and Smith,[63] Maier and Danielson[64] report results that confirm the conclusion that "democratic" or "integrative" or "employee-centered" leadership provides more opportunity for the subordinate to express his self. The findings reported by Katz, Mann, Kahn, Dent, and Likert are based upon tens of thousands of interviews and questionnaires in railroad, utility, auto, agricultural manufacturing, appliance manufacturing, clerical, government, research laboratory, labor union, and professional groups.

Finally, if one analyzes the "interactionists" approach as exemplified by Whyte,[65] one finds that the basic interaction patterns that characterize what he calls "organized cooperation" actually describe a situation in which the employees, foremen, and the union feel *less* dependent upon and submissive to the management. The union also feels that it is not being bypassed in order that it might be "busted." The union members feel less dependent upon their trade union officers and what dependence they do feel in this state of organized cooperation is fruitful (i.e., the officers are able to win demands from the management and satisfy the membership's needs).[66]

Successful employee-centered supervisors who were liked by the employees had superiors who:

1) Let them participate in decision-making.
2) Lets them know what he thinks of their work.
3) Frequently asks him for his opinion.[67]

Thus, for a supervisor to be an "employee-centered leader," it may be necessary that his superior be one. If not, training him in "good human relations" may not be too effective. More of this later.

A natural growth of employee-centered leadership is that the subordinates at all levels are increasingly brought into conferences to participate in decision-making. Research shows that, under certain conditions, groups are able to make more useful decisions than individuals make. Guetzkow and Kriesberg list the following advantages of group conferences.

1) Conferences aid in problem-discovery.
2) Conferences aid in problem-solving.

3) Conferences increase acceptance of decisions by:
   a. assuring colleague acceptance
   b. assuring superior's approval
   c. securing subordinate motivation
4) Conferences improve ability to execute decision.[68, 69]

Summarizing up to this point: If leadership is defined as "the ability to effectively influence the opinions, attitudes, and behavior of subordinates,"[70, 71] then the "ability" to influence others may exist because the individual has the power derived from (a) his formal leadership, or (b) his capabilities. In (b), the group perceives him as the best person to help them fulfill their needs (informal leadership).[72] Theoretically, a leader can lead without understanding the employees' needs because the organization gives him the power to do so. This kind of directive leadership focuses on the formal organization obtaining self-expression, and therefore acts to compound the human relations difficulties created by the formal organization and by management controls. But the individuals who make up and keep the organization alive must also gain what they believe is minimal self-expression. The "employee-centered," "democratic," "integrative," "collaborative," leaders are primarily leaders who place an increasing emphasis on the individuals' needs.

C. Participative Leadership and Management Control

Some readers may infer that the "natural" extension of democratic leadership is anarchy. Is there an attempt, they may ask, to turn over the administrator's prerogatives to the workers? Who will make the decisions? Doesn't the organization count?

Democratic leadership is not an absence of leadership. A do-nothing, let-the-boys-have-their-way type of leadership is *not* natural extension democratic leadership. Lewin points out that the people who arrive at the above conclusion are operating under the false assumption that democracy is something between autocracy and anarchy.

He writes:

The person who thinks in terms of one continuum has no choice but to consider democracy as something *between* autocracy, or frequently as a kind of sugar-coated or refined method to induce the group member to accept the leader's will. It is a prerequisite to democratic living and democratic education that this concept be destroyed. The democratic leader is no less a leader and in a way, has no less power than the autocratic leader. There are soft and tough democracies as well as soft and tough autocracies; and a tough democracy is likely to be more, rather than less, democratic. Like autocracy, democracy is fully aware of the role of power in group life and considers power a necessary and legitimate element of group superiority aloof from the rule—so characteristic, for instance, of the treatment of "natives" by the British colonial office—as from the religious zeal for one's own power so typical of the "sacred egoism" of totalitarian Fascism.

The difference between autocracy with a democratic front is still an autocracy.[73]

We know from experiments and field research that *laissez-faire* leadership creates *more* tension and anxiety than does *either* democratic or autocratic. Subordinates are frustrated from lack of leadership which in turn frustrates their need for clarity, sense of direction, and accomplishment. In experimental situations subordinates complained about the *laissez-faire* leaders: "He was too easy going." "He had too few things for us to do." *Laissez-faire* leadership created a feeling of chaos, confusion, and uncertainty.[74] Lippitt and Bradford conclude:

The picture of frustration, failure and insecurity was greater for this group (laissez-faire) than for any other. Because of no leadership there was no group to which to belong. Without leadership there was no work goal and thus low production and no sense of personal achievement. Adequate prediction of the future was impossible when there was no direction in the present.[75]

Nor are we suggesting that democratic leadership is *the* answer. At the beginning of the chapter we defined the function of leadership as helping the individual to obtain optimum self-actualization and the organization to fulfill its objectives. If we accept this proposition, then it follows logically that "employee-centered" or "democratic" leadership fulfills primarily the *individual's needs*.

But this is not all of the organization. What is also needed is leadership that tries to fulfill the demands of the organization.

D. INDIVIDUAL NEEDS VS. ORGANIZATIONAL REQUIREMENTS

Argyris,[76] analyzing the differences between formal organization vs. groups, focused on the members' needs and concluded it may be convenient to think of two types of social organisms existing on either end of a multi-dimensional continuum. On the one end is the group whose focus is on individual needs; on the other, the organization whose focus is on the attainment of organizational objectives. The former can develop into an organization and the latter into an "individual-need oriented group." However, if we think of these two phenomena on opposite ends of a continuum, it provides a simple model for an analysis of the conditions under which individual-need-centered groups will differ from *organizations* and vice versa.

As a beginning, a model containing two basic dimensions each with a subdimension is considered. Each of these dimensions is to be conceptualized as a continuum. On the one end (left) we place the ideal case of formal organization (FO). On the other end (right) is the ideal case of individual-need-centered group (I). One may hypothesize that the closer the conditions match the ideal in 1a. and 1b., 2a. and 2b. under FO, the greater is the probability that the results will apply to organization and the less is the probability that they will apply to individual-need-centered groups.

The converse of this hypothesis would also hold. The closer the research conditions match the ideal in 1a., 1b., 2a., and 2b. under I, the greater the probability that the results will apply to the individual-need-centered group and the smaller the probability that they will apply to organization.

FO	*I*
1a. At the outset, interpersonal relations are *prescribed* and they reflect the *organization's* idea of the most effective structure within which to achieve the *organization's* goals.	1a. At the outset the interpersonal relations *arise* from the members' interaction and reflect the *need* of *the members* to interact with each other in order to fulfill their *needs*.

FO   *I*

1b. The *leadership* role is assigned to the person whom the *organization* feels can best perform the *organizationally* defined duties.

1b. The *leadership* role is delegated to the individual whom the *members* believe will best fulfill their *needs*.

2a. The formal behavior in organization manifested by an individual is "caused" by the individual's acceptance of the *organizationally* defined reward and penalty (sanctions).

2a. All the behavior of individual members in the group is "caused" by the individual members' attempts to fulfill their *needs*.

2b. The *dependency* of the members upon the leader is *"accepted"* by the members because of the existing organizational sanctions.

2b. The *dependency* of the members upon the leader is created and accepted by the members because they believe it will fulfill their *needs*.

An example of how this model may be used may be found in a recent publication. Whyte[77] analyzes certain groups observed at the National Training Laboratory for Group Development at Bethel, Maine, and finds that instead of achieving certain officially specified goals (i.e., helping the delegates solve back-home problems) the groups wallowed in frustration, conflict, and disorganization. Whyte suggests that part of the reason for these results is the fact that the groups he observed had no recognized leader, goals, and structure. Under these conditions, Whyte continues, there will always be conflict, frustration, and confusion. In terms of our analysis it seems that the faculty members at Bethel who created the "groups" (i.e., told fifteen people to meet in a room at a specific time) tried to create the conditions that border more on the individual-need-centered groups mentioned above. Presumably they refused to lead, to make decisions, to be directive, to define a structure because they tried to get the delegates to evolve their own group structure and to elect their own leadership. In doing this, they (and the delegates) lost sight of the official goal of the meetings (to solve back-home problems). The members became preoccupied with the problems of creating a group.

Whyte suggests that the groups would have been more efficient if the official leaders at Bethel had helped the groups to establish some sort of structure or organization.[78] In effect, Whyte is making a plea for a stable structure. He believes that the goal of talking about back-home problems would be achieved more efficiently through such organization. Jacobson's[79] finding, that if a social organism is to mature it must *first* create a set of well-understood and stabilized rules and then develop good communications, confirms Whyte's point.

Both Whyte and Bethel have a point. Whyte observes that the delegates have a difficult time in evolving organization from an individual-need-centered group. But it does not necessarily follow that the Bethel faculty should make it easier for the delegates by organizing the group for the delegates. Assuming the faculty leadership is competent, it seems fair to generalize that the discussion groups never became organizations because the delegates were incapable of evolving such structures and still keeping the individual-need-centered aspects intact. Perhaps here is where the Bethel leadership became confused. Perhaps they (being the experts) should have known that organizational decisions not related to the individuals' needs tend not to be most effectively achieved in groups that are individual-need-centered. Therefore, they ought not to try to get certain tasks achieved without creating or helping the delegates to create the proper structure. On the one hand, faculty members want the individuals to create their own group, which means they must go through the process of being individual-need-centered. Therefore, the faculty led in such a way that at the outset the conditions of *individual-need-centered group* exist. This is most efficient for helping individuals achieve a "gut" experience in how to become more aware of themselves, their impact upon others, and the process of group development. However, this type of group is not effective in achieving the officially stated goals of solving back-home problems.

In other words, if the faculty members were to lead an individual-need-centered group, trying to increase the delegates' self-awareness, then the lack of structure and the frustration that

Whyte observed might become a topic for the group to discuss. Presumably this would increase the individual's growth and self-awareness. But it may also prevent the group from achieving the stated goals of solving back-home problems. It may be that the error the faculty made was to try to use an individual-need-centered type of structure for a problem that requires an organizational structure. Whyte, on the other hand, may be making an unwarranted implication that all groups are better off and more efficient if they have a stable interaction pattern.

Gordon[80] specifies the differences between the more traditional organizational leadership (leader-guided) and the leadership that we called individual-need-centered (group-centered). He suggests that group-centered leadership is maximized when the members (1) are free from dependence on a formal leader, (2) are permitted to determine their own goals and the skills they intend to use to achieve these goals, (3) are permitted to define and initiate for themselves any changes within their group, (4) are not led by any one individual all the time, and (5) are free to depose their leader (physically or psychologically) whenever they desire.

Gordon's suggestions raise significant questions about the adequacy of the present mode of organizational structure if group-centered leadership is to exist. They imply a redesigning of the chain of command and unity of direction principles. No longer would a few individuals be responsible for defining the groups' goals, evaluating its behavior, and providing the directions, rewards, and penalties. These activities would presumably be turned over to the group. Gordon suggests that a group-centered leader "allows the group to diagnose its own problems, to plan its own experiences, to make its own decisions, to make its own plans." How effective can this leadership behavior be in the context of an authoritarian organizational structure reinforced, in part, by management controls?

Hood, the President of Ansul Chemical Company, has helped to introduce a type of participative management that is close to the leadership philosophy defined by Gordon. Beginning with two management axioms (1) "people, not products, are the real competitive difference between companies," and (2) "people support what they help create,[81] Hood has helped to establish participation at all levels, and organizationally supported participation by reducing the decision-making point to the lowest possible level. In effect, this helps to decrease the subordinate's feeling of dependence upon his leader and to increase his control over his own immediate work environment.

The results include a definite increase in production and decrease in costs,[82] but equally important, reports Hood, it also helps to establish a climate conducive to freer, more creative communication, to develop more self-confidence in the group members as individuals and in the groups themselves, and to greatly increase individual self-involvement.

Another living industrial experiment where a leader is actually trying to behave more like an individually-need-centered leader, is the one being conducted by James Richard, the executive vice president of a firm employing about four hundred people. Richard[83, 84] finds that in behaving as a "collaborative" leader, he has been able to help people actualize themselves and at the same time the company has achieved and maintained an excellent financial condition. As a production superintendent he tried *not* to maintain order and control over his subordinates, *not* to keep things moving on the right track, and *not* to make decisions. As he writes:

To sum it up, instead of issuing orders, giving assignments, and following up results, he (collaborative leader) puts the problems raised by individuals and departments into the group's hands and leaves it to the group to handle them from there. He (collaborative leader) provides for the meetings, and the means of keeping track of events. Beyond that, he (collaborative leader) serves merely as a catalyst in the group, mirroring back the members' thoughts and feelings so that they can better understand them. The members, responding to this freedom, come to see the need for providing themselves with the factual information and the other tools needed to solve their problems.

Underlying his actions is the fundamental belief that there is more wisdom, good judgment, and creativity stored up in the group as a whole than there can be in any one individual, himself included. Therefore, he places all the authority he can in the men in the organization and concentrates on understanding their problems and finding solutions with them, not for them.

Not only do changes like these imply a new philosophy of management and organization, they also imply, as Hood and Richard attest, a different kind of leadership behavior, a different kind of leadership personality.

Argyris[85] confirms this conclusion in a follow-up study of "successful" leaders[86] (successful in the eyes of management). He concludes that the "successful" formal leaders seem to manifest the personality predispositions indicated below.[87] The frequency of choice of and the degree of importance attached to these predispositions is shown in Table I.

TABLE I*

Predisposition	Frequency of choice and degree of importance (in per cent)			
	R.I.	H.I.	E.H.I.	Total
1. Directive			100	100
2. Variety-seeking			100	100
3. Challenge-accepting			100	100
4. Problem-solving minded			100	100
5. Self-responsible			100	100
6. Self-controlled		22	78	100
7. Frustration-tolerant		22	78	100
8. Success-seeking		55	45	100
9. Expert		11	69	80
10. Self-motivated		11	78	89
11. Organizationally identified	11		66	77
12. Harmonious		11	66	77
13. Organizationally upward mobile	11		66	77
14. Power-minded		33	44	77
15. Industrious	33	44		77
16. Socially upward mobile	33			33
17. Humorous	22			22
18. Objective	11			11
19. Prestige-minded	11			11
20. Family-oriented	11			11
21. Remindful	11			11
22. Verbal	11			11

* Key: R.I.=regular importance; H.I.=high importance; E.H.I.=extremely high importance.

If Gordon's type of leadership and that implied in the model of the individual-need-centered group are to be used, then the executives above would have to change their predispositions as follows:

Directive. Instead of initiating action, the executive listens, draws out, and by careful questioning, helps the other person clarify his thoughts and arrive at his own decision.

Variety-seeking. No modification.

Challenge-accepting. The challenge now becomes understanding individuals rather than conquering them. Emotional problems as well as intellectual ones represent a challenge.

Self-responsible. The individual recognizes healthy dependencies but still wants to be his own boss.

Self-controlled. Instead of inhibiting the expression of his feelings and tensions, the executive expresses them as fully as he feels is necessary.

Tolerant to frustration. Instead of fighting against frustration to achieve his goal, the executive temporarily stops fighting to try to understand what is frustrating him and why. Careful analysis of emotional tensions is substituted for "guts" and "stamina" toward tension.

Success-seeking. Instead of trying to achieve goals quickly, the executive places a premium on *how much growth* and *self-insight* is achieved by individuals and the group in the course of reaching the goals.

Expert. The executive recognizes and accepts his limitations. He does not feel he must know everything about his work. On the contrary, he looks for, and feels contented when he finds, someone with whom he can team up.

Self-motivated. There is agreement to the extent that the person who is self-motivated does not criticize or condemn those who are not.

Organizationally identified. Instead of placing most emphasis on the organization, the executive would place most emphasis on the needs of the individual. If conflict occurs between organizational and individual needs, the latter are usually chosen.

Harmonious. The executive does not try to be harmonious. He makes no attempt to cover up, gloss over, minimize, or refuse to recognize conflict and tension. On the contrary, feelings are expressed and discussed so that their causes can be found and future conflict avoided.

Industrious. No modification.

Power-minded. The executive does not want to have others dependent upon him. He continually tries to minimize dependence.

Organizationally upward mobile. Instead of aspiring to move upward, the executive prefers to live in a group where all members have equal power.

E. LIMITATIONS OF PARTICIPATIVE OR EMPLOYEE- CENTERED LEADERSHIP

Assuming these changes in management behavior are possible, and assuming that Hood's and Richard's experience suggests that the necessary structural changes are also possible, the question arises are there any conditions under which the employees would not tend to behave in such a way that need-centered leadership would succeed? The basic characteristics of this leadership require the employees as individuals or as a group to make their own decisions in (a) their goals, (b) the best paths toward achieving their goals, (c) their level of aspiration, and (d) the maintenance of a cohesive group. Recalling the basic property of "needs" (psychological energy) it is clear that the employees will not behave effectively in this manner unless they *need* to do so. Individual-need-centered leadership assumes that the people with whom one is working are highly motivated, desirous of full self-actualization, and willing to be responsible for their behavior not only as individuals, but also as a group.

However, in Chapter IV it has been shown that an increasing number of employees are becoming apathetic, disinterested, and non-ego-involved; they are reducing the number and the potency of the needs that they wish to express while at work; they are maintaining and reinforcing these informal adaptive behaviors through small work group sanctions and formal trade unions; they are emphasizing material rewards, and acculturating their children in the same informal activities. Many employees do not manifest a strong need to be responsible for their own and their group's behavior. They have learned to be dependent, submissive, passive, and subordinate to the leader. *He* is responsible, from their point of view.

It is therefore possible to derive from the framework the hypothesis that as the informal adaptive activities increase in frequency and potency, the probability that individual-need-centered leadership will succeed tends to decrease. It is in this area that management representatives feel their greatest anxiety when discussing types of group-centered leadership. Many of them believe that the employees do not manifest enough self-responsibility for democratic, participative leadership to work. In their experience, when they make this suggestion, they tend to be asked by the adherents of democratic-type leadership if they have tried it, or they are covertly informed that this may be a defense on their part. No doubt both of these possibilities ought to be explored. However, the "pusher" for free and full expression in industry also ought to become aware that in many cases the management does not have a work force actively seeking expression on the mature ends of the continua described in Chapter II.

Odd as it may sound, those emphasizing the individual commit an error somewhat similar to that of those who emphasize the formal organization. Both assume an ideal personality type. The latter assume an ideal personality who will identify and lose himself in his work. The former assume a mature individual who will take on full responsibility for his own behavior and for the behavior of the group to which he actively belongs.

Morse defines individual "satisfaction to depend upon what the individual aspires for and how much he receives." She is careful not to assume that all individuals have high aspirations. "Thus," she continues, "a highly skilled job provides the opportunity for the individual to use complex abilities and this has a high environmental return for those with needs to utilize these skills. . . ."[89]

However, Jacobson et al[90] basing their definition partially on Morse's work hypothesize that satisfaction will tend to increase as the individual (1) obtains greater "intrinsic job satisfaction," (2) becomes more involved in his immediate work group, (3) identifies with his organization, (4) experiences satisfactory relations with his superiors, and (5) is satisfied with the reward system (material and nonmaterial). This hypothesis assumes that the individual is actively looking for greater job satisfaction, involvement in his work group and organization, close relationships with his superiors, and a just material and nonmaterial reward system. Evidence is presented in Chapter IV that an increasing number of employees are not actively seeking greater job satisfaction; do *not* need to belong to cohesive work groups; do *not* need to identify with the larger organization; and do *not* need psychological rewards.

The same difficulty may be pointed out with some of the hypotheses Mischler[91] derives from a definition of satisfaction which he calls "commitment." "An individual is committed to an organization to the extent that central tensions are integrated through organizationally relevant instrumental acts." He defines centrality as, "One aspect of the relationship of need dispositions to each other referring to the extent to which the entire structure would be altered by the alteration of a particular need disposition." "Instrumental acts" are "behavior which alters the (individual's) psychological field in the direction of a more stable structure." Integrative potential is a "property of a situation referring to the extent to which it permits instrumental acts to be carried out." Mischler suggests that the individual's degree of commitment will be directly correlated with such independent variables as: (1) the consistency with which achievement or nonachievement of the goal is followed by specific rewards or deprivations; (2) consistency of rewards with responsibilities; (3) knowledge by the member of whom he can look to for support; (4) importance of the position for the objectives of the organization; (5) relative certainty of advancement; and (6) proportion of working time spent in directing and evaluating the work of others.

Thus Mischler assumes that all individuals continually need (1) consistent rewards (a perfectly respectable learning theory hypothesis found valid if individuals are motivated to be mature), (2) support from others, (3) important positions, (4) relative certainty of advancement, (5) to evaluate others, and (6) intimate communication. As in the case above, these hypotheses will probably be confirmed if the individuals studied actively aspire toward the adult end of the growth continua described in Chapter II. As hypotheses for action, their validity may be increased if, after stating them, the condition is added "as long as the individual's adaptive behavior has not resulted in a desire to remain dependent, subordinate, passive."

It has been shown that middle management supervisors are able to learn to become dependent, passive, submissive, and subordinate to a directive leader.[92] With the help of an informal system where they could give vent to their pent-up feelings and with the use of defense mechanisms to suppress and distort those feelings that would threaten them if they were clearly acknowledged, the supervisors were able to obtain high morale scores with conventional methods of measuring morale) in spite of the conflict, frustration, failure, hostility, tension, and aggression that seemed prevalent. They would not change their leader "for love nor money" to quote one subordinate, "especially since with him we've made the greatest profits in our history" adds another, "which guarantees us a job" concludes a third supervisor.

Bailey[93] cites some interesting evidence of students who have become subordinate and passive as well as dependent upon the teacher. They expect him to behave in such a manner that they can remain in this psychologically immature state. Although he tried to help the students be self-responsible they kept insisting that it was his task as the leader (1) to point out important facts, (2) to prevent time from being wasted, (3) to organize and summarize group feelings, (4) to correct erroneous estimates and poor reasoning, (5) to supplement their (students') relatively meager experience with his lengthy and far superior knowledge, (6) to point out student shortcomings, and (7) to suggest concrete steps for the students to take to overcome their limitations.

It is possible that once individuals become accustomed to dependence they will learn to produce effectively if kept in this state. This may partially explain the studies which suggest that under directive leadership, production has been observed to increase much more than under the more participative leadership. Perhaps the employees have learned to be dependent and respond to directive leadership.

Morse and Reimer,[94] in a controlled field experiment, present evidence that production can be increased to a greater degree through directive leadership than through participative leadership. In two divisions of an organization they created an "autonomous" program where the employees had a greater say in the decision making. In two other divisions of the same organization performing the same work, they established a "hierarchically controlled" leadership pattern where the employees had a decreased say in the decision making. In none of the departments did the employees have control over the amount of work flowing into their department. After providing evidence that the two types of leadership patterns were in fact perceived by the employees, Morse and Reimer conclude:

1. The individual satisfaction of members increased significantly in the autonomous group and decreased significantly in the hierarchically controlled group. During the year and a half that the experiment was in effect, more girls quit from the hierarchically controlled groups than from the autonomous groups because of lack of satisfaction.

2. Productivity increased in both groups but to a *greater* extent in the hierarchically controlled groups.

3. In the hierarchically controlled groups the extra employees were discharged as production increased. In the autonomous groups motivation of the employees to produce was increased. Thus the employees did not feel the need for replacing the staff members who left the section. In addition, they were willing to make an effort to try to find new jobs of greater interest for some of their members who left.

If employees have learned to become dependent upon and centered toward a leader, one may predict that when they disagree strongly with each other, they may turn for help toward their directive leader. This leads to another set of conditions under which participative leadership will tend to have rough going in an authoritarian organizational structure. If the employees have learned to become dependent and submissive a transition period is needed for the change to a different leadership pattern. During this transition it is possible that productivity may decrease and an open dislike for the leader increase.

Reimer[95] cites such an example in an interesting field experiment in a large organization. He reports the employees resented an opportunity to become more autonomous. They did not believe that the management was willing to give them greater autonomy. Once they realized that the offer was sincere and genuine, they found their beginning behavior to be feeble, tentative, and frequently frustrating. Some became confused and anxious, especially over the fact that their decision-making authority and responsibility had greatly increased.

Likert,[96] Gordon,[97] and Richard[98] confirm the conclusion that employees and managers may resist employee-centered leadership because of the existing human relations climate. Richard, a production superintendent, when he first decided to become more employee-centered or "collaborative" was resisted by his foremen at the outset. A study of Richard's impact by Drs. Thomas Gordon and Robert Burns shows quite clearly that Richard was not liked at first. The men felt that he created confusion and that he was weak. However, two years later the picture is quite different. The net effect is that the foremen are very satisfied and making creative decisions that rival (and in many cases beat) the decisions made by top management on the same subject. Some of the greatest resistance to Richard came from members of his own top management who felt the whole idea was a wild, crazy scheme.

Singer's and Goldman's[99] findings that group discussions may be more effective if the leader begins by using a more directive type of leadership and slowly shifts to a more participative leadership may be explained by the transition concept.

F. REALITY LEADERSHIP

Recent research raises doubts that there is one best way to lead people. Fiedler[100] reports effective leaders do not try to understand their subordinates. They tend to be judgmental, critical, and nonaccepting of poor co-workers. This evidence is reenforced by the work of Torrance,[101] Cattell,[102] Martin, Darley, and Gross,[103] which suggests that too much emphasis on maintaining a friendly atmosphere can reduce the group's goal of achieving efficiency. Berkowitz[104] finds that groups with low cohesiveness can perform as effectively as groups with high cohesiveness. Vollmer and Kinney[105] suggest women tend to prefer autocratic leadership and men democratic leadership.[106] Case and Davison present evidence that effective leaders may have to go against public opinion and the opinions of their subordinates.[106A, 106B]

Roethlisberger et al point this out excellently in their discussion of "cultism." They note that their students (being trained as human relations specialists) tended to develop a "love" for one type of leadership versus another.

Roethlisberger writes:

In the beginning, for example, some of our trainees became enamored with the 'nondirective' approach. Using it indiscriminately, they tried to reflect the feeling of people at all times, places, and occasions, and then were startled to find that these attempts often were not perceived by these people in the way they intended. To change their behavior they felt would involve them in becoming inconsistent with their understanding of how they ought to behave (i.e., being nondirective); on the other hand, not to change their behavior would involve them in becoming inconsistent with another principle of behavior (i.e., being scientific in the sense of looking at the facts). As a result, there was much anguish, pain, and stewing.

Other beginners become enamored with being 'group-centered.' They shrink from exercising any leadership or from contributing any ideas that would seem to be imposing their will on the group. The group must decide everything by itself and of course there must be unanimity. Often beginners further assume that such groups are wholly self-contained and that there is not external environment to which they have to relate. Operating under these assumptions, again the beginner finds that often certain things happen which are not mentioned in the books about being 'group-centered.' The members of the group become confused and frustrated. The leader becomes immobilized. The accomplishment of the goals is in jeopardy. Negative rather than positive feelings between members of the group arise. Here again the beginner finds himself in conflict. Should he remain true to his "principles of group-centeredness" and hope that from all this confusion and frustration learning will result, or should he do something and risk the possibility of being 'autocratic'?[107]

Apparently the confusion is found in industry. Roethlisberger continues:

In many places persons in positions of responsibility were trying hard to be *client-centered*, *employee-centered*, *group-centered*, *subordinate-centered*, and *person-centered* when they were in situations where they also had to be *organizationally-centered*, *production-centered*, *superior-centered*, *decision-centered*, and *task-centered*.

Why do these problems arise? Because, suggests Roethlisberger, many people try to apply the leadership insights as absolute principles of behavior rather than to incorporate them first as simple guides for helping diagnosis. Also they tend to apply "human relations principles" derived from studies made of only one dimension of reality. Since real life is a multi-dimensional world, their behavior becomes inadequate. Finally, people tend so hard *to be* something (e.g., participative, democratic) that they lose their capacity to observe and to learn.

Effective leadership depends upon a multitude of conditions. There is no one predetermined, correct way to behave as a leader. The choice of leadership pattern should be based upon an accurate diagnosis of the reality of the situation in which the leader is imbedded. If one must have a title for effective leadership, it might be called *reality-centered leadership*.[108] Reality-centered leadership is not a predetermined set of "best ways to influence people." The only predisposition that is prescribed is that the leader ought to first diagnose what *is* reality and then to use the appropriate leadership pattern. In making his diagnosis, he must keep in mind that all individuals see reality through their own set of colored glasses. The reality he sees may not be the reality seen by others in their own private world. Reality diagnosis, therefore, requires self-awareness and the awareness of others. This leads us back again to the properties of personality. A reality-oriented leader must also keep in mind the worth of the organization. No one can make a realistic appraisal if for some reason he weighs one factor in the situation as always being of minimal importance.

The above may help to explain the results of Hemphill's[109] study of twenty-two college departments. He reports that those departments with the best reputations for good administration have chairmen who are described as above the average on both Consideration and Initiating Structure . . .[110] Apparently optimal amounts of both of these types of behavior are required in order that a department earn a reputation for good administration.

These results are confirmed by Halpin[111] who finds that the more respected leaders concern themselves with developing warm relationships with members of their units *and* with organizing and initiating new ways to solve departmental problems. Cleven and Fiedler,[112] Fiedler[113, 114] in studies conducted in the military and in industry report that the more critical and analytic (rather than the more accepting) supervisors tend to have the more productive groups.

Kahn and Katz[115] also conclude that a balance is required in the use of the different types of leadership patterns. They report that a "soft" leader who abdicates his formal organizational responsibility can have an adverse effect on both productivity and morale. They report, "A moderate amount of emphasis on production is required to avoid *both* low production and low morale. But beyond a certain point, higher productivity by means of pressure appears to be obtainable only at the expense of morale."[116] Bach reports that a client-centered type of leadership can help individuals to express themselves. However, if a group is to develop and maintain a continuing climate of growth, a more directive leadership is needed to control the "pathogenic" (destructive) forces that also seem to arise within the group when individuals actualize themselves.[117]

Unfortunately there are too few studies of reality-centered leadership. One reason is that the field of organizational behavior has developed by evolving extreme positions.[118] First came the formal organizational experts. Then came the human relations experts with their emphasis on the individual. Lately, the pendulum is swinging toward the center so that the researcher does not go into the field with an assumption that one organism is better than the other. The health of the *total* organization now becomes the focus with thought given to how the components may adapt, within their limits, in order that the *whole* organization (formal and informal) may live a healthy life.

VIII

The Development of Effective Executive Behavior

In the previous chapter, specific changes in the executive's behavior are recommended to decrease the basic conflict, frustration, and failure which the healthy agents down the line are hypothesized to be experiencing. The executive reading the analysis may then raise the question, "How are these changes to be implemented?" This question focuses on an important problem, commonly called, "executive development."[1] It is difficult to provide concrete answers regarding the effective development of executives.[2] Rainio, in a review of some research literature on leadership, is able to list nearly 100 leadership traits and to show that there is little agreement among researchers concerning their degree of importance.[3] Excellent analyses exist by Stogdill,[4] Gouldner,[5] Krech and Crutchfield,[6] Gebb,[7] and Jennings[8] (to mention a few) who criticize these lists of traits, but when faced with the task of providing a conclusion they suggest that leadership behavior depends primarily upon the situation and not upon any inherent leadership abilities, although some traits may be common to all leaders. Carter typifies this middle-of-the-road conclusion when he states, "As a general statement, it would appear that leadership is neither completely general nor completely specific to the situation."[9]

More recently, increasing criticism from two directions has been focused on executive development programs. Mace,[10] Stolz,[11] and

Chapman[12] for example, highly criticize the formalized programs which make as their central focus not the executive, but such techniques as "replacement tables," "manning charts," and "personnel evaluation forms." Briefly, their main argument is that the focus of executive development programs should be the individual self-development of every executive in the organization. The second group of critics are certain social scientists who have been trying to evaluate the impact of these programs upon the participants. A penetrating analysis by Mann,[13] backed by experimental evidence from Fleishman,[14] and supported by Mahler and Monroe,[15] suggests that the present programs are not successful in helping individuals change their attitudes, their behavior, and their leadership philosophies in such a way that a difference is perceived by their subordinates, a difference which makes a difference in both the executive's and subordinates' behavior while on the job.[16]

Anshem, in two recent articles, discusses the differences between the "in company" versus the "university" programs[17] and has cautioned management about need for attention to several factors in their use of both programs. He suggests that management tends to make such errors as (1) sending some men to those programs without having any clear-cut objectives in mind, (2) refusing to send some individuals until it is too late, (3) sending the wrong personality to the course, and (4) being unaware of the back-home problems that they might create when the "retreads" return with new aspirations and expectations only to find that the ones who did not go tend to perceive them as "crown princes" who have been singled out for advancement in the company.[18]

Although little published research exists, there is increasing activity in evaluating these kinds of courses by studying the men "before" and "after." Much more needs to be done in terms of systematic evaluation of the courses, but even if accurate "before" and "after" studies were in existence, to be of value they would clearly have to relate the "after" changes (or no changes) to some particular phase of the course. Some men change and some do not. It is most urgent to know *why* this is the case. Is it the personality of the student? Perhaps it is the trainer? Or maybe the role-playing? How about the case studies? Until questions like these can be answered, we shall have no way of knowing whether the "changes" or "no changes" that are observed are due to the course. Some preliminary research suggests that in some executive development courses the informal bull sessions seem to be an important factor in creating change. If so, perhaps the courses might be altered to make better use of bull sessions.

A. FOUNDATIONS FOR EFFECTIVE LEADERSHIP AND HUMAN DEVELOPMENT

Can the framework outlined in this analysis shed any light upon the problem of "effective leadership behavior" and "the human or personality development of executives?"[19]

The first guide suggested by the framework is that the individual's behavior is so interlocked with the organization (formal and informal aspects) that executive development must focus on development of the human personality *in a particular organizational context*.[20] This means the proper development of an executive requires consideration of both the nature of personality *and* the nature of the situation in which the executive behaves.

Can anything be derived from our knowledge of the two basic components (personality and organization) which can provide specific insights into the meaning of effective leadership behavior and the directions toward its development?

A general definition of effective leadership may be a good place to begin. A fundamental proposition derived from the framework presented is that many of the "human problems" in organizations originally are caused by the basic incongruence between the nature of relatively mature individuals and healthy formal organizations. Assuming that both must "fuse," if the organization's goals are to be achieved, and knowing that both will always strive for self-actualization, it follows that effective leadership behavior is "fusing" the individual and the organization in such a way that both simultaneously obtain optimum self-actualization. This process of the individual "using" the organization to fulfill his needs and simultaneously the organization "using" the individuals to achieve its demands has been called by Bakke *the fusion process*.[21]

B. Basic Skills of Effective Leadership

The analysis also shows that the fundamental incongruence between these two components may not be solved by simply changing the formal structure (job enlargement) or directive leadership because the employees have already adapted to these activities by creating informal activities which feed back to influence their behavior to prevent any changes in a "constructive" direction. For example, the employees may adapt to dependence and submissiveness through apathy and disinterest. This, we have seen, tends to make management behave in ways that reinforce the employees' feelings of dependence. Soon the employees become acculturated to being dependent and submissive. Once this occurs it is difficult to install job enlargement and participative leadership because they require employees who need to be independent and active. It has been shown that in order to maximize fusion (i.e., the optimum simultaneous expression of the individual and the organization) a reality-oriented or reality-centered leadership behavior is required. The executive must first diagnose the situation and then decide what is effective behavior in this situation. This leads us to conclude that effective leadership requires effective diagnostic skill.

How effective a diagnostician can an executive be? What factors exist "in" the executive *and* "in" the organizational context that inhibit effective diagnosis? From the framework already presented the following factors can be said to exist "in" the organization which act to inhibit effective diagnosis: (1) barriers of secrecy between formal and informal aspects of organization; (2) distorted upward and downward communication; and (3) apathetic, disinterested, "double loyal" employees who adapt to conflict, frustration, and failure by "not giving a damn," "taking it easy," "not burning themselves out," "letting management take on all the responsibility," asking for more material rewards, and de-emphasizing in their own minds the importance of the human rewards.

Five basic human skills have been identified on the basis of the analysis. Skill in self-awareness, in effective diagnosing, in helping individuals grow and become more creative, in coping with dependent-oriented, apathetic, disinterested employees and in surviving in a competitive world of management which, as one executive suggests, "is not a dog eat dog world," although he readily admits to being nibbled at a few times.

Turning to the literature, several examples of research in human relations training confirm the importance of at least three of the basic skills inferred from the framework. Weschler, Klemes, and Shepherd[22] emphasize self-awareness, awareness of impact upon others, basic principles of personality, leadership, group dynamics, helping individuals reduce their tensions to become more creative, and finally, helping groups become more creative.

Bradford[23] summarizing ten years of numerous researches in human relations training concludes that effective training includes (1) understanding of group problem-solving and decision-making processes, (2) understanding forces within group coercing behavior, (3) understanding conditions facilitating group growth, (4) understanding the needs of the individual participants, and (5) their unique relationships to the group.

Roethlisberger,[24] emphasizing more the importance of individual growth and self-awareness, suggests that one needs to learn how to listen, to recognize his own and other people's feelings, to ask questions that help to understand a situation. In terms of our categories, Roethlisberger emphasizes self-awareness and impact upon others, diagnostic skills (e.g., listening to others, recognizing others' and one's own feelings), and the skill to help oneself and others to develop, which includes the development of a philosophy of life.

Roethlisberger summarizes the differences in content between the more traditional training programs and the one described above as follows:

1. Instead of seeking for techniques by which practitioner A can influence the behavior of B, should we look first to see how in a concrete situation the behavior of A does influence the behavior of B and vice versa and how A takes this into account?
2. Instead of trying to inculcate practitioner A with the proper attitudes, values, and beliefs, should we look first to see how in a concrete situation A deals with his own attitudes, values and beliefs as well as those of others? How does he take these factors into account? Is there not something here that A can learn and does learn?

3. By looking at the behavior of skillful practitioners and seeing how they take into account the effect of their own behavior upon others, could we perhaps find out the uniformities that reside in and are associated with the skillful practice of human relations in concrete situations?

4. By looking at our own behavior in our own dealings with others in specific situations, could we learn to see the determinants and consequences of understanding and misunderstanding in our own daily activities and the part we may play in them? Through such an approach could we improve our practice?[25]

There are three important characteristics basic to the results stated up to this point. First, none of them takes a particular point of view. They are not "for" management or the employees or the union. Any individual, no matter what socio-economic-political group he belongs to, may find these results helpful. Secondly, the research results focus on helping an individual, group, or organization (all of which are organisms) to develop. The research focuses on understanding, as clearly and as completely as possible, the organism as a whole on whatever level it exists. This focus is congruent with a principle of effective diagnosing that, whatever the unit being diagnosed, the diagnostician must have the feeling that the unit has a right to a healthy, growing life. Third, if one accepts the first two characteristics, one will find that his self-concept and his own private world will tend to have a minimum impact in biasing the individual unknowingly towards any given direction that may be need-fulfilling for him.

Nowhere in the lists does one find a suggestion that the executive ought to learn how to "sell" the company to the employees, or "how to behave with kid gloves," or "the thirty best ways to get things done through people." On the contrary, as is recommended above, self-awareness and diagnoses are emphasized. Knowledge about the dynamics of individuals, groups, and the organization are also included. Developing human skills to help others grow and become more creative form the basis of one of these lists. Clearly these topics if learned will tend to decrease the basic conflict between the individual and the organization by helping the former become more self-aware, independent, and self-responsible.

Conspicuous, however, by their absence in the literature are research results on the skill of dealing with dependent-oriented employees and the skill of surviving in a psychologically competitive world full of upward mobile rivals aspiring for the few positions open on the top. In the former category, one might conceivably help the executive become more aware of the forces that seem to motivate a person to be indifferent, apathetic, and dependent. Along with this awareness, the executive would need to learn the many complex and subtle defense mechanisms used by people who have accepted a position of dependence. In fact, an executive in an organization might find it profitable to learn the process by which people choose to follow. Too frequently, leadership is studied as the only active process. "Creative followership" is a subject neglected for too long a period of time. Anyone acquainted with organizations has observed many examples of subordinates *leading* their boss in such a way that the boss thinks he is leading them!

Another very important research area practically untouched is related to the skills of surviving in a psychologically and socially competitive world. For example, how may an executive be helped to develop "frustration tolerance," the ability "to express hostility diplomatically," the ability "to understand and cope with acts and rules of competitive warfare," and the ability "to understand the necessity for unfavorable decisions"?

To be sure, neither of these two skill areas fits nicely into the management (or the cultural) ideal of "good management." Nor in discussing these skills is the scientist taking the position that they are good or bad. The scientist observes two important sets of conditions existing in the world of organizational behavior and merely attempts to infer the necessary skills if human beings are to adapt to these conditions. If some individuals do not like these skills, they will not solve the problem by not offering the "needy" executive an opportunity to learn them. The only way the problem can be solved is for the conditions (psychological dependence and competitive world) to be modified or eliminated.

C. The Roots of Directive Leadership Behavior

Having enumerated a number of human skills, the next question is with which one ought the training begin. Chapter II pointed out that an individual may not understand others unless he first understands himself. It follows, therefore, that the first step in an executive program is to help the executive become more skillful in how to become more aware of himself and his impact upon others.

Nothing is said that suggests that, once the executive gains adequate self-awareness, he must change. The "training" experience offered the executive should focus on helping him understand himself and leave it up to him how he will use this new insight. The objective should be to help the individual have greater feelings of tolerance for himself. This will lead naturally to greater tolerance of others, for the way we evaluate others, we have seen, is based on our own self-concept. Finally, since the door to self-awareness is locked from the inside, no executive should be required to take such a course.

In Chapters III and V evidence is presented to suggest that the greatest proportion of executive behavior observed in industry is "directive," "autocratic," and "pressure oriented." It seems useful therefore to present some of the existing psychological research on how the directive, authoritarian personality is hypothesized to develop. This information should prove valuable not only in planning an effective "training" experience to develop self-awareness and human skill but also in pointing up the basic difficulties involved in achieving these objectives.

Erich Fromm,[26, 27] in two penetrating analyses of authoritarian leadership, cites a basic sense of weakness as one of the motivating factors to make a person become authoritarian. "It is the expression of the inability of the individual self to stand alone and live. It is the desperate attempt to gain secondary strength where genuine strength is lacking."[28] In a more recent analysis Fromm adds a number of other factors influencing authoritarian behavior. A strong internalized conscience coupled with a fear of external laws, public opinion, mores. The "prime offense in an authoritarian situation is rebellion against authority's rule. Thus those that break rules are held in contempt.

One of the most detailed research projects on the authoritarian personality has been conducted by a group of investigators at the

University of California.[29] According to these and other investigators some of the more critical factors are as follows. The authoritarian personality:

1) Compulsively follows rules and regulations to the point of irrationality.

2) Believes that obedience and respect are crucial and the first characteristic to teach children.

3) Believes that business and the manufacturer rather than the artist or professor are more important to society.

4) Believes that a leader is someone who has power, is capable of being submissive towards his superiors and dominating towards those below him.

The paradox of submission and aggression is explained by the hypothesis that to allay anxiety, to avoid punishment, the authoritarian leader represses his hostility toward his boss and by a process of reaction-formation[30] develops an uncritical, idealized attitude toward the boss, which is one reason why authoritarian leaders believe in conformity.

5) Believes that others, as well as he, should not express aggression and hostility toward authority.

6) Releases his pent-up feelings by projecting his hostility toward a scapegoat (e.g., unions, lazy workers, minority groups, and workers).

7) Tends to think in rigid dichotomies. He thinks in "black or white" terms.

8) Tends to be more concrete in his thinking. Ambiguity threatens him. He sticks close to the everyday details of life.

9) Tends to be more narrow-minded about change.

10) Overcomes any feelings of guilt about his own aggressiveness toward his subordinates by being "paternalistic," granting personal favors and thereby increasing the subordinates' feelings of indebtedness.

Thus an authoritarian leader respects power and needs it. He is willing to submit and expects his subordinates to submit. He tends to feel the people on top are smarter than the people below. He dislikes changes especially those that imply he may lose any of his power. Helping the authoritarian directive leader to become more aware of himself and his impact upon others will not be easy.

D. Some Guideposts for Developing Executive Behavior

Assuming it is agreed that basically authoritarian directive leaders (and others) ought to be developed, what is the most effective climate for this development to be achieved? More concretely, what guideposts can be used in defining the educational processes by which self-awareness, diagnostic skill, skill in coping with dependent-oriented employees, and skill to survive in a competitive management world can be developed? There are six basic guideposts derivable from the framework that may influence the choice of "educational experience" to be offered to the executive. They are:

1. If an individual is to educate his "whole" self, his *behavior* becomes a fit subject to learn about and to understand.

2. Anybody who aspires to positions of power over *people* in organizations, if he is to succeed, is responsible for becoming more aware of his self and the systematic knowledge that exists about human behavior; he needs to become proficient in *human skill in living* (e.g., the ability to listen, to diagnose human situations, and to help himself and others become more aware of their involvement in human situations). Basic to these requirements, the individual must develop a philosophy of life and of leadership which is thought through to the point where it can be used to guide him in his behavior under varying conditions; to evaluate his and others' behavior; and to guide him to seek new knowledge about and understanding of human behavior.[31]

3. Self-insight and human skill in living can be learned only through living in, and learning from, the stream of "life events" we call experience. Experience *per se* never teaches anyone human relations skills. It is always up to the person to utilize experience properly if he is to learn, which explains why two individuals can grow up in the same environment, one becoming a minister and the other a criminal. A professor may teach about democracy and behave in a most undemocratic manner. He is not learning from his experience. Similarly, an executive can work for thirty years

in a company but claim only five years' experience. After the first five years he stops learning anything new. At best he simply re-experiences the old. The basis for this generalization is found in the property of personality called the self-concept (Chapter II). At that time we learned that one can understand himself only by inter-acting in a particular manner with and understanding others. This interaction and understanding should lead to self-awareness which is the desired goal.

4. Exactly what is meant by "a particular kind of experience"? What types of experiences are necessary to develop self-awareness? Just about any human situation can provide the basic components. The critical requirement is that the individuals in the situation be capable of learning. One reason why this requirement is difficult to fulfill is that most such learning requires individuals who are willing not only to learn but also to express their true feelings and to respond to others' feelings with a minimum of defensiveness. Katz defines the conditions necessary for learning as follows:

a. The man must sincerely *want* to improve his human relations skill.
b. He must be willing to face up squarely to his own inadequacies, with-out rationalizing or minimizing them.
c. He must be provided with a permissive atmosphere which shields out censure or ridicule when he exposes his weaknesses.
d. He must have someone whom he trusts, who is interested in helping him improve his performance, and who is himself sufficiently skilled that he is *able* to help without imposing his values on the trainee.
e. He must be provided with direct experiences in working with others, where he can learn and practice the news skills he acquires.[32]

5. We understand ourselves primarily through others and we understand others primarily through ourselves. Understanding does not exist unless the result is an acceptance of and a deep emotional respect for ourselves (or others). To understand is *not* to forgive, for if we understand, there is nothing to forgive. Some might feel that this may lead to self-complacency and a static personality; however, this is not so. Rather, the principle suggests that human changes are made most constructively when there is a high respect for and an understanding of whatever is to be changed. It is not true that changes resulting from discomfort, distaste, dislike, and

disagreement are most effective. It is true, however, that these are the most frequent motivations for change.

6. No one starts from scratch in human relations training. All of us have our own feelings, values, needs, and prejudices which greatly influence our behavior. Therefore, the emphasis in human relations training should really be on *re-education* or redevelopment of executives.[33] This is not simply a play on words. Re-education points up the important fact that the first step in self-development is *not* the acquisition of new ideas, new attitudes, and new skills. Rather it begins with a careful examination of the presently held ideas, attitudes, and skills in order that the individual may gain insight into *why* he believes what he does, he feels the way he feels, and behaves as he does. Re-education emphasizes that the "old" must be "unfrozen" before the "new" can be acquired.[34] Such emphasis has important implications in training. For example, many trainers believe that their courses are a success if the men leave with at least one new idea, one new attitude, and one new skill. During a recent executive development program, a "student" came up to the faculty member and said, "Today I have learned something about myself that I should have known twenty-five years ago. I am so glad that I came." Although the instructor felt quite happy, he did admit that he wished he could help that individual learn *why* it took him twenty-five years to learn this bit of information. (For example, what part did his personality, the work situation, the employees play in keeping him from learning?) If he could do this, he would be helping the individual continue to learn *after* having left the course.

These propositions have far-reaching implications for the design of courses related to helping individuals develop themselves. For example, the trainer's behavior as well as the student's becomes a fit subject for discussion. In the case of the former, the trainer may no longer plan his "teaching attack" by presenting his material in such a way that (in his opinion) "the students think that they come up with the answers themselves." This "training behavior" of leading the "executive horses" to water and getting them to drink without their being aware of it (if this is possible) may now become a fit subject matter for discussion by the students as well as the faculty.

Similarly, the students' behavior in the training session becomes an important focus. Executives have been observed to analyze beautifully and verbally solve a case that focuses on "understanding the other person" and five minutes later show little or no ability to use this knowledge in a hot argument with the man across the table!

Recently I conducted an informal examination at one of Europe's most respected schools for executive development. Some of the faculty members were asked how they felt about creating experiences in which the participants could become more aware of themselves and their impact upon others. "Oh, by all means, this is very important," they replied. "Then why is there no room for that in your programs?" I asked. "But there is," they replied. "You see, we have found that it is not a good idea to make a special point of this type of learning. We want it to go on all the time during all the discussions of all the different subjects." Another faculty member added, "If you look into our small groups, you'll find these chaps, once they get to know each other, pull no punches." Still another trainer adds (with the kind of a smile that made me feel he would wince if he were in such a group), "I am amazed at how these fellows have a go at it. They tell each other exactly how they feel." The participants confirm the faculty's reports. "The boys let you have it in a jolly nice way." Another states, "Our course is long enough so that we learn to let our hair down, especially outside the meetings, during the informal sessions. It's been a great help to me."

Firsthand observations confirmed the reports. In a joking, careful, diplomatic manner, the participants "let go once in a while" and "remind" each other of their impact. Thus they are learning more about themselves. But a careful analysis of the *process* by which the learning occurs during the sessions suggests that the participants are not learning any new way of helping each other to become more aware of their selves. In fact, they are simply repeating the interpersonal habits they have already found useful in the plant. For example, they wait until they are "a bit fed up with John" and then they "politely" tell him so. Many times they wait until *after* the group meetings when, over a drink, they discuss a "personal" problem. Does not this type of behavior go on every day in the plants? Are these not the kinds of methods that **cause** difficulties? Since people believe that they are unable to help each other become more aware of each other's impact without arousing hostility and negative feelings, they try to help a person become aware of himself "diplomatically" and "definitely over a drink" *after* the meeting. Do we not need to help executives develop human skill to deal with these human problems as they arise and without becoming so defensive that they must saturate themselves with some kind of liquor which they hope will calm down the recipient and which can be used as an excuse by the executive if he fails?

Imagine a group of top managers discussing a particular case similar to those made popular by the Harvard Business School. The group is trying to assess the nature and causes of the problems "in" the case and make concrete recommendations for their solution. An observer reports this session as follows:

During the first 15-20 minutes each member offers his opinion freely to the group. In all cases the opinions given start off by such statements as: "*The* mistake made here is. . . ." "*I* don't think Mr. X behaved correctly. He should have. . . ." "*The* crux of the problem is. . . ." "I can't help feeling the whole mess is due to. . . ."

These statements are value judgments. They evaluate someone's behavior as good or bad. Research tells us that once people make such value judgments, they shall tend to "see" this particular judgment in everything the fellow does. People tend, in short, to behave in such a way as to confirm their evaluations.

A problem arises since the managers are predisposed to evaluate each other in the same way they evaluate the people in the case. (This assumes that the case brings out the manager's "natural" behavior.)

The prediction is confirmed. Soon, the members of the group begin to criticize, to evaluate each other. For example: "I don't agree with you at all . . ." "No, Bill, I think you're wrong . . ." "If we really read in between the lines. . . ." (Probably meaning if people would only read things as he does.) "I want to oppose Mr.——— for a few minutes. . . ."

As the discussion continues, the members begin to take sides and try to gain support for their judgments. "I agree with Bill and Tom" and "I would simply like to say that in my opinion John is correct . . ." are typical statements made during this stage. It isn't long before one observes a "bloody good session where the boys really let their hair down and tell each other off."

The question arises, what *are* these participants learning? The leader never helps them to focus on their behavior. Instead he informs them how well they have discussed the case, that there are no right or wrong answers, and next week they will turn to the next case. Thus the leader helps the executives to focus on the case which is before their own eyes. How about the executives' *own behavior*, which is not only before their eyes but *caused* by their interactions with each other?

We could continue asking such questions, but space does not allow. One interesting problem is the pressure that most executive development programs apply on the students. "We're not running a country club," points out one director. "This is serious business," suggests another. If our observations are correct, the pressure seems to motivate the men to work hard. Soon they begin to feel that the course is a rough one. Once they perceive the course as tough, then "getting through it" becomes a sign of success. Soon the students rave about how good the course is and how pressured they were to learn. Again, we may ask the question, what are the students learning by living in such a situation? My inquiries suggest that they learn among other things that raising the standards high and placing pressure on people really makes them work. Is this the lesson that ought to be taken back to the plant? One may even ask if the executives have not already learned this lesson well.

E. GUIDEPOSTS REGARDING THE ROLE OF THE STAFF SPECIALIST IN EXECUTIVE DEVELOPMENT

Katz suggests[35] that the four basic obstacles to the proper development of human skill in living are that the individuals tend (1) not to know what to look for in a given administrative situation, (2) to pass judgment on what they observe rather than to note it objectively, (3) not to have available all the information they need to make a proper decision, and (4) not to organize that which they know correctly. These barriers Katz suggests lead to important problems in training sessions. For example, the individuals tend (1) not to support statements with factual evidence, (2) to take an all-or-nothing, either-this-or-that attitude falling back upon extremes, stereotypes, and rigid preconceptions, (3) to ignore unpleasant conclusions, (4) to attempt complicated situations with one hypothesis, and (5) to ignore those factors that do not support their point of view.

How must the human relations staff expert behave in order to help individuals develop? The first step is to bring the executives together in a small group because as Thelen suggests they are the most effective medium for self-development. These small groups ought to be organized in such a way that the members be well enough acquainted that they can communicate fairly readily; that there be enough range of temperament that they challenge each other; that they have among them enough skills of group process (socialization skills) that they can work together; that they have enough resources and enthusiasm for the achievement problem that they keep on going on that; and that they have a secure enough role in the total group that they do not waste much energy comparing themselves to or belittling the other subgroups. And finally, that the difficult members are in groups that can handle them either by containment, giving of security, or meeting them on their own terms.[36]

Having formed the group, let us now focus on the behavior of the human relations staff specialist. McGregor[37] points out that basically the staff specialist will succeed if he is perceived as a source of help, if he is able to understand the "private world" of the executive being helped, if he is able to help the executive to choose successful and rewarding behavior patterns, and if he can help the executive gain self-confidence in his own leadership behavior so that he no longer needs the staff specialist.

Gordon[38] suggests that a human relations specialist in an organization will help to develop others if he helps people only if they express a need for help, if he focuses on problems the executives feel are important, if he helps them to discover the most appropriate solutions for their problems, if he avoids "using" information given to him by one individual to influence the behavior of another, and if he is willing to leave when the executives no longer desire his presence.

Sampson[39] is in substantial agreement with the above in suggesting that a human relations specialist should be skilled as a discussion leader who stimulates true learning not by subtle manipulation but by providing the climate within which people feel free to be fully expressive. Second, the human relations specialist should be capable of helping the group develop into a cohesive self-functioning unit where the necessity for the human relations specialist is greatly decreased. Third, the human relations specialist acts as a resource person or consultant to the group providing it with information when the group requests it and at its pace.

Perhaps the most intensive discussion of the role of the staff specialist based upon an extensive search of the literature and experimentation is found in Thelen's[40] recent book. He defines the role of the trainer as follows:[41]

1. *The balance between work and emotion.* At all times the trainer is interested in the "way things are going." His basic characterization is in terms of the balance between "work" and "emotionality." Group work can be seen and felt, and can also be recognized by a variety of criteria. Thus people, when the group is working, listen to each other. The comments of each individual show that he heard and understood the previous comments, and that he understood from them what the speaker meant not what he wanted to imagine the speaker meant. Further, people seem to know how to contribute the sort of comment which is needed. In other words, there is a clear understanding of the member role even though it may not have been discussed. Also, there is a sense of "getting some place," a sense of purpose and movement.

The signs of lost effort include: trivial conversation, apathy, unusual politeness, incoherence, too much regard for the feelings of others, too rapid talking, talking at cross purposes, individually oriented confessions, hostility greater than the situation calls for, efforts to find out what the leader wants, making long lists on the blackboard, looking up past history of the group—and a host of other symptoms of avoidance, resistance, disorganization, attack, and disintegration.

2. *The trainer helps set conditions.* The trainer distinguishes between

"doing" and "thinking" activities. It is understood that the group is to plan and carry out activities and to reflect upon the results. During the planning and reflecting stages, the trainer intervenes to test the realism and feasibility of plans, and the validity and implications of conclusions. He serves as a resource person to make the planning and reflecting effective. But in the carrying out of a plan—such as role-playing several styles of leadership, or having working subgroups, or interviewing each other, or having "free discussion"—the leader does not intervene.

On the other hand, when the group has been acting out its conflicts through an unfocused bull session, anxieties have been mounting; the group may hope that by continuing to flounder it will somehow come up with a resolution of its emotional problems (which are responsible for the ambiguity and, therefore, the floundering) but it knows that usually it will not. Under these conditions, the trainer may call for a thinking period to look back at "what we have been doing." The purpose, of course, is to provide a structured work task which can pull the group back together, and to work toward the development of competence and readiness to deal with anxiety. And the work task is to diagnose the problem.

3. *The trainer speaks to the group.* His remarks about individuals are confined to behavior presented by design during "acting out" periods, when the purpose is to demonstrate interpersonal dynamics. The trainer during work periods is constantly pulling the group together by seeing all together, by seeing all problems as group problems. Thus the behavior of a deviate individual is per se no problem; the problem is that the group does not know how to respond to particular types of communications. Anger or bullying of individuals is seen not as a response to the members' own anxieties set off by the more or less accidental behavior of the deviate. In the same way, during a work situation, deviate behavior that is disturbing must nonetheless be seen as "speaking for the group." Otherwise, why is the group upset by it?

4. *The trainer helps the group understand.* The steering of the group into needed activities can be done through two kinds of interpretation: one is in terms of learning theory; the other is in terms of psychiatric theory. Both are based on diagnosis of the state or relationship between work and emotionality in the group.

Learning theory is useful for planning: e.g., "We have just been formulating a lot of ideas about how the leader influences the group, and it now seems to me that the logical next step is to set up a situation in which we can see these behaviors and find out if they have the effects we think they will." The concepts here are that ideas need to be assimilated through the experiences of applying them; that learning is a kind of inquiring based on problem-solving models.

Psychiatric theory is useful for diagnosis: e.g., "We seem generally agreed that we saw Richard and Henry as leaders, that they were in a sense spokesmen for the group; but they appeared to be in competition with each other which suggests that the group as a whole has mixed feelings about the problem." The concepts here are not so much concerned with the way in which learning takes place as with describing the dynamics of the situation.

Either type of interpretation can be used at certain times. The most successful type is usually not recognized by the group as an interpretation at all.

5. *The trainer helps the group "grow"*. The trainer may believe he sees what needs to be done next, or the diagnosis which should be made. How shall he decide whether to speak up? There are several general policies that need to be considered. The first is that an insight achieved by the trainer at a particular time may occur to someone else at the same time so perhaps the trainer should wait.

Second, the trainer should enter the discussion only when he knows what he is doing and why; this cuts down an astonishing number of impulses to talk.

The third notion is that the trainer must forever be helping the group to take such responsibility for itself as it is ready for. This means standing aside enough to let the group experiment with new skills, including ones for which they have in the past looked to the trainer.

The fourth notion is that the training value of the experience must be protected. For example, if the group is all set to role-play a scene and several individuals start a big argument over "whether role-playing is valid," the trainer has to decide whether the resistance to role-playing means that the plan to role-play needs further discussion, or whether to go ahead on the grounds that the factors expressed as resistance to role-playing will come out much better in the scene itself. Usually he latter is the case and the subsequent discussion adds insight in a way that dealing directly with the resistance could not.

6. *The trainer knows his limitations*. Every trainer has certain blind spots or certain emotional conditions in which he cannot help the group. In such cases he can explain what is called for and ask if someone will take a shot at it.

7. *The trainer does not try to be a "member."* The trainer's job is to deal with the group not with individuals. Thus, for example, a good deal

of member behavior originates in the need to find a position in the group and to deal with feelings about certain members. This should not be the source of the trainer's behavior. He does not need to establish his position because it is defined from the very start, and he does not need to be concerned over his relationship to individuals because he is stimulated only by conditions within the total group. He must be sufficiently free of personal entanglements to respond to the interactions between members, but his behavior is expressed toward the whole group.

The important message found in all these suggestions is that the specialist must not only say the right things—but above all, he must also behave in the manner he is suggesting the executives should consider. Thus the specialist continually strives to help the "students" become independent of him. He strives to help them to grow, to define their own program, their own objectives. Instead of directing (overtly or covertly), he focuses on being a group servant, on bringing hidden feelings out, on summarizing, on defending others' needs to express themselves, on keeping the program within limits of reality, and on helping each member become more aware of his own behavior.[42] These behaviors provide a real living experience for the executive on how to decrease dependence, subordination, and passivity in a group. If they are truly learned (i.e., they become emotionally as well as intellectually accepted), the executives have taken the first major step toward reducing the conflict between the individual and the organization.

IX

Summary and Conclusions

A new behavioral science "field" is developing which focuses on understanding human behavior in on-going organizations. We may call it *organizational behavior*. Organizational behavior can stake out a claim as a basic behavioral science because of the heavily documented empirical observation that most of life is organized. There are those who would go so far as to imply that organization is basic to all life.[1]

The basis for this framework is found in the simple observable fact that most social organizations, at the time of their inception, contain at least two basic components. They are the individual and the formal organization. These basic components when they are fused give birth to the social organization. The properties of each component must be known if the impact of their simultaneous interaction is to be determined. Consequently, the analysis begins with a discussion of the basic properties of the human personality and of the formal organization. Once these properties are described and their probable impact analyzed, we conclude that the needs of healthy individuals (in our culture) tend to be incongruent with the maximum expression of the demands of the formal organization. The latter is seen as a set of formal strategies, something like a set of football plays. The assumption is made that if the plays are followed according to plan and if there is no opposition (or if the opposition is overwhelmed) one will always score a touchdown (i.e., the organization's demands will be met). Unfortunately, if the analysis is correct, the formal plays not only meet opposition in the form of the individuals' feelings, but actually create them because they require behavior that tends to frustrate, place in conflict, and create failure for the psychologically healthy individual. The healthy individual, if he is to maintain a minimum degree of health, responds by creating his own set of plays (informal ones). These informal plays (i.e., the informal adaptive behavior discussed in Chapter IV) tend to provide opportunities for the individual, among other things:

1. To decrease his feelings of dependence, submissiveness, subordination, and passivity toward management.

2. To decrease the probability that he is subject to arbitrary unilateral action by the people in power, thereby increasing the possibility that he can find opportunity to be self-responsible.

3. To express his pent-up feelings ranging from outright aggression and hostility to passive internalization of tensions that are caused by the formal organization, directive leadership, management controls, and pseudo human relations programs.

4. To create his own informal world with its own culture and values in which he can find psychological shelter and a firm anchor to maintain stability while in the process of constantly adjusting and adapting to the formal organization (and directive leadership). By creating the informal world he can also take an active role in influencing the formal organization.

Thus the informal organization helps to decrease the basic causes of conflict, frustration, and failure. It is true that as the informal behavior achieves its purpose it may tend at times to take on the characteristic of being different from, and antagonistic to, the behavior desired by the agents of the formal organization. *However, it is a basic conclusion of this analysis that the apparently incongruent behavior on the part of the employees coerced by the informal organization is necessary if healthy individuals are to maintain a minimum level of health and if the formal organization is to obtain optimum expression of its demands.* To put this another way, if there existed no informal organization, the employee would soon find himself full of pent-up tension. The human personality can absorb only a certain amount of tension. Past a point (which varies with individuals) the individual loses his human efficiency. He becomes more primitivized (i.e., more like a child).[2] Once this point is reached the employee not only loses his capacity to produce with relative efficiency but, being full of tension, having regressed, and being predisposed to aggression, also becomes more difficult to understand and to administer.

Bakke was the first to emphasize that the informal and formal activities of the organization constitute the total organization. He states:

> . . . as factors influencing human behavior, the formal and informal systems *are not separable.* . . . Without denying the danger of inconsistency and conflict between the formal and informal systems, we would suggest that the social system to which participants in an organization react, and which is an effective determinant of their behavior, is a synthesis of both formal and informal elements. People do not live in the midst of now one, now the other set of elements. They experience the system as a whole, a whole which is continually, though slowly, being modified by the daily adjustments of participants.[3]

Accepting the proposition that organization includes all the behavior of the participants, Bakke then points out that this must include all those human activities that may be classified as formal and informal, response and initiation, outwardly directed and inwardly directed, normal and deviational.[4, 5, 6]

An examination of a large sample of the existing management literature leads us to conclude that many managers diagnose the informal behavior as "bad." Basing their actions on the logic of formal organization, they try to neutralize or do away with the informal behavior through directive leadership, management controls, and pseudo human relations programs. An analysis of these responses suggests that they tend only to "compound the felony" that the formal organization is committing every minute, every hour of the day, because they tend to increase the employees' feelings of dependence, submissiveness, and subordination. The employee reacts to the management's responses by increasing and strengthening his informal organization. Clearly, this creates a circular process. The agents of the formal organization try to decrease the informal organization. In the eyes of the employees, this behavior increases the need for strengthening and defending the informal organization. The moment the employees try to strengthen the informal organization, the management reacts by strengthening their original responses which in turn leads the employees to strengthen the informal organization.

A second conclusion that follows from the above is that *in every formal organization (and its derivatives of directive leadership, management controls, and pseudo human relations programs) lie the roots of disorganization.* The process of disorganization is partially inhibited by the informal organization. The analysis also suggests that the process towards disorganization may be inhibited by the use of job and role enlargement, employee-centered and reality-centered leadership. These activities theoretically would tend to decrease the feelings of dependence, submissiveness, subordination, and lack of use of one's abilities that many of the healthy employees experience when they first begin their work career. Theoretically, activities such as these should decrease the necessity for the informal organization. Herein lies an important area for research. There are those who would maintain that an organization does not necessarily require an antagonistic informal organization *if* it creates the right kind of formal organization (i.e., the kind which includes the characteristics of the informal organization). There are even a few who would suggest that an antagonistic informal organization is basically as unhealthy as cancer is to the human body. Much more research needs to be done before the answers to these difficult questions are obtained. Unfortunately the behavioral scientists have little to say on this subject and even less on how one may try to create a formal organization which may be used by anybody (management, unions, government, education) and which does not rely for part of its health on a basically antagonistic sub-system.

Summary of Primary Findings

The primary findings are listed below as propositions. Taken as a whole, they should be viewed as a grand hypothesis (again with the emphasis on hypothesis) that requires careful testing through controlled systematic research. Organizational behavior theory is in its beginning stages. It is hoped that this analysis is of some help in the long difficult process of developing systematic frameworks that are conceptually rigorous, empirically verifiable, and which mirror reality faithfully and accurately.

Proposition I. *There is a lack of congruency between the needs of healthy individuals and the demands of the formal organization.*

If one uses the traditional formal principles of organization (i.e., traditional chain of command, task specialization) to create a social organization, and

if one uses as an input, agents who tend toward a mature state of psychological development (i.e., they are predisposed toward relative independence, activeness, use of important abilities),

one creates a disturbance because the needs listed above of healthy individuals are not congruent with the requirements of formal organization, which tends to require the agents to work in situations where they are dependent, passive, and use few and unimportant abilities.

Corollary 1. The disturbance will vary in proportion to the degree of incongruency between the needs of the individuals and the requirements of the formal organization.[7]

An administrator, therefore, is always faced with an inherent tendency toward continual disturbance.

Proposition II. *The resultants of this disturbance are frustration, failure, short time perspective, and conflict.*

If the agents are predisposed to a healthy, more mature self-actualization:

1. They will tend to experience frustration because their self-actualization will be blocked.

2. They will tend to experience failure because they will not be permitted to define their own goals in relation to central needs, and the paths to these goals.

3. They will tend to experience short time perspective because they have no control over the clarity and stability of their future.

4. They will tend to experience conflict because, as healthy agents, they will dislike frustration, failure and short time perspective

which is characteristic of the present job. However, if they leave they may not find a new job easily, and/or even if a new job is found, it may not be much different.

Proposition III. *Under certain conditions the degree of frustration, failure, short time perspective, and conflict will tend to increase.*

The resultants of the disturbance in the organization will tend to increase in degree:

1. As the individual agents increase in degree of maturity (as operationally defined in Chapter II), and/or
2. As the degree of dependence, subordination, and passivity increase, these tend to increase:
    a. As one goes down the chain of command
    b. As directive leadership increases
    c. As management controls are increased
    d. As human relations programs are undertaken but improperly implemented and/or
3. As the jobs become more specialized, and/or
4. As the exactness with which the traditional formal principles are used increases.

Proposition IV. *The nature of the formal principles of organization cause the subordinate, at any given level, to experience competition, rivalry, inter-subordinate hostility, and to develop a focus toward the parts rather than the whole.*

Because of the degree of dependence and subordination of the subordinates upon the leader, and because the number of positions above any given level always tend to decrease, the subordinates aspiring to perform effectively[8] and to advance will tend to find themselves in competition with, and receiving hostility from each other.

Because according to the formal principles, the subordinates are directed toward and rewarded for performing their own task well, the subordinates tend to develop an orientation toward their own particular part rather than toward the whole.

This part-orientation increases the need for the leader to coordinate the activity among the parts in order to maintain the whole. This need for the leader, in turn, increases the subordinates' degree of dependence and subordination. This creates a circular process whose impact is to maintain and/or increase the degree of dependence and subordination plus the rivalry and competition for the leader's favor.

Proposition V. *The employee adaptive behavior maintains self-integration and impedes integration with the formal organization.*

If the input is composed of healthy individuals, and if the make-up of the organization includes the basic disturbances hypothesized in propositions I, II, III, and IV, then individuals will tend to adapt by: (1) Leaving the organization. (2) Climbing the organizational ladder. (3) Manifesting defense reactions such as (daydreaming, aggression, ambivalence, regression, projection). (4) Becoming apathetic and disinterested toward the organization, its make-up and goals. This leads to such phenomena as employees reducing the number and potency of the needs they expect to fulfill while at work, and employees goldbricking set rates, restricting quotas, making errors, cheating, and slowing down. (5) Creating informal groups to sanction the defense reactions and the apathy, disinterest, and lack of self-involvement. (6) Formalizing the informal groups. (7) Evolving group norms that perpetuate the behavior outlined in (3), (4), (5), and (6) above. (8) Evolving a psychological set that human or nonmaterial factors become increasingly unimportant while material factors become increasingly important. (9) Acculturating youth to accept the norms discussed in (7) and (8).

Proposition VI. *The adaptive behavior of the employees has a cumulative effect, feedbacks into the organization, and reinforces itself.*

All these adaptive reactions reinforce each other so that they have not only their individual impact on the system, but also a cumulative impact. Their total impact is to increase the degree of dependence and submissiveness and increase the resulting turnover, apathy, and disinterest. Thus a feedback process exists where the adaptive mechanisms become self-maintaining.

The continual existence of these adaptive mechanisms tends to make them norms or codes which, in turn, act to maintain the adaptive behavior and to make it "proper" behavior for the system. If this is valid, employees who may desire to behave differently will tend to feel deviant, different, not part of the work community (e.g., rate busters).

The individual and cumulative impact of the defense mechanisms is to influence the output-input ratio in such a way that a greater input (energy, money, machines) will be required to maintain a constant output.

Proposition VII. *Certain management reactions tend to increase the antagonisms underlying the adaptive behavior.*

Those managements that base their judgment on the logics of the formal organization and their self-concept, will tend to dislike the employee adaptive behavior. They also will tend to diagnose the problem behavior of the employee to be the fault of the employee. These managements should tend to take those "corrective" actions that are congruent with their self-concept and the logics of formal organization. These actions tend to be: (1) Increasing the degree of directive leadership. (2) Increasing the degree of management controls. (3) Increasing the number of pseudo human relations programs.

The first two modes of reaction tend to compound, reinforce, and help maintain the basic disturbance outlined in Proposition I. It follows, therefore, that the behavior included in Propositions IV, V, and VI will also be reinforced. (This is the behavior management desires to change in the first place.) The third mode of reaction tends to increase the distance and mistrust between employee and management because it doesn't jibe with the realities of the system within which the employee works.

The present employees influence the attitudes of future employees. They will tend to behave according to their self-concept, thus acculturating the future employees (future input) to the nature of the internal system and the adaptive behavior.

One must conclude that the management behavior described in Proposition VII acts primarily to influence the output-input ratio so that a much greater input is required to obtain the same constant output, or that a disproportionately higher input will be necessary for a given increment of increased output.

Proposition VIII. *Other management actions can decrease the degree of incongruency between the individual and formal organization.*

The trend in the output-input ratio may be reversed by decreasing the basic antagonism between the individual and the formal organization. One way is to use a new input of individuals who do not aspire to be healthy mature adults.[9] A second way is to change the nature of the formal organizational structure, directive leadership, and management controls.[10]

Evidence is presented that job and/or role enlargement is one effective method to change the organization structure.

Individual-centered (or employee-centered) leadership is one possible way to modify the directive leadership.[11]

Proposition IX. *Job or role enlargement and employee-centered leadership will not tend to work to the extent that the adaptive behavior (propositions III, IV, V and VI) has become imbedded in the organizational culture and the self-concept of the individuals.*

Proposition X. *The difficulties involved in proposition IX may be minimized by the use of reality-oriented leadership.*

A Closing Note

The objectives of this book have been to integrate the relevant behavioral science research by the use of a systematic framework in such a way that some insight can be obtained as to why people behave as they do in organizations, as well as to point out some possible areas for further research. No claim is made that the framework used in this analysis is "the" framework. The best one can hope for is that some will find it useful and others will be inspired by its limitations to create newer and better frameworks. It can indeed be rewarding if a book is able to provide the impetus for research that soon outdates its conclusions.

Appendix

Some Basic Categories of a Theory of Organization

If informal organization is accepted as necessary in order to maintain the formal organization and permit it to achieve its goals, one is led to conclude that organization, as Bakke[1] has pointed out, includes all the formal and informal activities. No longer may a researcher assume he is studying, or a manager assume he is administering "the" organization if the former studies only the informal *or* formal activities and if the latter manages and supports only the formal activities.

Accepting the notion that an organization includes *all* the behavior of *all* the participants, a number of categories may be evolved that seem to be necessary for a theory of organizational behavior.

If one is to focus on all the behavior in an organization, how should this behavior be classified? On the basis of the analysis up to this point, the following categories may be derived concerning the source of behavior.

1. According to the analysis, a basic component of organization is the individual who is viewed as an organism constantly seeking self-actualization. In all organizations some behavior will be caused by the idiosyncratic needs of the individual. This behavior may be called "individually caused" or "individual" behavior. The key to understanding this behavior is that it is caused by the individual fulfilling his needs. He (and/or a competent observer) perceives that he is responsible for this behavior.

2. The second major component continually seeking self-expression is the formal organization. In all organizations some behavior will be caused by the formal structure (formal policies and practices) of the organization. This may be called *formal behavior*.

The key to understanding formal behavior is that the employees perceive that they are not responsible for behaving the way they do; the formal structure and those who control it are responsible.

3. A third category of behavior is derived from the resultants of the employees' attempt to *adapt* and *adjust* to their work invironment. The individual behavior which the employees manifest as they are adapting and adjusting does not have organizational or group sanctions to guarantee its existence. Because of the power the formal administrator has over the employees, the latter's individual behavior can be jeopardized arbitrarily and without warning by administrative action. In order to provide some "life insurance" and stability to this need-fulfilling behavior the work group sanctions it. It may be called *informal behavior*. Informal behavior is need-fulfilling behavior sanctioned by the group. The key to understanding informal behavior is that the individual perceives the work group and work norms as responsible for the way he is behaving.

A number of useful categories may be derived by combining the above with some of the properties of personality discussed in Chapter II. The reader may recall that all individuals view the world of reality through their own set of personality-determined glasses. Individuals always live in their own "private world." Different individuals may perceive formal, informal, and other individual behavior differently. Moreover, from the property that personality is always growing (the self-concept keeps changing) it also follows that an individual may perceive the same behavior differently at different stages of development. A theory of organization, therefore, will find it useful to differentiate between *perceived* and *actual* behavior. *Perceived behavior* is simply any given individual's perception of reality. *Actual behavior* is simply behavior that a number of competent observers report reliably and from which predictions can be made that are subsequently confirmed.

It is a property of personality that all individuals evaluate experience according to their self-concept. They may accept experience if it is congruent with their self-concept or they may reject it if it is not. A theory of organizational behavior, therefore, will also have to deal with behavior that is *accepted* and *desired* and behavior that is *rejected*.

Those readers familiar with the work by Massarik, Tannenbaum, Kahane, and Weschler may have recognized by this time that the categories above are similar to those proposed by these researchers. Their category of prescribed behavior includes our formal and informal behavior. The remainder are identical (perceived, actual, desired, and rejected). Using the above categories, Massarik et al, have been able to construct a number of diagnostic indices of organizational effectiveness. For example:

1. *Indices of Understanding.* Indices of understanding measure the extent to which the prescribed relations are correctly perceived.

2. *Indices of Normative Conformity.* Indices of normative conformity measure the extent to which actual behavior conforms to the prescribed and/or to perceptions of the prescribed.

3. *Indices of Affective Conformity.* Indices of affective conformity measure the extent to which actual behavior conforms to desires and rejections.

4. *Indices of Satisfaction and Dissatisfaction.* Indices of satisfaction and dissatisfaction measure the extent to which prescribed, perceived, or actual relations also are desired or rejected.

5. *Indices of Affective Atmosphere.* Indices of affective atmosphere measure the state of balance that exists in an organizational unit between affectively positive and affectively negative choices (rejected).

6. *Indices of Centralization.* Indices of centralization measure the extent to which choices (prescribed, perceived, actual, desired, or rejected) are concentrated in a particular person or in a particular group of persons.

7. *Indices of Pervasiveness.* An index of pervasiveness measures the extent to which any one relation connects a pair or pairs of specific individuals in a number of activities. In other words, this index tells us how pervasive ties between two individuals are, as we examine several activities in which the persons may interact. It is possible to construct one index of pervasiveness for each relation. There exists an index of prescribed pervasiveness, perceived pervasiveness, actual pervasiveness, desired pervasiveness, and rejected pervasiveness.[2]

Throughout the discussion above, we have been continually referring to behavior and to the individual. It is clear that no individual manifests nor perceives all the behavior that occurs in an organization. For example, no one individual manifests all the formal or informal behavior nor is he the cause of all the individual behavior observable in organizations. A theory of organizational behavior, therefore, will also find it necessary to have concepts that "chop up" behavior into the size manageable by and referable to individuals.

The most frequently used concept to satisfy this requirement is the concept of role. The research groups at the Urban Life Research Institute (Tulane), Personnel Research Board (Ohio State), Social Science Research Center (Michigan), the Labor and Management Center (Yale), and the Human Relations Research Group (California, Los Angeles) are a few examples of those utilizing some form of role theory. In most cases, the scientists using the concept role include in it the behavior *expectancies,* the *actual* behavior, and the *reciprocal* relationships to other roles.

These three properties of the role concept flow from the analysis made above. It has been shown that there may be a difference between actual behavior and the perceptions of others. Jacobson et al.,[3] following Newcomb,[4] chose to call the actual behavior, "role behavior," and the perceptions that others share of the behavioral expectations of a particular position, "social role." Their concept of "personal role" focuses on what we have called individual behavior.

Once the organizational behavior is "cut up" in terms of units which are capable of describing individual behavior, it is possible to make specific predictions regarding the conditions under which conflict will tend to occur in an organization. For example, Rohrer et al.[5] are able to hypothesize that organizational disturbances will tend to occur when the formal structure is at variance with the informal structure, or when the formal structure is at variance with the psychological role.

In all the above approaches to role behavior, there does not exist a unitary concept which will include the total number of roles as organized and played by the individual. The advantages of a unitary concept are enough that some thought to its creation and systematization would be useful. For example, with a unitary concept of role one may begin to ask the question, "How does an individual perceive and integrate the various roles in his life so that he may be adjusted and adapted?" Asking this question leads us naturally to the very rich research that exists in perceptual psychology.[6] Along with using vague words, diagrams, or lights, the perceptual psychologist might find it useful to focus on the roles the individual perceives at any given moment in his life. Another advantage of a unitary concept would be that the conflict and frustration for any given individual as well as for aggregates of individuals can be derived logically.

Bakke and Argyris[7] have taken such a step. They categorize organizational behavior as follows: The formal behavior assigned by the organization is called a *formal task*. The informal behavior assigned by the work group is called an *informal task*. The individual need-fulfilling, self-actualizing behavior is called a *personal act*. A role, therefore, may be defined as the totality of formal tasks, informal tasks, and acts as organized by the individual.

Argyris[8] has shown that some individuals have highly stabilized roles, i.e., the parts and their organization do not continually change to the point where the individual's behavior is continually altered. It would be interesting to test the implications of this research. It implies that a role is as stable as the individual's self-concept. From what is known about the self-concept it might be possible to predict the way an individual will tend to organize his role if one knows the individual's self-concept and the work environment in which he is imbedded. Relating the self-concept to role may be a fruitful way to discover exactly how the personality affects the environment and how the environment affects personality.

The same study reports that it is impossible to obtain statistically significant correlations between the number of formal tasks, or the number of informal tasks, or the number of acts in an individual's role and his "degree of self-expression" while at work. Individuals with three formal tasks seem to have the same variances in self-expression (morale) as do the individuals with twenty to forty formal tasks. This study reports, however, that meaningful predictions could be made about the individual's self-expression and their future behavior (i.e., whether they will leave or not) based upon an understanding of the way the individual has *organized* the formal and informal tasks and acts rather than upon their mere number. If preliminary findings like these prove to be valid, the beginnings of a rigorous ladder may be found by which the different levels of behavior in organizations can be related. One might begin with biological organization, traverse to the psychological organization (self-concept) then on to the small and large social organizations. Once having understood these he can abstract aspects of these into a meaningful organization called a role which would lead him back to the individual level. This feedback closes the circle and an unbroken connection from the individual up to the large organization and back to the individual is obtained.

Other concepts that may perform this important linking function between various levels of analyses are those of social ranking and status symbols.[9] Social rankings are the evaluations people make of their experiences. (E.g. some experiences are "bad," others are "good"; some are useful, others are "useless.") Status symbols are created in order to perpetuate the rankings. Chapter II points out that evaluations may be viewed as attempts by the individual to defend his self-concept in order that he may continue his self-actualization (i.e. to fulfill his needs, to adjust, and to adapt).

Why cannot this function of rankings be presumed to be true for all types of social organizations or parts of organizations which are themselves organisms? Perhaps social rankings and their concomitant status symbols function to facilitate the self-actualization of the social organization. Why is it not possible to hypothesize that the agents of formal organization create and then use such status symbols as desks, rugs, chairs, telephones, decorating, and size of room[10, 11, 12] to help the formal organization achieve its goals, maintain itself internally, and adapt to its external environment?

The agents of formal organization may reason (consciously or unconsciously) that status symbols such as desks and rugs may act as stimuli for those from within and those in the external environment to recognize the discreteness of the formal organization. Similarly, the high rankings given to rate-setters and conformers and the low rankings given to rate-busters (Chapter IV) could be viewed as evolving from the employees' interacting in their specific work situation and trying to actualize themselves. Rate-setters who keep production down are "good" because they prevent the possibility of overproduction and possible unemployment. Thus they are given high rankings. Rate-busters are "bad" because they increase the possibility of unemployment and therefore they receive low rankings.

Why the agents of any particular system (e.g. the formal or informal) decide to pick a particular set of symbols to denote status may be related to their personalities, to the culture within which they exist, and to the particular situation being observed. Research into these aspects would lead to insight into how the individual, organization, and culture interact and transact to maintain themselves and each other.[13]

To put this hypothesis in another manner, is it not possible that status rankings and status symbols can be created by individuals (acting for their own need fulfillment) or by individuals (acting as agents for a given organization-unit) in order that the unit in question (1) is provided with characteristics to accent its internal homogeneity so that (2) its dissimilarity with other units can be more easily perceived which may (3) facilitate the members' and nonmembers' recognition of this unit and thereby (4) lead to freer and more spontaneous interaction. These four factors co-existing and functioning as hypothesized would tend presumably to assist in prolonging the life of the unit (whether it be individual, small group, or the total organization).[14]

If this analysis is valid then one may find it useful to study the conditions under which employees are attracted to organizations and vice versa through the use of social rankings and status symbols. One might hypothesize that an individual will find most satisfying that department whose existing pattern of social rankings and status symbols is congruent with his self-concept and the rankings he is predisposed to create for his own self-actualization. One might also conduct studies of how individuals with personalities antagonistic to the rankings and symbols within a department become frustrated when placed in the department or if they are given power over the department's activities attempt to change the ranking pattern. Another set of studies could be conducted to discover how frustrated, dissatisfied members of a unit, who perceive no possibility of leaving the unit, create rankings which help them to modify the nature of the unit or at least to make their immediate job situation more tolerable. Still other studies could focus on the "birth" and "growth" of a ranking from the moment an individual conceives of the ranking to satisfy his needs and how this is transmitted to a small group and to a larger unit. In such studies, status symbols and social rankings could become useful linking concepts between the several levels of analysis one must transgress.

Circularity In and Explanation of Organizational Behavior. The property of circularity the reader may recall is also built into the organization postulate used in this analysis. The necessity for circularity derives from the property that the components are continually interacting with and transacting upon each other in such a way that they exist because of their pattern of interactions and transactions. Bernard, many years ago, described this state of affairs when he said:

> The ancient emblem that represents life by the circle formed by a snake biting its tail gives a sufficiently just picture of the state of affairs. In effect, the organization of life in complex organisms does form a closed circle, but one that has a head and a tail, in the sense that all the phenomena of life are not equally important although all take part in the completion of the *circulus* of life. Thus the muscular and nervous organs maintain the activity of the organs that make blood, but the blood in turn nourishes the organs that produce it. There is in this an organic or social solidarity that keeps up a kind of perpetual motion, until a disturbance or cessation of the action of a necessary vital element shall have broken the equilibrium or brought about a trouble or stoppage in the play of the bodily machine.[15]

This concept of multi-level parts simultaneously interacting and transacting upon another leads also to the concept of multiple causality. It is no longer feasible to speak of simple causal chains such as A then B. We now must consider the possibility that many variables affect B, and B in company with other variables affects A.

A somewhat crude example may be obtained of the importance of circularity multi-level variables being multiple-caused in the study by the writer of a bank. Very briefly, a particular type of personality is found to be attracted to and remains in the bank. The "right type" as he is called, tends to have a self-concept which results in his expressing (1) a strong desire for security, stability, predictability in his life; (2) a strong desire to be left alone and to work in relative isolation; and (3) a strong dislike of aggressiveness and for hostility in himself and others.

Since most of the officers come from the ranks, their leadership behavior is congruent to their self-concept (right type). A passive or "weak" leadership coupled with the extremely good job security forms the basis for satisfactions for the right type. To put this another way, the right type creates passive leadership which in turn feeds back to perpetuate the right type, which complex joins with job security to form the basis for personal satisfaction for the employees.

However, since wages are low and advancements infrequent, the right type also feels frustrated and dissatisfied. Because of the personal dislike for aggression and hostility in himself and others, the right type internalizes his dissatisfaction. But knowing that dissatisfaction means needs in tension and that needs in tension mean psychological energy is being expended and that psychological energy must find some expression, it is understandable when we observe the employees adapting by disliking the officers and setting low work standards. However, because both employees and officers are basically the right type, the former do not express their dissatisfactions about the bank openly and the same is true about the officers expressing their dissatisfaction with the employees' behavior. The employees, in turn, noting no penalty for their informal adaptive behavior, continue it, and reinforce it. Thus work norms are evolved to the effect that the bank is a "good place to work" because one need not work hard and one is left alone. These norms are communicated by the employees to the people outside the bank. Soon the bank is perceived as a place where wages are not good; where the work is not hard; where the officers let you alone; and where with patience one can have a secure job. This "organizational charter" tends to attract the right type of prospective employee. Even if a "wrong type" were attracted, he would tend to be filtered out by the interviewing officers who, as the data show, hire those individuals whose behavior is congruent to their (officers') self-concept. We have now closed the circle for we are right back where we started from with the right type employee. The system is now a self-perpetuating one where each factor interacts with and trans-acts upon the other forming a pattern which has perpetual life.

We may now see why organization is said to be composed of multi-level interacting and trans-acting, multiple-caused factors which exist in such a pattern that they will tend to perpetuate themselves and the pattern if not molested. For example, in the analysis of the organization of the bank we find personality factors (individual level) causing leadership and group structures (small group level) which in turn feed back to reinforce the personality factors. Organizational policies and practices (formal organizational level: e.g., "low wages," "never fire an employee," "upgrade slowly") lead to personality dissatisfaction (individual level) which in turn leads to informal adaptive behavior (informal organizational level) which, because it is not affected by leadership, leads to new work norms (informal organizational level) which in turn helps to maintain passive leadership. The new work norms act to create a living organizational charter (informal organizational level) which is different from the one desired by the officers (formal organizational level). Nevertheless, it is communicated to the external environment. Individuals whose self-concept is congruent to the informal charter are attracted to the bank (individual level). The admission into the system of the "right" type is assured by the fact that officers tend to hire, and bank policies tend to support their choice of, the right type (individual and formal organizational level). If for some reason an aggressive, hostile individual enters the system, because of the factors demonstrated above, he will tend to perceive himself as atypical and be unhappy and soon desire to leave.

Output-Input System Analysis. How may one best conceptualize such a complicated circular pattern? Perhaps the easiest way is to consider an organization as a system with a particular input feeding into a "steady state" of components (organization) and an output. If we were to accept such a model then one might conceptualize organizational effectiveness in terms of output-input ratio. The greater the output for any given (or decreasing) input the more effective is the organization. Fundamentally this means that the output-input ratio is influenced by the nature of the input and the nature of the system (i.e., the steady state of the components). If output is to be modified, presumably the system and/or the input must be modified.

Focusing upon the steady state of the system for a moment, it is composed of many definable sub-systems of different complexities and makeup. Some are composed of individuals; others of group and individuals and still others of individuals, group and organizational (formal and informal) components. A substantial number are composed of individuals and machines (e.g., the bookkeepers and their bookkeeping equipment),[16] some of individuals and formal organizational policies (e.g., right type, passive leadership and the policies of low pay, infrequent discharge, and advancement) finally some of individuals, formal organizational factors, and informal organizational factors (e.g., right type, leadership, and employee adaptation).

Another interesting characteristic is that the sub-systems have their own output which influences the final output but is not viewed as being included directly in the final output of the total organism. Thus low work standards and dissatisfaction are outputs resulting from a combination of factors. The outputs may also form a sub-system to create still other outputs. Low work standards, dissatisfaction, and passive leadership combine to give the bank a particular reputation in the community. This model of input-output feeding back into the input and into the system, is no doubt oversimplified and much more research needs to be done in this area.

It may be that the output-input model will help to integrate some of the existing theoretical schemes regarding organizational behavior. For example, Hemphill and Westie's[17] interesting dimensions of group structure may be viewed as follows. Such factors as flexibility, hedonic tone, control, intimacy, and viscidity, may be considered as resultants of the steady state of the internal system. On the other hand, homogeneity, size, and permeability might be conceptualized as input. Stability may be an output that finds expression outside the system.

Argyris and Bakke's[18] concept of organizational processes might be integrated in the same manner. Thus the perpetuation process deals with inputs. The work flow, authority, reward, penalty, and communication deal with the system. The evaluation and identification process would be resultants of the internal system finding expression primarily in the internal system. The identification process would also find expression in the output which directly influences the environment.[19]

The model for analysis of group behavior by Cattell[20, 21] seems to be congruent with the above model. Cattell defines syntality factors as those that deal "with performance of the group acting as a whole," and which "can be measured without any observations on the *internal* interaction of the group." These syntality variables are similar to those we call output factors. Structure variables deal with "the particulars of internal structure and interaction." These seem to be similar to the factors that we have called components of the internal system and resultants that do not represent the expression of the group as a whole. Finally his population variables seem to be similar to what we have called input factors.

References

PREFACE

1. Mosteller, Frederick, See his book review pertaining to this topic in *The American Anthropologist*, Vol. 58, No. 4, August 1956, p. 736.

2. Lewin, Kurt, *A Dynamic Theory of Personality* (New York: McGraw-Hill, 1935), especially pp. 1-42.

3. For a provocative exception, see Chamberlain, Neil W., *Management in Motion* (New Haven: Labor and Management Center, Yale University, 1950).

CHAPTER I

1. Greenleaf, Robert K., "Behavioral Research; Factor in Tomorrow's Better Management," American Telephone and Telegraph Company, address, February 3, 1955, Chicago Industrial Relations Association.

2. Argyris, Chris, *The Present State of Human Relations Research* (New Haven: Labor and Management Center, Yale University, 1954).

3. Cassirer, E., *Substance and Function and Einstein's Theory of Relativity* (Chicago: The Open Court Publishing Company, 1923).

4. Du Bridge, L. A., Science and National Security (Pasadena, 1949), p. 4

5. Einstein, Albert, "On the Generalized Theory of Gravitation," *Scientific American*, Vol. 182, No. 4, April 1950.

6. For an interesting lay discussion of the advantages and limitations of this approach, see Engel, Leonard, "What Einstein Was Up To," *Harper's*, Vol. 211, No. 1267, December 1955, pp. 69-74.

7. Argyris, Chris, and Miller, Frank, under the direction of Hoslett, S. D., *The Impact of Budgets on People* (New York: Controllership Foundation, Inc., March 1952).

8. Heisenberg, W., *The Physical Principles of the Quantum Theory* (Chicago: University of Chicago Press, 1930).

9. Bridgman, P. W., "The Task Before Us," *Proceedings of American Academy Arts and Sciences*, Vol. 83, Chap. 3, p. 101.

10. For an interesting example of how one top executive's impact is viewed by others, see Coughlin, Robert, "The Ugliest Man Since Abe Lincoln," *Life*, August 10, 1953, pp. 86-100.

11. Argyris, Chris, *The Present State of Human Relations Research, op. cit.*, Chap. I.

12. I put the word problems in quotes because I do not assume that management's judgment on what the problems *are* is necessarily correct.

13. Argyris, Chris, *Human Relations in A Bank* (New Haven: Labor and Management Center, Yale University), Reprint 21; or *Harvard Business Review*, September-October 1954, pp. 63-72.

14. Sheviakov, George V., and Redl, Fritz, *Discipline,* Dept. of Supervision and Curriculum Division, N.E.A., 1944, p. 63.

15. Roethlisberger, Fritz, *Training for Human Relations* (Boston: Harvard Graduate School of Business Administration, 1954), p. 156.

16. *Ibid.,* pp. 142, 143.

17. *Ibid.,* pp. 142, 143.

18. Argyris, Chris, and Miller, Frank, under the direction of Hoslett, S. D., *The Impact of Budgets Upon People, op. cit.*

19. An increasing number of top executives and scholars are trying to define an effective philosophy for management. A few of the more recent examples are:

Niebuhr, Reinhold, "The Cultural Crisis of Our Age," *Harvard Business Review,* Vol. 32, No. 1, January-February 1954, pp. 33-38.

Randall, Clarence B., *Freedom's Faith* (Boston: Little, Brown, 1954).

Spates, Thomas G., "Filling the Spiritual Gap in American Labor Relations," *Addresses on Industrial Relations,* pp. 1-12, Bureau of Industrial Relations Bulletin, University of Michigan, 1955.

"The American Businessman and World Place," *Saturday Review,* January 23, 1954, pp. 24-48.

Heron, Alexander, *Reasonable Goals in Industrial Relations.* (Palo Alto: Stanford University Press, 1954).

Tead, Ordway, *The Art of Administration,* (New York: McGraw-Hill, 1951).

Abrams, Frank W., "Management's Responsibilities in a Complex World," *Harvard Business Review,* Vol. 29, No. 3, May 1951, pp. 29-34.

Colliers, Abram J., "Business Leadership and a Creative Society," *Harvard Business Review,* Vol. 31, No. 1, January-February 1953, pp. 29-38.

Demos, Raphael, "Business and the Good Society," *Harvard Business Review,* Vol. 33, No. 4, July-August 1955, pp. 33-44.

Ohmann, O. A., "Skyhooks," *Harvard Business Review,* Vol. 33, No. 3, May-June 1955, pp. 33-41.

Pamp, Frederic E., Jr., "Liberal Arts as Training for Business," *Harvard Business Review,* Vol. 33, No. 3, May-June 1955, pp. 42-50.

20. Griswold, A. Whitney, *Essays on Education* (New Haven: Yale University Press, 1954).

21. Hacker, Louis M., *The Shaping of the American Tradition* (New York: Columbia University Press, 1947).

22. Nickerson, Albert J., "Climbing the Managerial Ladder," *Saturday Review,* November 21, 1953, p. 38.

23. Later on I hope to show that you have just read an example of poor interviewing.

24. Sometimes it is possible to have thirty years of living in a company with only five years' experience. After the first five years very little that is new is learned. One keeps having basically the same experiences.

25. Roethlisberger, Fritz, "Training Supervisors in Human Relations," *Harvard Business Review,* Vol. 29, No. 5, September 1951, p. 48.

26. Einstein, Albert, and Enfeld, Leopold, *Development of Modern Physics* (New York: Simon and Schuster, 1938).

27. Krech, David, and Crutchfield, Richard, *Theory and Problems of Social Psychology* (New York: MacGraw-Hill, 1948), p. 4.

28. Carr, Lowell J., *Situational Analysis* (New York: Harper, 1948).

CHAPTER II

1. The relevant literature in clinical, abnormal, child, and social psychology; personality theory; sociology; and anthropology. The "trait" theory by Allport, Cattell's factor analytic approach, and Kretschmer's somatotype framework are not included. For a lay description see Argyris, Chris, *Personality Fundamentals, op. cit.*

2. Management never hires simply a hand, states psychiatrist Temple Burling. They always hire a whole person. *You Can't Hire A Hand* (Ithaca: New York State School of Industrial and Labor Relations, Cornell University), Bulletin No. 2, February 1950.

3. Too much tolerance for tension can also be a sign of difficulties.

4. Merit rating devices (and many psychological tests) not only violate the very nature of personality, they violate some of the most basic principles of measurement. If we assume for a moment that parts of a personality can be added, the mathematicians tell us that the scores that most tests come up with are very shaky. Coombs, Clyde H., "Theory and Methods of Social Measurement," Chapter II in *Research Methods in the Social Sciences*, (ed.) Leon Festinger and Daniel Katz, (New York: The Dryden Press, 1953), p. 12. Stevens, S. S., "Mathematics, Measurement and Psychology," in Stevens, S. S., (ed.), *Handbook of Experimental Psychology* (New York: Wiley, 1951), Chapter I.

5. This section draws heavily from Ruesch, J., and Bateson, G., *Communication: The Social Matrix of Psychiatry* (New York: Norton, 1952), pp. 248-249.

6. Allport, Gordon W., "The Trend in Motivational Theory," *American Journal Orthopsychiatry*, Vol. 23, No. 1, January 1953, p. 117.

7. Goldstein, Kurt, "The Effect of Brain Damage on the Personality," *Psychiatry*, Vol. 15, No. 3, August 1952, p. 251.

8. For an interesting analysis of needs see, Sanford, Nevitt. "Surface and Depth in the Individual Personality," *Psychological Review*, Vol. 63, No. 2, November 1956, pp. 349-359.

9. There are many comments that have to be made if a thorough discussion is to be given concerning tests. Space does not permit us to do so. Krech, David, and Crutchfield, Richard, *Theory and Problems of Social Psychology, op. cit.;* White, Robert W., "What is Tested by Psychological Tests?" *Relation of Psychological Tests to Psychiatry,* by Hoch and Zubin, (New York: Grune and Stratton, 1952).

10. For an excellent discussion of the use of psychological tests, see Haire, Mason, "Use of Tests in Employee Selection," *Harvard Business Review*, Vol. 28, No. 1, January 1950, pp. 42-51.

11. Rogers, Carl R., *Client-Centered Therapy* (Boston: Houghton Mifflin, 1951), pp. 497-507.

12. Hogan, Richard A., "A Theory of Threat and Defense," *Journal Consulting Psychology*, Vol. 16, No. 6, December 1952, p. 419.

13. Lindgren, Henry Clay, *The Art of Human Relations* (New York: Hermitage, 1953), pp. 86-87.

14. Newcomb, Theodore, *Social Psychology* (New York: Dryden Press, 1950), pp. 361 ff.

15. For a discussion of the impact of failure on employees, see Chapter III.

16. This should provide us with a clue as to why it is difficult for a person to give help (therapeutic) to others without having undergone some therapy which will provide him with a basis of knowing himself.

17. Kasper, August M., "The Psyche Doctor, The Soma Doctor and the Psychosomatic Patient," *Bulletin of the Menninger Clinic,* Vol. 16, No. 3, May 1952, p. 80.

18. White, Robert W., *Lives in Progress* (New York: Dryden Press, 1952).

19. Kluckhohn, Clyde, and Murray, H. A., "Personality Formation: The Determinants," in *Personality,* (ed.) by above authors (New York: Knopf, 1949), pp. 35-37.

20. Jacques, Elliot, *The Changing Culture of a Factory* (London: Tavistock Publications, Ltd., 1951).

21. Erikson, E. H., *Childhood and Society* (New York: Norton, 1950). See also Kotinsky, R., *Personality in the Making* (New York: Harper, 1952), pp. 8-25.

22. Bronfenbrenner, Urie, "Toward an Integrated Theory of Personality," in *Perception,* by Robert R. Blake and Glen B. Ramsey (New York: Ronald Press, 1951), pp. 206-257.

23. This is similar to Erikson's "Sense of autonomy" and Bronfenbrenner's "state of creative interdependence."

24. White, Robert W. *Lives in Progress, op. cit.,* pp. 339 ff.

25. Lewin and Kounin believe that, as the individual develops needs and abilities, the boundaries between them become more rigid. This explains why an adult is better able than a child to be frustrated in one activity and behave constructively in another. See Lewin, Kurt, *A Dynamic Theory of Personality* (New York: McGraw-Hill, 1935); and Kounin, Jacob S., "Intellectual Development and Rigidity," in *Child Behavior and Development* (ed.) Barker, R., Kounin, J., and Wright, H. R. (New York: McGraw-Hill, 1943), pp. 179-198.

26. White, Robert W., *op. cit.,* pp. 347 ff.

27. Lewin also cites the billions of dollars that are invested in insurance policies. Lewin, Kurt, "Time Perspective and Morale," in *Resolving Social Conflicts* (New York: Harper, 1948), p. 105.

28. Bakke, E. W., *The Unemployed Worker* (New Haven: Yale University Press, 1940), pp. 23-24.

29. Rogers, Carl R., *Client-Centered Therapy, op. cit.*

30. Bakke, E. W., *op. cit.,* p. 247.

31. Bakke, E. W., *op. cit.,* p. 29.

32. Another related but discrete set of developmental dimensions may be constructed to measure the protective (defense) mechanisms individuals tend to create as they develop from infancy to adulthood. Exactly how these would be related to the above model is not clear.

33. In subsequent sections, it will be shown that an organization has the same limitation imposed upon its self-actualization.

34. See Chapters V and VIII.

35. It is possible that adults may be found who report that they prefer jobs that permit them to be in a world similar to the infant's. These adults

could be immature or neurotic or they could be defending themselves by not desiring self-expression while at work. Both possibilities will be considered in the following chapters.

CHAPTER III

1. Simon, Herbert A., "Recent Advances in Organization Theory," Chapter 2 in *Research Frontiers in Politics and Government* (Washington 6, D. C.: Bookings Institution, 1955), p. 30.

2. Urwick, L., *The Elements of Administration* (New York: Harper, 1953).

3. *Ibid.*, pp. 36-39.

4. Koontz, Harold, and O'Donnell, Cyril, *Principles of Management* (New York: McGraw-Hill, 1955), p. 24.

5. Arensberg, Conrad M., and McGregor, Douglas, "Determination of Morale in an Industrial Company," *Applied Anthropology*, Vol. 1, Chap. 2, January-March 1942, pp. 12-34.

6. Stodgill, Ralph M., and Koehler, Kathleen, *Measures of Leadership Structure and Organization Change* (Columbus, Ohio: Personal Research Board, Ohio State, 1952).

7. *Ibid.*, pp. 36-39.

8. For a provocative discussion of Taylor's philosophy, see Bendix, Reinhard, *Work and Authority in Industry* (New York: Wiley, 1956), pp. 274-319.

9. *Ibid.*, pp. 36-39.

10. Argyris, Chris, *The Present State of Research in Human Relations, op. cit.*, Chap. I.

11. Urwick, L., *The Elements of Administration* (New York: Harper, 1944).

12. Mooney, J. D., *The Principles of Organization* (New York: Harper, 1947).

13. Holden, Paul E., Fish, Lounsbury S., and Smith, Hubert L., *Top Management Organization and Control* (New York: McGraw-Hill, 1951).

14. Fayol, Henri, *General and Industrial Management* (New York: Pitman, 1949).

15. Dennison, Henry S., *Organization Engineering* (New York: McGraw-Hill, 1931).

16. Brown, Alvin, *Organization of Industry* (Englewood Cliffs, N. J.: Prentice-Hall, 1947).

17. Gulick, Luther, and Urwick, L., *Papers on The Science of Administration* (New York: Institute of Public Administration, 1927).

18. White, L. D., *Introduction to the Study of Public Administration* (New York: Macmillan, 1939).

19. Gauss, J. M., White, L. D., and Demack, M. E. (eds.) *The Frontiers of Public Administration* (Chicago: University of Chicago Press, 1936).

20. Stene, E. D., "An Approach to a Science of Administration," *American Political Science Review*, Vol. 34, December 1940, pp. 1124-1137.

21. Hopf, Harry Arthur, "Management and the Optimum," an address before the Sixth International Congress for Scientific Management, London, July 15-18, 1935; reprinted by Hopf Institute of Management, Ossining, N. Y., 1935.

22. Taylor, F. W., *Scientific Management* (New York: Harper, 1948).

23. Gillespie, James J., *Free Expression in Industry* (London: The Pilot Press, Ltd., 1948), pp. 34-37.

24. Simon, Herbert A., *Administrative Behavior* (New York: Macmillan, 1947), pp. 80-81.

25. Davis, L. E., Canter, R. R., and Hoffman, J. H., "Current Job Criteria," unpublished paper, University of California, Berkeley, California.

26. Marks, A. R., *An Investigation of Modification of Job Design in an Industrial Situation and Their Effects on Some Measure of Economic Productivity*, unpublished Ph.D. dissertation, Dept. of Engineering University of California, Berkeley, California, November 1954.

27. For an interesting discussion see Friedman, Georges, *Industrial Society* (Glencoe, Ill.: The Free Press, 1955), p. 54 *ff*.

28. *Ibid.*, p. 201. Friedman reports that 79 per cent of Ford employees had jobs for which they could be trained in one week.

29. Wilensky, Harold L., and Lebeaux, Charles W., *Industrialization and Social Welfare* (New York: Russell Sage Foundation, November 1955), p. 43.

30. Martin, Norman H., "Differential Decisions in the Management of an Industrial Plant," *Journal of Business*, University of Chicago, Vol. 29, No. 4, October 1956, pp. 251-252.

31. May, Rollo, "Historical and Philosophical Presuppositions for Understanding Therapy," in O. H. Mowrer, *Psychotherapy Theory and Research* (New York: Ronald Press, 1953), pp. 38-39.

32. Williams, Douglas, "Effects of Competition between Groups in a Training Situation," *Occupational Psychology*, Vol. 30, No. 2, April 1956, pp. 85-93.

33. Deutsch, M., "The Effects of Cooperation and Competition Upon Group Process," *Human Relations*, Vol. 2, 1949, pp. 129-152.

34. Levy, Stanley, and Freedman, Lawrence Z., "Psychoneurosis and Economic Life," *Social Problems*, Vol. 4, No. 1, July 1956, pp. 55-67.

35. The validity of these principles is questioned by a recent study. Heckscher concludes that the principles of unity of command and unity of direction are *formally* violated in Sweden. "A fundamental principle of public administration in Sweden is the duty of all public agencies to cooperate directly without necessarily passing through a common superior. This principle is even embodied in the constitution itself, and in actual fact it is being employed daily. It is traditionally one of the most important characteristics of Swedish administration that especially central agencies, but also central and local agencies of different levels, cooperate freely and that this is being regarded as a perfectly normal procedure." Gunnar Heckscher, *Swedish Public Administration at Work*, SNS, Stockholm, Sweden, 1955.

36. First defined by V. A. Graicunas in an article entitled "Relationship in Organization," in *Papers on the Science of Administration* (ed.) Gulick, L., and Urwick, L., *op. cit.*, pp. 183-187.

37. Urwick, L. F. *Scientific Principles and Organization*, (New York: American Management Association), Institute of Management Series, No. 19, 1938, p. 8.

38. Dale, Ernest, *Planning and Developing the Company Organization Structure*, Research Report, Ch. 20 (New York: American Management Association, 1952).

39. Worthy, James C., "Organizational Structure and Employee Morale," *American Sociological Review*, April 1950, pp. 169-179.

40. Suojanen, W. W., "The Space of Control Fact of Trouble," *Advanced Management*, Vol. 20, No. 11, November 1955, pp. 5-13.

41. Healey, James H., "Coordination and Control of Executive Functions," *Personnel*, Vol. 33, No. 2, September 1956, pp. 106-117.

41A. Miller, George A., "Communication and Information as Limiting Factors in Group Formation," mimeographed, Harvard University, March 1957.

42. Urwick, L. F., "The Manager's Span of Control," *Harvard Business Review*. May-June, 1946.

43. Urwick, L. F., "The Span of Control—Some Facts About the Fables," *Advanced Management*, Vol. 21, No. 11, Nov. 1956, pp. 5-15.

44. Simon, Herbert A., *Administrative Behavior* (New York: Macmillan 1947), pp. 26-28.

45. Whisler, Thomas L., "The Assistant-To: The Man in Motley," *Journal of Business*, Vol. 29, No. 4, October 1956, p. 278.

46. Martin, Norman H., *op. cit.*, p. 254.

47. Whyte, William F., "On the Evolution of Industrial Sociology," Mimeographed copy of paper presented at the 1956 meetings of the American Sociological Society.

48. Brennan, Mal, *The Making of a Moron* (New York: Sheed and Ward, 1953), pp. 13-18.

49. Mr. Brennan's emphasis.

50. Bavelas, Alex, "Communication Patterns in Task-Oriented Groups." Chapter X in *The Policy Sciences* (ed.) by D. Lerner and H. L. Lasswell (Palo Alto: Stanford University Press, 1951), pp. 193-202.

———, "A Mathematical Model for Group Structures," *Applied Anthropology*, Vol. VII, 1948, pp. 16-30.

51. Leavitt, H. J. "Some Effects of Certain Communication Patterns on Group Performance," *Journal of Abnormal Sociol Psychology*, Vol. 46, 1951, pp. 38-50.

52. Heise, G. C. and Miller, G. A. "Problem-Solving by Small Groups Using Various Communications Nets," *Journal of Abnormal Social Psychology*, Vol. 46, 1951, pp. 327-335.

53. Shaw, Marvin E., and Rothchild, Gerard H., "Some Effects of Prolonged Experience in Communication Nets," *Journal of Applied Psychology*, Vol. 40, No. 5, October 1956, pp. 281-286.

54. A "wheel" structure is similar to the structure that is created by the use of the principles of chain of command and space of control. One individual becomes the "boss" of the structure.

55. However, they also point out that once the other structures "got going," they were as efficient (in terms of time required to achieve the task) as the wheel. Guetzkow, Harold, and Simon, Herbert A., "The Impact of Certain Communication Nets Upon Organization and Performance in Task-Oriented Groups," *Management Science*, Vol. 1, April-July 1955, pp. 233-250.

56. Arensberg, Conrad M., "Behavior and Organization: Industrial Studies," (eds.) John H. Rohrer and Musafer Sherif, *Social Psychology at the Crossroads* (New York: Harper, 1951), p. 340.

57. Bakke, E. Wight, *Citizens Without Work, op. cit.*, p. 90.

58. ——— *Ibid.*, p. 91.

59. Blau, Peter M., *The Dynamics of Bureacracy* (Chicago: University of Chicago Press, 1955), pp. 167 ff.

60. *Ibid.*, pp. 172-173.

61. Gibb, Cecil A., "Leadership," in *Handbook of Social Psychology*, (ed.)

Gardner Lindzey (Reading, Mass.: Addison-Wesley, 1954), pp. 887-920. (Italics mine.)

62. Blau, Peter M., *Bureaucracy in Modern Society* (New York: Random House, 1956).

63. Bierstedt, Robert, "The Problem of Authority," in Morroe Berger, Theodore Abel, and Charles H. Page (eds), *Freedom and Control in Modern Society* (New York: Van Nostrand, 1954), pp. 67-81.

64. Carter, Launor, "Leadership and Small Group Behavior," in M. Sherif and M. O. Wilson (eds.); *Group Relations at The Crossroads* (New York: Harper, 1953), p. 279.

65. Fleishman, Edwin A., "The Description of Supervisory Behavior," *Journal of Applied Psychology*, Vol. 37, No. 1. Although I was unable to obtain it, E. F. Harris' thesis is also reported to include valuable data. It is entitled, "Measuring Industrial Leadership and Its Implications for Training Supervisors," Ph.D. thesis, Ohio State, 1952. It should be pointed out that Fleishman's study was not limited to the impact of the formal structure. It includes leadership patterns. This aspect will be discussed in Chapter VI.

66. Weber, Max, *The Theory of Social and Economic Organization*, A. M. Henderson (tr.) and Talcott Parsons (ed.) (New York: Oxford, 1947).

67. For an interesting discussion of Weber's and others' work, see Merton, Robert K., Gray, Ailsa P., Hackey, Barbara and Selvin, Hanan C., *Reader in Bureaucracy* (Glencoe, Illinois: The Free Press, 1952).

68. Gouldner, Alvin (ed.). *Studies in Leadership* (New York: Harper, 1950), p. 75.

69. *Ibid*, p. 57.

70. *Ibid*, p. 58.

71. Merton, Robert K., "Bureaucratic Structure and Personality," *Social Forces*, 1940, printed also in *Studies in Leadership, op. cit.*, pp. 67-68.

72. Walker, Charles C., and Guest, Robert H., *The Man on the Assembly Line* (Cambridge: Harvard University Press, 1952).

73. Personal Communication. Publication in progress.

74. Turner, Arthur N., "Management and the Assembly Line," *Harvard Business Review*, September-October, 1955, pp. 40-48.

75. Argyris, Chris, *Organization of a Bank, op. cit.*, and *Human Relations in a Hospital, op. cit.*

76. *New York Sun*, December 1954.

77. Lewisohn, Sam, *Human Leadership in Industry* (New York: Harper, 1945).

78. Ruttenberg (one of the originators of the idea of the Guaranteed Annual Wage, while an economist for the CIO Steel Workers and now a plant president), insists that if "pay by the year" becomes effective the employees must take on management responsibilities. *Harper's*, December 1955, pp. 29-33.

79. Argyris, Chris. *An Analysis of the Human Relations Policies and Practices in England, Norway, Holland, France, Greece, and Germany*, OEEC Dept. of Management Reports, Paris, France, 1955.

CHAPTER IV

1. *Labor-Management Relations in Illini City*, Vol. I, The Case Studies; Vol. II, Explorations in Comparative Analyses. (Champaign, Ill.: The Institute of Labor and Industrial Relations, 1953 and 1954).

2. A recent preliminary attempt may be found in Howard R. Bowman, *The Business Enterprise as a Subject for Research,* Social Science Research Council, Pamphlet II, May 1955.

3. Newcomb, Theodore M., *Social Psychology* (New York: Dryden Press, 1950), pp. 360-364.

4. Lewin, Kurt, "Behavior and Development as a Function of the Total Situation," in Darwin Cartwright (ed.), *Field Theory in Social Science* (New York: Harper, 1951), pp. 238-303.

5. Miller, N. E., "Experimental Studies of Conflict," in *Personality and the Behavior Disorders* (New York: Ronald Press), Vol. 1, pp. 430-465.

6. Barker, Roger, Dembo, Tamara, and Lewin, Kurt, *op. cit.*

7. Dollard, John, *op. cit.*

8. Bakke, E. W. *Adaptive Human Behavior* (New Haven: Labor and Management Center, Yale University, 1950), pp. 50-51.

8ª. Lewin, Kurt, *et al,* "Level or Aspiration," in J. McV. Hunt (ed.), *Personality Behavior and Disorders* (New York: Ronald Press, 1944), pp. 333-378.

9. Lippitt, Ronald, and Bradford, Leland, "Employee Success in Work Groups," *Personnel Administration,* Vol. 8, Chap. 4, December 4, 1945, pp. 6-10.

10. To the extent that the individual needs to experience dependence, submissiveness, passiveness, and so forth, the individual will tend to be satisfied in the situation and not feel failure, frustration, and conflict.

11. Nevertheless, it is important to note that one way to help individuals to adapt is for the administration to provide as many opportunities for upward mobility as possible. True, everybody cannot become a boss. However, not everyone wants to become one, for this is only one way of adapting to the organization.

The importance of advancement as a mechanism for healthy adaptation is confirmed in certain countries of Europe, where the workers' desire to overthrow the "capitalists" or to maintain a noncapitalistic political party in power increases as the opportunity for economic, social, and political advancement decreases. The lack of upward mobility creates a definite feeling on the part of many workers that Marxian theory is right; namely, there are those who have and those who do not have. The fact that societies are structured so that people in power in industry are also the people in power outside of industry leads many workers to feel that the overthrow of those in power is the only solution.

It is not a coincidence to find in America, where upward mobility is higher (although not as high as some Americans think), that workers and trade union leaders act more like capitalists than workers.*

* See, for example, Bendix, Reinhard, *et al,* "Social Origins and Occupational Career Patterns," Report 53, Institute of Industrial Relations, University of California, Berkeley, 1954. Bendix, Reinhard, and Lipset, Seymour, "'Karl Marx' Theory of Social Classes," in *Class, Status and Power* (Glencoe, Ill.: The Free Press, 1953).

12. Guest, Robert H., "A Neglected Factor in Labor Turnover," *Occupational Psychology,* Vol. 29, October 1955, pp. 217-231.

13. Guest, R. H., "Work Careers and Aspirations of Automobile Workers," *American Sociological Review,* Vol. 19, No. 2, April 1954.

14. Mann, Floyd, and Baumgartel, Howard, *Absences,* Survey Research Center, Human Relations Program, Series 1, Report 2, December 1952, pp. 10

and 16. Low frequency of absences is also related to leadership pattern. This is discussed in Chapter VI.

15. Metzner, Helen, and Mann, Floyd, "Employee Attitudes and Absences." *Personnel Psychology*, Vol. 6, No. 4, Winter 1953, pp. 467-485.

16. Segerstedt, Torgny T., and Lundquist, Agne, *Man In Industrialized Society*, S.N.S., Stockholm, Sweden, April 15, 1956, pp. 10-11.

17. Gordon, Robert A., *Business Leadership in the Large Corporation* (New York: Brookings Institution), p. 313.

18. Copeland, Melvin J., *The Executive at Work* (Cambridge, Mass.: Harvard University Press, 1952).

19. Griffin, Clara E., *Enterprise in a Free Society*, (Chicago: Irwin and Co., 1949), p. 72.

20. Cited in "What Makes the Boss Work?" *Fortune*, Vol. 37, April 1948, p. 212.

21. National Industrial Conference Board, *Effects of Taxes upon Corporate Policy*, 1943, pp. 9-10.

22. Hickman, Addison C., and Kuhn, Manford H., *Individuals, Groups and Economic Behavior* (New York: Dryden Press, 1956), Chapters 2 and 3.

23. Warner, W. L., and Abegglen, J., *Big Business Leaders in America*, (New York: Harper, 1955), pp. 72-82.

24. Argyris, Chris, "Some Characteristics of Successful Executives," *Personnel Journal*, Vol. 32, No. 2, June 1953, pp. 50-55.

25. ———, "Top Management Dilemma: Company Needs vs. Individual Development," *Personnel*, Vol. 32, September 1955, pp. 123-134.

26. ———, *Executive Leadership* (New York: Harper, 1952).

27. Whyte, William H., Jr., "How Hard do Executives Work?" *Fortune*, January 1954.

28. Spencer, Lyle M., "Ten Problems that Worry Presidents," *Harvard Business Review*, Vol. 33, No. 6, November-December 1955, pp. 75-84.

29. Newcomer, Mabel, *The Big Business Executive* (New York: Columbia University Press, 1955), Chap. 9.

30. Talbott, H. S., *Time*, November 10, 1952, p. 109.

31. Argyris, Chris, *Executive Leadership, op. cit.*

32. Merton, Robert K., and Kitt, Alice S., "Reference Group Theory and Social Mobility," in *Class Status and Power: A Reader in Social Stratification* Reinhard Bendix and Seymour M. Lipset (ed.) (Glencoe: The Free Press, 1953), pp. 409-410.

33. Martin, Norman H., and Strauss, Anselm L., "Patterns of Mobility Within Industrial Organizations," *Journal of Business*, Vol. 29, No. 2, April 1956, pp. 101-110.

34. Two studies related to the problem of sponsoring are Everett C. Hughes, "Queries Concerning Industry and Society Growing out of Study of Ethnic Relations in Industry," and Orvis Collins, "Ethnic Behavior in Industry," in *Human Relations in Administration* (ed.) Robert Dubin, (New York: Englewood Cliffs, N. J.: Prentice-Hall, 1951).

35. Martin, Norman H., and Strauss, Anselm L., *op. cit.*, p. 108.

36. Hollingshead, A. B., Ellis, R., and Kirby, E., "Social Mobility and Mental Illness," *American Sociological Review*, Vol. 19, No. 5, October 1954, pp. 557-584.

37. Dynes, Russell R., Clarke, Alfred C., and Dinitz, Simon, "Levels of

Occupational Aspiration: Some Aspects of Family Experience as a Variable," *American Sociological Review*, Vol. 21, No. 2, April 1956, pp. 212-215.

38. *Ibid.*

39. Argyris, Chris, *Human Relations in a Bank, op. cit.*

40. For a recent anecdotal description of defensive reactions between management and employees, see H. Meltzer, "Roads to Misunderstanding in Industry," *American Journal of Orthopsychiatry*, Vol. 26, No. 2, April 1956, pp. 394-400.

41. Unless otherwise noted, they are taken from interviews obtained in actual plant situation by the author.

42. Roy, Donald, "Quota Restrictions and Goldbricking in a Machine Shop," *American Journal of Sociology*, Vol. LVII, March 1952, pp. 427-442.

43. Argyris, Chris, "Human Problems in a Hospital," mimeographed report (New Haven: Labor and Management Center, Yale University, 1955).

44. We are speaking of situations where workers know they will not be laid off in the short or long run and still they resist.

45. Centers, Richard, "Attitude and Belief in Relation to Occupational Stratification," *Journal Social Psychology*, Vol. 27, May 1945.

46. See Great Britain Industrial Fatigue Research Board Reports Nos. 25, 30, 32, 52, 56, 69, 88, and 90.

47. Mayo, Elton, "The Basis of Industrial Psychology," *Bulletin of Taylor Society*, Vol. 9, 1924, pp. 249-259.

48. Friedman, George, *op. cit.*, p. 146.

49. Lynd, R. S. and Lynd, H. M. *Middletown* (London: Constable, 1929), p. 75.

50. Argyris, Chris, *Organization of a Bank, op. cit.*, pp. 159-161.

51. Wyatt, S., Frost, L., and Stack, G. F., *Incentives in Repetitive Work: A Practical Experiment in a Factory*, Great Britain Industrial Health Research Board, Report No. 69, 1934; No. 56, 1929; No. 52, 1928; No. 32, 1924.

52. Wyatt, S. "Boredom in Industry," Harry W. Karn and B. von Heller Gilmer (eds.), *Readings in Industrial and Business Psychology* (New York: McGraw-Hill, p. 246).

53. Fromm, Erich, *The Sane Society*, (New York: Rinehart, 1955), p. 288.

54. Leggo, Christopher, "Attitudes Which may be Adopted in the Dubious Compensation Claim in California," *Industrial Medicine and Surgery*, Vol. 20, pp. 364-368, August 1951.

55. Barker, R. G., Dembo, Tamara, and Lewin, Kurt. *Frustration and Regression*, University of Iowa Studies in Child Welfare, 1941, Vol. 18. John Dollard *et al, Frustration and Aggression* (New Haven: Yale University Press, 1939).

56. The Yale Technology group report that the largest number of employees who remain on the assembly line tend to internalize the tensions caused by the assembly line.

57. Because of high wages, job seniority, job security, and so forth.

58. Child, Irvin L., and Waterhouse, Ian H., "Frustration and the Quality of Performance," *Psychological Review*, Vol. 59, September 1952, pp. 351-362.

59. Dollard, John, et al, *op. cit.*

60. Barker, Roger, et al, *op. cit.*

61. "Job Attitudes: Review of Research and Opinion Report No. 1," Psychological Service of Pittsburgh, April 1955, p. 2. The researchers also suggest

that morale goes up as the workers grow older. In terms of our analysis, this increased "morale" may be due to the fact that the worker has become apathetic, disinterested, and does not permit frustrating experiences to bother him.

62. Chinoy, Ely, *Automobile Workers and the American Dream* (Garden City: Doubleday, 1955).

63. Dahlstrom, Edmund, *Internal Communication*, S.N.S., Stockholm, Sweden, June 1956, pp. 318-319.

64. Davis, Louis E., and Josselyn, P. Dudley, "How Fatigue Affects Productivity," *Personnel*, Vol. 30, No. 1, July 1953, pp. 56-59.

65. *Ibid.*, pp. 56-59.

66. Fromm, Erich, *The Sane Society*, *op. cit.*, p. 290.

67. Fromm, Erich, *The Sane Society*, *op. cit.*, p. 290.

68. This may explain why Reynolds reports that the great majority of workers do not aspire to supervisory positions. Lloyd G. Reynolds, *Labor Economics and Labor Relations* (Englewood Cliffs, N. J.: Prentice-Hall, 1949).

69. Dubin, Robert, "Industrial Workers' World: A Study of the 'Central Life Interests' of Industrial Workers," *Social Problems*, January 1956, pp. 131-142.

70. *Personnel*, Vol. 33, No. 4, January 1957, p. 236.

71. Fromm, Erich, *The Sane Society*, *op. cit.*, p. 180.

72. Cartwright, Dorwin, and Zander, Alvin, *Group Dynamics* (Evanston Illinois: Row, Peterson, 1953), p. 82.

73. As we shall see in Chapter V, there are factors other than formal organization which have a similar impact. We are studying these factors one at a time, although in real life they exist simultaneously.

74. Lewin, Kurt, et al "Level of Aspiration," in (ed.) J. McV. Hunt, *Personality and Behavior Disorders*, *op. cit.*, pp. 333-378.

75. Lippitt, Ronald, and Bradford, Leland, "Employee Success in Work Groups," *op. cit.*, pp. 6-10.

76. Max Weber many years ago reported cases of slowdown and restriction of output in his research, "Gesammelte Aufsätze zur Soziologie und Sozialpolitik" (Tübingen: J. C. B. Mohr, 1924, "Zur Psychophysik der Industriellen Arbeit") p. 155.

77. Homans, George, *The Human Group* (Harcourt Brace, 1950), pp. 53-59.

78. Roy, Donald, "Work Satisfaction and Social Reward in Quota Achievement," *American Sociological Review*, Vol. 18, No. 5, October 1953, pp. 507-514.

79. Dalton, M. Collins, O., and Roy, D., "Restriction of Output and Social Cleavage in Industry," *Applied Anthropology*, Vol. 5., No. 3, Summer 1946.

80. Roy, Donald, "Quota Restrictions and Goldbricking in a Machine Shop," *American Journal of Sociology*, Vol. 57, No. 5, March 1952, pp. 427-442.

81. Moore, David G., "Employee Attitude Surveys in the U. S.," Industrial Relations Center, March 1953, p. 9. The Center has "attitude-tested" hundreds of thousands of employees in airlines, meat packing, retailing, railroads, and manufacturing groups of all types and descriptions.

82. *Ibid.*, p. 10.

83. Renck, Richard, "Morale in Four Key Groups In Industry," *Occasional Papers*, Chap. 7, Industrial Relations Center, University of Chicago, 1955.

84. Brown, J. A. C., *The Social Psychology of Industry* (Pelican Book, 1954), p. 87.

85. Vitelis, Morris, *Motivation and Morale in Industry* (New York: Norton, 1953), p. 51.

86. Drucker, P. F., *The New Society* (New York: Harper, 1950), p. 83.

87. Mathewson, S. B., *Restriction of Output Among Unorganized Workers* (New York: Viking Press, 1931).

88. *Ibid.*, p. 146.

89. Rosmussen, G., and Zander, A., "Group Membership and Self-Evaluation," *Human Relations*, 1954, Vol. 7, pp. 293-351.

90. Stotland, E., Thorley, S., and Zander, A., "Group Expectation and Self-Evaluation," unpublished manuscript. Research Center for Group Dynamics, University of Michigan.

91. Zander, A., "The Effect of Group Variables on Individual Behavior and Adjustment," Ann Arbor Research Center for Group Dynamics, Progress Report, Prof. No. M-701 for period October 1, 1953-April 15, 1955 (mimeographed).

92. Lieberman, Seymour, "The Relationship Between Attitudes and Roles: A Natural Field Experiment," Survey Research Center, University of Michigan. Read at the American Psychological Meetings, New York, September 1954, (manuscript form). The reasons for apathy toward the union are discussed in the next section.

93. Whyte, William, *Money and Motivation* (New York: Harper, 1955), p. 262.

94. Homans, George C., "The Western Electric Researchers," in *Human Factors in Management*, (ed.) Schuyler Dean Hoslett (New York: Harper, 1951, rev. ed.), pp. 235-236.

95. Dalton, M., Collins, O., and Roy, D., "Restriction of Output and Social Cleavage in Industry," *Applied Anthropology*, Vol. 5, No. 3, Summer 1946.

96. Chapter IV.

97. Coleman, John R., "The Compulsive Pressures of Democracy in Unionism," *American Journal of Sociology*, Vol. LXI, No. 6, May 1956, p. 522.

98. McGregor, Douglas, "Conditions of Effective Leadership in the Industrial Organization," *Journal Consulting Psychologists*, Vol. 8, 1944, pp. 55-63.

99. Brooks, Robert R. R., *When Labor Organizes* (New Haven: Yale University Press), 1938.

100. Important research exists that views the establishment of trade unions more in terms of "institutions" promoting themselves among the workers than in terms of the stabilization of small informal groups. For example, see the works of E. W. Bakke, Clark Kerr, and Arthur M. Ross.

101. Twentieth Century Fund, *How Collective Bargaining Works: A Survey of Experience in Leading American Industries* (New York: The Fund, 1942).

102. Bakke, E. Wight, "Why Workers Join Unions", *Personnel*, American Management Association, Vol. 22, No. 1, pp. 2-11.

103. Rosen, H., and Rosen, R. A., *The Union Member Speaks* (New York: Prentice Hall, 1955).

104. Tannenbaum, Arnold S., and Kahn, Robert L., *Organizational Control Structure*, University of Michigan Survey Research Center, unpublished manuscript, November 1955.

105. Straus, G., "Control by the Membership in Building Trade Unions," *Amer. J. Soc.*, Vol. LXI, No. 6, May 1956, pp. 527-535.

106. Lipset, S. M., Traw, M. and Coleman, James, *Union Democracy: The Inside Politics of the International Typographical Union* (Glencoe, Ill.: Free Press, 1956).

107. Sayles, Leonard, and Strauss, George, *The Local Union* (New York: Harper, 1953).

108. Seidman, Joel, "Democracy in Labor Unions," *Journal of Political Economy*, Vol. LXI, No. 3, June 1953, pp. 221-231.

109. Lipset, Seymour M., "The Political Process in Trade Unions: A Theoretical Statement," in Berger, M., Abel, T., and Page, C. H., (eds.) *Freedom and Control In Modern Society* (New York: D. Van Nostrand, 1954).

110. Kopald, Sylvia, *Rebellion in Labor Unions* (New York: Bone and Liveright, 1924).

111. Howe, Riving, and Widick, B. J., *The UAW and Walter Reuther* (New York: Random House, 1949).

112. Hardman, J. B. S., "The State of the Movement," in J. B. S. Hardman and M. F. Neufeld (eds.) *The House of Labor* (New York: Prentice Hall, 1951).

113. Taft, Philip, "Democracy in Trade Unions," *American Economic Review*, Vol. XXXVI, 1946, pp. 359-381.

114. ———— "Internal Characteristics of American Unionism," *Annals of the American Academy of Political and Social Science*, Vol. CCLXXIV, 1951, pp. 94-100.

115. ————. "Understanding Union Administration," *Harvard Business Review*, Vol. XXIV, 1946, pp. 245-257.

116. Shister, Joseph, "The Focus of Union Control in Collective Bargaining," *Quarterly Journal of Economics*, Vol. LX, 1946, pp. 513-545.

117. Coleman, John R. "The Compulsive Pressures of Democracy in Unionism," *American Journal of Sociology*, Vol. LXI, No. 6, May 1956, pp. 519-526.

118. Miller, G. W., and Young, J. E., *American Journal of Economics and Sociology*, Vol. 15, No. 1, October 1955, pp. 44-45. See also G. Popiel, "Bureaucracy in the Mass Industrial Union," *American Journal of Economics and Sociology*, Vol. 15, No. 1, October 1955, pp. 49-58.

119. Recent group dynamics research implies that "closed shop" condition can lead to member surface involvement rather than deep involvement. Cartwright and Zander (*op. cit.*, p. 143) summarizing a number of studies conclude: "The group whose members are not allowed to leave will develop more overt or noninvolved conformity.

119A. Miller, Glen W., and Rosen, Ned, "Members Attitudes Toward the Shop Steward," *Ind. Lab. Rel. Rev.*, Vol. 10, No. 4, July 1957, pp. 516-531.

120. For an interesting example see Tannenbaum, Arnold S., "Mechanisms of Control in Local Trade Unions," *British Journal of Sociology*, Vol. VII, No. 4, December 1956, pp. 307-313.

121. Rosen and Rosen, *op. cit.*, p. 121.

122. a. Purcell, Theodore V., "Dual Allegiance to Company and Union," *Personnel Psychology*, Vol. 7, No. 1, March 1954, pp. 48-58, b. *The Worker Speaks His Mind: On Company and Union* (Cambridge: Harvard University Press, 1954).

123. a. Stagner, Ross, "Dual Allegiance as a Problem in Modern Society,"

Personnel Psychology, Vol. 7, No. 1, March 1954, pp. 41-47. b. *Illini City* (2 vols.), (Champaign, Ill.: University of Illinois, The Institute of Labor and Industrial Relations, 1953, 1954).

124. Kerr, Willard A., "Dual Allegiance and Emotional Acceptance-Rejection in Industry," *Personnel Psychology,* Vol. 7, No. 1, March 1954, pp. 59-66.

125. The exception is when the union is truly democratic; then, of course, it has a different organizational structure.

126. Anther cause of trade unionism is the employees' mistrust of, and lack of confidence in, management. This problem is analyzed when we come to discuss leadership.

127. Blum, Fred H., *Toward A Democratic Work Process* (New York: Harper, pp. 94-99).

128. Smith, Gudmund J. W., and Lund, Andreas, "Women Workers in Industry," S.N.S. Stockholm, Sweden, 1954.

129. Ling, T. M., Wilson, V. W., Briggs, L. A., "An Investigation into the Readjustment to Work of Psychiatric Cases, *International Journal of Sociological Psychiatry,* Vol. 1, No. 2, Autumn 1955, pp. 18-27.

130. Ling, T. M., and Wilson, V. W., "A Survey of Occupational Problems in a Neuroses Centre," *British Medical Journal,* Vol. 2, September 1952, p. 558.

131. Chinoy, Ely, *Automobile Workers and the American Dream* (New York: Doubleday, 1955).

132. Friedman, Eugene, and Havighurst, Robert J., *The Meaning of Work and Retirement* (Chicago: University of Chicago Press, 1954).

133. *Ibid.,* p. 27.

134. Riegel, John W., *Employee Interest in Company Success* (Manuscript form.) To be published by the University of Michigan Press.

135. Viteles, M. S. *Motivation and Morale in Industry* (New York: Norton, 1953). (Reported in the Public Opinion Index for Industry in 1947.)

136. Jaques, Elliot, *Measure of Responsibility* (Cambridge, Mass.: Harvard University Press, 1956), p. 31.

137. Fromm, Erich, *The Sane Society op. cit.,* p. 295.

138. Underlining mine.

139. *Ibid.,* p. 295.

140. Drucker, Peter F., *Concept of the Corporation* (New York: John Day 1946), p. 179.

141. Purcell, Theodore V., "Dual Allegiance to Company and Union," *op. cit.;* Sayles, Leonard, and Strauss, George, *The Local Union, op. cit.;* Stagner, Ross, "Do Management Attitudes Determine Union Management Relations," *Current Economic Comment,* February 1955, pp. 3-9, e.g., "Regardless of management attitude, higher wage rates tend to make for a more favorable climate of opinion at the rank-and-file level." Viteles, *op. cit.,* shows ample evidence for the increasing importance of job security for the workers in spite of an expanding economic enterprise. p. 315.

142. Reynolds, Lloyd, *The Structure of Labor Markets* (New York: Harper, 1951).

143. I add this condition because I know of cases where the employees disliked their wages but remained primarily because of the excellent possibilities for a personality satisfaction on the job and their dislike of changing. *Organization of a Bank, op. cit.* Also many middle management executives, although

dissatisfied with their salaries, feel it is disloyal to management to create a union.

144. *Job Attitudes: Review of Research and Opinion, Report No. 2,* Psychological Service of Pittsburgh, April, 1955, p. 10.

145. See research reports entitled, "Job Attitudes and Performance," and "Agent Attitude," Research Report 1954—11 File No. 440 Hartford, 1954, Life Insurance Agency Management Association.

146. *Personnel* Vol. 33, No. 4, January 1957, p. 326.

147. Kahl, Joseph, "Educational and Occupational Aspirations of 'Common Man' Boys," *Harvard Educational Review,* Vol. 23, No. 3, Summer 1953, p. 202.

148. Bakke, E. W., *op. cit.,* pp. 20-21. (italics Professor Bakke's).

149. Bakke, E. W., *op. cit.,* p. 90.

150. Davis, Allis, "The Motivation of the Underprivileged Worker," in (ed.) Whyte, William F., *Industry and Society* (New York: McGraw-Hill, 1946).

151. Guest, Robert, "Work Careers and Aspirations of Automobile Workers," *American Sociological Review,* Vol. 19, No. 2, April 1952, pp. 155-163.

152. *Ibid.,* p. 163.

153. Hyman, Herbert, "The Value Systems of Different Classes," in (ed.) Bendix, Reinhard, Lipset, Seymour M. *Class Status and Power* (Glencoe, Ill.: Free Press, 1953), p. 438.

154. Chinoy, Ely, "The Tradition of Opportunity and the Aspiration of Automobile Workers," *American Journal of Sociology,* Vol. LVII, 1952, p. 454.

155. Hollingshead, A. B., *Elmtown's Youth* (New York: Wiley, 1949), p. 286.

156. Galler, E. H. "Influences of Social Class on Children's Choices of Occupations," *Elementary School Journal,* Vol. LI, 1951, pp. 439-445.

157. Centers, Richard, "Children of the New Deal," *International Journal of Opinion and Attitude Research,* No. 4, 1950, pp. 315-317; 322-335.

158. Archibald, Catherine, *Wartime Shipyard* (Berkeley: University of California Press), pp. 157-167; 173-177.

159. Fromm, Erich, *Escape From Freedom* (New York: Rhinehart, 1941), pp. 29-32.

160. Italics mine.

161. Riesman, David, *The Lonely Crowd* (New Haven: Yale University Press, 1950), p. 19.

162. Barker, Roger, Dembo, T., and Lewin, Kurt, *op. cit.*

163. Argyris, Chris, *Organization of a Bank, op. cit.; Human Problems in a Hospital, op. cit.*

164. Clarke, Alfred C., "The Use of Leisure and Its Relation to Levels of Occupational Prestige," *American Sociological Review,* Vol. 21, No. 3, June 1956, pp. 301-307.

165. *Ibid.,* p. 307.

166. Komarovsky, Mirra, "The Voluntary Associations of Urban Dwellers," *American Sociological Review,* Vol. 9, 1946, p. 687.

167. Goldhamer, Herbert, "Some Factors Affecting Participation in Voluntary Associations," unpublished Ph.D. thesis, University of Chicago Libraries, 1942.

168. Scott, J. C., "Membership Participation in Voluntary Associations," unpublished Ph.D. thesis, University of Chicago Libraries, 1948.

169. Blum, Fred H., *op. cit.,* pp. 100 ff.

170. Frumkin, Robert M., "Occupational and Major Mental Disorders", in

(ed) Rose, Arnold M., *Mental Health and Mental Disorder* (London: Routledge and Kegan Paul, 1956), pp. 155 ff.

171. Connely, Gordon, and Field, Harry, "The Non-Voter; Who He is, What He Thinks," *Public Opinion Quarterly*, Vol. 8, 1944, pp. 175-187.

172. Lazarsfeld, P. F., Berelson, B. and Gaudet, Hazel, *The People's Choice* (second edition, New York: Columbia University Press, 1948), pp. 4-51.

173. Rosenberg, Morris, "Some Determinants of Political Apathy," *Public Opinion Quarterly*, Vol. XVIII, No. 4, Winter 1954-55, pp. 349-366.

174. *Ibid.*, p. 364.

175. Generally speaking, the frustration and conflict should *decrease* as we go up the chain of command and/or as the individual is less mature.

176. Job security can become so important that when the individual loses it, he may have low morale in spite of the fact that his wages are high. Byron A. Grave and Willard A. Kerr, "Specific Evidence on Origin of Halo Effect in Measurement of Employee Morale," *Journal of Sociological Psychology*, Vol. 34, 1951, pp. 165-170.

177. Mayo, Elton, and Lombard, George F., *"Teamwork and Labor Turnover in the Aircraft Industry of Southern California"* (Cambridge, Mass.: Harvard University, Graduate School of Business, 1944).

178. Morse, Nancy C., *Satisfactions in the White Collar Job* (Ann Arbor: University of Michigan Press, July 1953), p. 123.

179. Abstracted from Brown, James A. C., *The Social Psychology of Industry* (Balbemone Penguin Books, 1954).

CHAPTER V

1. Williams, Douglas, and Peterfreund, Stanley, *The Education of Employees: A Status Report* (New York: American Management Association), pp. 13-16.

2. Hower, Ralph M., "Final Lecture, Advanced Management Program," in (ed.) Kenneth R. Andrews, *Human Relations And Administration* (Cambridge, Mass.: Harvard University Press, 1953), pp. 99-100.

3. Roethlisberger, Fritz, "A New Look for Management," *General Management Series*, No. 141, (New York: American Management Assn.), June 1948, pp. 11-12.

4. *Ibid.*, pp. 11-12.

5. Hower, Ralph, *op. cit.*, p. 100.

6. *Ibid.*, *p.* 100.

7. Roethlisberger, Fritz, *op. cit.*, p. 11-12.

8. Youmann, E. Grant, "The Administrative Mind," *Public Personnel Review*, Vol. 15, No. 2, April 1954, pp. 72-76.

9. Moore, John F., "Too Much Management, Too Little Change," *Harvard Business Review*, Vol. 35, Chap. 1, January-February, 1956, pp. 41-49.

10. Argyris, Chris, and Miller, Frank B., under the direction of Schuyler Dean Hoslett, *The Impact of Budgets On People* (New York: Controllership Foundation, Inc., 1952), p. 16.

11. Argyris, Chris, and Taylor, Graham, "The Member-Centered Conference as a Research Method, II," *Human Organization*, Vol. 10, No. 1, Spring 1951, pp. 22-27.

12. *Personnel Journal*, Vol. 33, No. 1, May 1954, p. 3.

13. Newman, M. H., and Logan, James P., *Management of Expanding Enterprises* (New York: Columbia University Press, 1955), p. 45.

14. *Ibid.*, p. 46.

15. *Ibid.*, p. 69.

16. Martin, Virgil, "Self-Examination for Progressive Management," *Occasional Papers in Management*, No. 7, November 1955, (Chicago: Industrial Relations Center, University of Chicago), pp. 6-7.

17. McMurry, Robert N., "Man-Hunt for Top Executives," *Harvard Business Review*, Vol. 32, No. 1, January-February, 1952, p. 47.

18. Argyris, Chris, *Executive Leadership* (New York: Harper, 1953), p. 33.

19. Argyris, Chris, *Human Relations Problems in the Nursing Division*, Research Report (New Haven: Labor and Management Center, Yale University, 1955), mimeographed.

20. Dunham, Charles V., "Meeting the Human Problems Which Accompany Organization Changes," (Ann Arbor: Bulletin No. 23, Bureau of Industrial Relations, University of Michigan, 1955), Series, p. 3.

21. Lippitt, Ronald, and White, Ralph, "The 'Social Climate' of Children's Groups," in Barker, R. G., Kounin, J., Wright, H., (eds.), *Child Behavior and Development* (New York: McGraw-Hill, 1943), pp. 485-508.

22. White, Ralph, and Lippitt, Ronald, "Leader Behavior and Member Reaction in Three 'Social Climates' ", in Cartwright, D., and Zander, A., *Group Dynamics* (Evanston: Row, Peterson, 1953), pp. 585-611.

23. Lippitt, R., and White, R., *op. cit.*, pp. 607-609.

24. Adams, R. G., "The Behavior of Pupils in Democratic and Autocratic Social Climates," *Abstracts of Dissertations*, Stanford University, 1943-1946, pp. 19-21, pp. 83-86.

25. Mowrer, O. H., "Authoritarianism vs. Self-government in the Management of Children's Aggressive Reactions as Preparation for Citizenship in a Democracy," *Journal of Social Psychology*, Vol. 10, 1939, pp. 121-126.

26. Robbins, Florence, "The Impact of Social Climates Upon a College Class," *School Review*, Vol. 60, 1952, pp. 275-284.

27. Bavelas, Alex, "Morale and the Training of Leaders," in G. Watson (ed.) *Civilian Morale* (Boston: Houghton Mifflin, 1942), pp. 143-165.

28. Preston, Malcolm G., and Heintz, Roy K., "Effects of Participatory vs. Supervisory Leadership on Group Judgment," *Journal of Abnormal and Social Psychology*, Vol. 44, 1949, pp. 345-355.

29. Jacobson, E., Kahn, R., Mann, F., and Morse, Nancy, (eds.) "Human Relations Research in Large Organizations," *Journal of Social Issues*, No. 3. 7, 1951, Katz, D., Kahn, R. R., Jacobson, R., Morse, Nancy, and Campbell, A., "The Survey Research Center's ONC Program," in H. Guetzkow (ed.) *Groups, Leaders, and Men* (Pittsburgh: Carnegie Institute of Technology), p. 51.

30. Worthy, James C., "Factors Influencing Employee Morale," in (ed.) Hoslett, S. D., *Human Factors in Management* (New York: Harper, 1951), pp. 313.

31. Fleishman, Edwin A., Harris, Edwin F., and Burtt, Harold E., *Monograph 33*, Bureau of Educational Research, Ohio State University, 1955, pp. 7-8.

32. Campbell, Clyde M., *Practical Applications of Democratic Administration* (New York: Harper, 1952), pp. 107-108.

33. Holden, P. E., Fish, L. S., and Smith, H. L., *Top Management Organization and Control, op. cit.*

34. Villers, Raymond, *Dynamics Of Industrial Management* (New York: Funk and Wagnalls, 1954), pp. 66-67.

35. Hodges, Henry G. *Management* (Boston: Houghton Mifflin, 1956), pp. 162.

36. Martin, A., Manufacturing Dep't. of General Electric Co.). Paper presented before the Boston Chapter, National Association of Cost Accountants, January 19, 1931.

37. Whyte, William F., *Money And Motivation* (New York: Harper, 1955), p. 37.

38. Only the list of factors in this column are taken from Whyte.

39. Discussed in Chapters II and III.

40. *Ibid.*, p. 37.

41. *Ibid.*, pp. 261-262.

42. The fear of an unknown future is discussed in detail by Roger, Barker, Wright, Beatrice and Gonick, Mollie, in *Adjustment To Physical Handicap And Illness* Social Science Research Council, Bulletin 55, 1946, pp. 28-32.

43. Abruzzi, Adam, "Formulating a Theory of Work Measurement," *Management Science*, Vol. 2, No. 2, January 1956, pp. 114-130.

44. Jasinski, Frank, "Use and Misuse of Efficiency Controls," *Harvard Business Review*, July-August, 1956.

45. Dalton, Melville, "Industrial Controls and Personal Relations," *Social Forces*, Vol. 33, No. 3, March 1955, pp. 244-249.

46. Bakke, E. W., "Sources of Conflict Among Functional Groups in Danish Industry," *Nordisk Sommer Universitet*, 1953, pp. 214-215.

47. Segerstedt, Torgny, and Lundquist, Agne, *Man in Industrialized Society, op. cit.*, p. 11.

48. Argyris, Chris, and Miller, Frank, under the direction of Schuyler Hoslett, *op. cit.*, p. 10.

48A. Berowitz, Leonard, and Levy, Bernard I., "Pride in Group Performance and Group Task Motivation," *Journal of Abnormal and Social Psychology*, Vol. 53, No. 3, November 1956, pp. 300-306.

49. Whyte, William F., *Money and Motivation* (New York: Harper, 1955).

49A. Professor Douglas McGregor pointed out that Merit rating and management performance schemes as traditionally practiced also tend to make people feel more dependent, subordinate, and submissive.

50. Recent research suggests that feelings of loyalty are not necessarily related to productivity. Likert, Rensis, *Motivation: Common Care of Management, op. cit.*, p. 5.

51. Mayo, Elton, *The Human Problems of An Industrial Civilization* (Boston: Division of Research, Harvard Business School), 1946.

52. Roethlisberger, F. J., and Dickson, W. J., *Management and the Worker* (Cambridge: Harvard University Press, 1949).

53. For an interesting critique, see Kerr, Clark, and Fisher, Lloyd H., "Plant Sociology: The Elite and the Aborigines" (ditto paper). See Conrad Arensburg's and Geoffrey Tootell's reply entitled "Plant Sociology: Real Discoveries and New Problems," in the book tentatively entitled *Common Frontiers of the Social Sciences*, (eds.) Lazarsfeld and Kamaransky, accepted for publication by the Free Press, Glencoe, Ill.

54. See reports of Project #178, European Productivity Agency, Paris, France, 1954-1955, by Chris Argyris.

55. The material is based upon one year's travel in Europe holding "diagnostic discussions" with small groups of top managers, trade union leaders, government officials. The individual countries will be combined into a forthcoming over-all European report tentatively entitled "Human Relations Practice and Policies."

56. Whyte, William H., Jr., *Is Anybody Listening?* (New York: Simon and Schuster, 1952), pp. 6-7.

57. For some studies on how to make such programs more effective see:

a. Pigors, Paul, *Effective Communications in Industry,* (New York: National Association of Manufacturers), 1949.

b. Hoslett, Schuyler Dean, "Barriers to Communication," *Personnel,* September, 1951.

c. *Communications in Employment Relations,* Research and Technical Report No. 14, Industrial Relations Center, University of Minnesota, July, 1953.

d. For a realistic appraisal of certain communication policies, see Habbe, Stephen, *Communicating with Employees,* Studies in Personnel Policy 129, New York, National Industrial Conference Board, Inc., 1952.

58. *Management Review,* Vol. XLIV, No. 5, May 1955, p. 336.

59. Stagner, R., Flebbe, J. D. R., and Wood, E. V., "Working on the Railroad: A Study of Job Satisfaction," *Personnel Psychology,* Vol. 5, 1952, 293-306.

60. Katz, Daniel, Kahn, Robert L., "Some Recent Findings in Human Relations Research," Survey Research Center, University of Michigan, pp. 10-11.

61. Lystad, Mary H., and Stone, Robert C., "Bureaucratic Mass Media: A Study in Role Definition," *Social Forces,* Vol. 34, No. 5, May 5, 1956, pp. 356-361.

62. *Personnel Journal,* Vol. 34, No. 4, September 1955, p. 143.

63. Marrow, Alfred J., *Living Without Hate* (New York: Harper, 1951), p. 22.

64. Hovland, Carl I., Janis, Irving L., and Kelley, Harold, *Communication and Persuasion* (New Haven: Yale University Press, 1953), pp. 269-270.

65. *Ibid.,* pp. 272 and 277.

66. Smith, B., Bruner, J. S., and White, R. W., *Opinions and Personality* (London: Chapmas and Hall, 1956).

67. *Ibid.,* p. 277.

68. Crutchfield, Richard S., "Conformity and Character", *American Psychology,* Vol. 10, 1955, pp. 191-198.

69. Rogers Carl R., "Implications of Recent Advances in Prediction and Control of Behavior", *Teachers College Record,* Vol. 57, No. 4, February 1956, pp. 316-322.

70. Argyris, Chris, and Miller, Frank, under the direction of Schuyler Hoslett, *op. cit.,* p. 10.

70A. Merton, Robert K., "Patterns of Influence," in Paul F. Lazarsfeld and N. Stanton, editors, *Communication Research,* 1948-49, N.Y. Harper & Brothers, 1949.

70B. Katz, Elihu, Lazarsfeld, Paul F., *Personal Influence: The Part Played by People in the Flow of Mass Communication,* Glencoe, Illinois, The Free Press 1955.

70C. Berelson, Bernard., Lazarsfeld, Paul F., and McPhee, William N., *A Study of Opinion Formation in a Presidential Campaign*, Chicago, University of Chicago Press, 1954.

70D. For an excellent summary and insightful analysis see, Katz, Elihu, "The Two-Step Flow of Communication," *Public Opinion Quarterly*, Vol. xxi, No. 1, Spring 1957, pp. 61-78.

71. "Consultative Management," *Management Record*, Vol. XVII, No. 11, November, 1955, National Industrial Conference Board, Inc., pp. 438-439.

72. Italics mine.

73. The experiments of Lippitt and White, which are probably the most frequently quoted, suggest that autocratic leadership can be more productive but at a human cost of lower morale. Asch confirms these results (see *Handbook of Social Psychology, op. cit.*, pp. 1806 ff.).

74. Schacter, S., Ellertson, N., McBride, D., and Gregory, D., "An Experimental Study of Cohesiveness and Productivity," *Human Relations*, Vol. 4, 1951, pp. 229-238.

75. *Communications Training for Supervisors*, Supervisory Development Service, June 1955, American Management Association. The Supervisory Development Service is bringing together in these "sourcebooks" some of the best management material available.

76. Kutner, Bernard, "Elements and Problems of Democratic Leadership," in A. Gouldner (ed.) *Studies in Leadership, op. cit.*, p. 460.

77. Gordon, Thomas, *Group-Centered Leadership* (Boston: Houghton Mifflin, 1955), pp. 124 ff.

78. *Ibid.*, pp. 152-155.

79. Dahlstrom, Edmund, *Internal Communication S. N. S.*, Stockholm, Sweden, November, 1955.

80. Whyte, William H., *Is Anybody Listening?* (New York: Simon and Schuster, 1952), p. 44.

81. Argyris, Chris. *Executive Leadership, op. cit.*

82. Perry, D., and Mahoney, T. A., "In Plant Communications and Employee Morale," *Personnel Psychology*, Vol. 8, August 1955, pp. 339-348.

83. Katz, Daniel, and Kahn, Robert L., *Some Recent Findings in Human Relations Research*, Survey Research Center, University of Michigan, pp. 10-11. Italics mine.

84. Dunham, Charles V. "Meeting the Human Problems Which Accompany Organizational Changes," Bureau of Industrial Relations, Bulletin No. 23, University of Michigan, 1955, pp. 5, 6, and 7.

85. Except those formalized. For example, certain activities sanctioned by the union (i.e., strike).

86. Mellinger, Glen D., "Interpersonal Trust as a Factor in Communication," *Journal of Abnormal and Social Psychology*, Vol. 52, No. 3, May 1956, pp. 304-309. Naturally, in Mellinger's results, A could be the Subordinate and B the Leader.

87. Another possibility is to study plants in different cultures. In Europe, I was impressed by the similarity of the *in plant* problems that the manager, trade unionists, workers and researchers mentioned between the U.S. and such countries as England, Norway, Sweden, Holland, France, and Germany. My engineer-plant manager companion, Professor A. B. Cummins of Western

Reserve University, has compiled quantitative (unpublished) data supporting this impression.

88. Hower, Ralph M., *op. cit.*, pp. 100-101.

89. Hill, J. M. M., and Trist, E. L., "A Consideration of Industrial Accidents As A Means of Withdrawal From the Work Situation", *Human Relations*, Vol. VI, No. 4, 1953, pp. 357-380.

90. ―――, "Changes in Accidents and other Absences With Length of Service", *Human Relations*, Vol. VIII, No. 2, 1955, pp. 121-152.

91. Castle, Peter, F. C., "Accidents, Absence, and Withdrawal from the Work Situation," *Human Relations*, Vol. IX, No. 2, 1956, pp. 223-233.

92. Noland, William E., "Foreman and Absenteeism," *Personnel Journal*, Vol. 24, No. 2, June, 1945, pp. 73-77.

CHAPTER VI

1. Gardner, Burleigh B., and Whyte, William F., "The Man in the Middle: Position and Problems of the Foreman," *Applied Anthropology*, Vol. 4, No. 2, Spring 1945, pp. 19-20.

2. Gardner, Burleigh B., *Human Relations in Industry* (Chicago: Richard Irwin, 1945), pp. 45 ff.

3. Wray, D. E., "Marginal Men of Industry, The Foreman," *American Journal of Sociology*, January, 1949, p. 298.

For those interested in a study of what types of activities foreman tend to engage in during the day, see, Wallace, W. L., and Galleagher, J. V., *Activities and Behaviors of Production Supervisors*, PRS Report 946, Dept. of the Army, April 1952. Unfortunately, the study lacks any description of the psychological dimensions (e.g., do foremen frustrate or place their workers in failure) and any attempt at correlating what foremen do with some criterion. Nevertheless, it is a useful piece of work if one is interested in a description of certain nonpsychological activities of foremen.

4. Lieberman, Seymour, "An Analysis of Role Change in a Factory Situation," mimeographed, Institute of Social Research, University of Michigan.

5. Arthur, Guy B., "The Foreman's Place in Management," *Personnel Journal*, Vol. XXVI, No. 2, p. 44.

6. Moore, Wilbert E., *Industrial Relations and the Social Order* (New York: Macmillan, 1951), p. 162.

7. Renck, Richard, "Morale in Four Key Groups in Industry," *Occasional Papers*, University of Chicago, Industrial Relations Center, Chap. 7, November 1955, p. 28.

8. Argyris, Chris, *A Theoretical Formulation in Human Relations in Industry*, M. A. Thesis, Kansas University, 1949.

9. Seeman discusses similar possibilities by conceptualizing with the "criterion group," i.e., the group that matters for the individual. For example:

(1) *Agreement within criterion group.* This refers to the situation where the definition of the leader's role is characterized by substantial agreement within the criterion group on behaviors which are contradictory or mutually difficult to achieve under given institutional conditions.

(2) *Disagreement within the criterion group.* Briefly, this refers to a situation in which the members of a criterion group disagree as to what is appropriate behavior under a given set of conditions.

(3) *Disagreement between criterion groups.* The classic example is the "man-in-the-middle" view of the foreman in industry. He is seen as one who is caught between conflicting definitions of his role by top management and by his subordinates. An empirical example in the Air Force studies is found in the fact that superiors prefer the Structure-in-Interaction behavior while subordinates prefer high Consideration behavior.

Seeman, Melvin, "Role Conflict and Ambivalence in Leadership," *American Sociological Review,* Vol. 18, No. 4, August 1953, pp. 373-380.

10. Kahn, Robert L., "An Analysis of Supervisory Practices and Components of Morale," *Groups, Leadership and Men* (Pittsburgh: Carnegie Press, 1951), pp. 86-89.

11. Mann, Floyd C., and Dent, James K., "The Supervisor: Member of Two Organizational Families," *Harvard Business Review,* Vol. 32, No. 6, November-December, 1954, pp. 103-112.

12. Kahn, Robert L., and Katz, Daniel, "Leadership Practice in Relation to Productivity and Morale," (ed.) Cartwright, D., and Zander, A., *Group Dynamics, op. cit.,* pp. 612-628.

13. Selekman, Benjamin, *Labor Relations and Human Relations* (New York: McGraw Hill, 1949), pp. 35 ff.

14. Roethlisberger, Fritz, "The Foreman: Master and Victim of Double Talk," *Harvard Business Review,* Spring 1945, pp. 284 ff.

15. Gross, Ira B., Jr., "When Foreman Joined the CIO," *Personnel Journal,* 1940, p. 276.

16. Gardner and Whyte, *op. cit.* pp. 18-19.

17. Gardiner, Glenn, *When Foreman and Steward Bargain* (New York: McGraw Hill, 1945).

18. Labor Bulletin 66, *Foreman's Guide to Labor Relations,* Washington, D.C.: U.S. Department of Labor.

19. Newton, T. G., "Barriers to Leadership on the Foreman's Part," *Addresses on Industrial Relations,* Bureau of Industrial Relations, Bulletin No. 22, 1954, p. 3.

20. Mills, C. Wright, *White Collar,* (New York: Oxford University Press, 1953).

21. Lewin, Kurt, *Conceptual Representation and Measurement of Psychological Forces,* (Durham: Duke University Press, 1939).

22. For a systematic study of the impact of overlapping antagonistic situations see Barker, Roger, Wright, Beatrice, and Gonnick, M., *Adjustment to Physical Handicap and Illness,* Social Science Research Council Bulletin No. 5, 1946, pp. 28-44.

23. *Ibid.*

24. Pelz, Donald C., "Leadership Within A Hierarchical Organization," *Journal Social Issues,* Vol. VII, No. 3, 1951, pp. 49-55.

25. Pelz, D. C., "Influence: Key to Supervisory Leadership," *Personnel* Vol. 29, No. 3, November 1952, pp. 209-217.

26. Bonuses tend to confirm the foreman's trend to an increasing emphasis on monetary rewards.

27. "Not enough," according to the foreman. Published Statement by Foremen's Association of America, *Personnel Series,* American Management Association, No. 87, 1944, p. 22.

28. See, for example, budget study by Argyris, Miller, under the direction of Hoslett, *op. cit.*, and *Executive Leadership* by Argyris, *op. cit.*

29. Zalesnick, A., *Foreman Training in a Growing Enterprise*, Dev. of Research (Boston: Graduate School of Business Adminstration, Harvard University 1951).

30. Fleishman, Edwin A., Harris, Edwin F., and Burtt, Harold E., *op. cit.*

31. Surface, James R., "Resistance to Training," *Harvard Business Review*, Vol. 32, No. 2, March-April, 1954, pp. 73-78.

32. Guest, Robert H., "Of Time and the Foreman," *Personnel*, Vol. 32, No. 6, May 1956, pp. 478-487.

33. Jasinski, Frank J., "Human Relations Training: The Missing Link," *Personnel*, Vol. 32, No. 6, May 1956, pp. 508-515.

34. See *Study of Budgets and Executive Leadership, op. cit.*

35. For the foreman's point of view, see series of articles in *Advanced Management* (March and June, 1953) on "Human Problems of Foremen."

CHAPTER VII

1. It is important to re-emphasize the fact that the problems described up to this point assume that relatively mature individuals are brought in as agents of the organization.

2. Unfortunately, behavioral science research is at its weakest in this section. Comparatively little "developmental" research is available that can provide concrete information as to how the basic problems can be decreased in an actual organizational situation.

3. Walker, Charles R., "The Problem of the Repetitive Job," *Harvard Business Review*, Vol. 28, No. 3, May 1950, p. 54.

4. Walker, Charles R., and Guest, Robert, *The Man on the Assembly Line, op. cit*, pp. 151-152.

5. *Ibid*, pp. 151 and 152.

6. Schwab, Robert E., "Motivation and Human Relations Principles," *American Management Association*, 1953, pp. 30-39.

7. Katz, D., and Kahn, R., *op. cit.*, p. 20.

8. Hoppock, R., *Job Satisfaction* (New York: Harper, 1935).

9. Super, B., "Occupational Level and Job Satisfaction," *Journal of Applied Psychology*, 1939, 23, pp. 547-564.

10. Marks, A. R., *An Investigation of Modification of Job Design in an Industrial Situation and their Effects on Some Measures of Economic Productivity* (Ph.D. dissertation, Berkeley: Department of Engineering, University of California, 1954).

11. Worthy, James C., *op. cit., p.* 319.

12. Geographically the units are scattered through all sections of the U.S., in communities ranging from cities of under 5000 to the largest metropolitan centers. These units include retail stores, mail order plants, factories, warehouses, and offices; in size they range from fewer than twenty-five employees to more than 10,000.

13. As measured by the questionnaire developed by Sears Roebuck.

14. Wyatt, S., and Langdon, J. N., (assisted by F. G. L. Stock) *Fatigue and Boredom in Repetitive Work* (Great Britain: Industrial Health Research Board), Rep. No. 77, p. 68.

15. Other articles describing the impact of job enlargement along the work-flow process are:

a. Baldamus, W., "Type of Work Motivation," *The British Journal of Sociology,* Vol. II, No. 1, March 1951, pp. 44-58.

b. "Broadening the Job," *Time,* Vol. 63, April 12, 1954, p. 100.

c. Davis, L. E., and Canter, R. R., "Job Design," *The Journal of Industrial Engineering,* Vol. VI, No. 1, January 1955, p. 306.

d. Elliot, J. D., "Increasing Office Productivity Through Job Enlargement," American Management Association, *Office Management Series,* No. 134, 1954.

e. "Job Enlargement—a Safety Tool?" *Occupational Hazards,* Vol. 16, No. 10, August 1954, pp. 21, 69-70.

f. Largemann, J. K., "Job Enlargement Boosts Production," *Nation's Business,* Vol. 42, No. 12, December 1954, pp. 34-37, 79.

g. Raube, S. A., "The Problem of Boredom," *Conference Board Management Record,* Vol. 10, No. 12, December 1948, pp. 567-575.

h. Viteles, M. S., "Man and Machine Relationship," in R. B. Ross (ed.) *Proceedings of 1950 Annual Fall Conference* (New York: Society for Advancement of Management), 1951, pp. 129-138.

i. Walker, J. and Marriott, R. "A Study of Some Attitudes to Factory Work," *Occupational Psychology,* Vol. XXV, No. 3, July 1951, pp. 181-191.

j. Wharton, D., "Removing Monotony from Factory Jobs," *American Mercury,* Vol. 79, October 1954, pp. 91-95; also in *Reader's Digest,* "Workers Don't Have to be Robots," Vol. 65, October 1954, pp. 85-88.

k. Wright, D. R., "Job Enlargement," *Wall Street Journal,* March 13, 1954, p. 1. I am indebted to A. E. Turner of the Yale Technology Project for many of these above references.

16. Mann, Floyd C., and Hoffman, Richard L., "Individual and Organizational Correlates of Automation," *Journal of Social Issues,* Vol. 12, No. 2, 1956, (mimeographed manuscript).

17. *Ibid.,* p. 19.

18. Bibby, Danse L., "An Enlargement of the Job for the Worker," *Proceedings of the 17th Conference Texas Personnel and Management Association,* October 20-21, 1955. (Austin: University of Texas), pp. 29-31.

18A. Krugman, Herbert E., "Just Like Running Your Own Little Store," *Personnel,* Vol. 34, No. 1, July-August 1957, pp. 46-51.

19. Argyris, Chris, *Organization of a Bank, op. cit.,* and *Human Problems in a Hospital, op. cit.*

20. Jacques suggests the span of time during which an employee is authorized to make his own decisions without evaluations from his superiors (which is a measure of self-responsibility in our language) can be used as a basis of wage and salary determination, see *Measurement of Responsibility, op. cit.*

21. Golden, Clinton S., and Ruttenberg, Harold J., *The Dynamics of an Industrial Democracy* (New York: Harper, 1942).

22. McCormick, Charles P., *Multiple Management* (New York: Harper, 1938).

23. Ellis, Edward T., "Multiple Management," *Proceedings Texas Personnel and Management Association,* October 1955, pp. 43-48.

24, 25. Given, William, *Bottom-up Management* and *Reaching-out Management* (New York: Harper, 1949 and 1953, respectively).

26. If handled incorrectly, this type of job enlargement can have negative

effects. For example, management labor committees can be used to bypass the supervisor. See Campbell, H., "Some Effects of Joint Consultation on the Status and Role of the Supervisor," *Occupational Psychology*, Vol. 27, No. 5, October 1953, pp. 201-206.

27. McCormick, for example, reports 12% increase in production in first two years. Turnover reduced 3% and absenteeism was 7% less than the average during wartime.

28. Scanlon, Joseph N., "Profit Sharing Under Collective Bargaining: Three Case Studies," *Industrial and Labor Relations Review*, Vol. 2, No. 1, October 1948, pp. 58-75.

29. Shultz, George P., "Worker Participation on Production Problems," *Frontiers of Personnel Administration*, Dept. of Industrial Engineering, Columbia University, June 1951, pp. 77-88.

30. Scanlon, Joseph N., "Adamson and His Profit-Sharing Plan," *American Management Association, Production Series*, No. 172, 1947, pp. 10-12.

31. Shultz, George P., and Crisara, Robert P., *The Lapointe Machine Tool Company and the United Steelworkers of America*, National Planning Association Case Study No. 10, Causes of Industrial Peace, November, 1952, p. 35.

32. Gilson, Thomas Q., and Lefcowitz, Myron J., "A Plant Wide Productivity Bonus in a Small Factory: Study of an Unsuccessful Case," (Ithaca, N. Y.: Industrial and Labor Relations Review) Cornell University, January 1957.

33. Gillespie, James J., *Free Expression in Industry, op. cit.*, pp. 94-96. For two interesting examples in Europe, see the work of Marcel Barbu of the Boimondau watch factory found in Claire H. Bishop's *All Things Common* (New York: Harper, 1950), and E. Jacques, *The Changing Culture of a Factory* (London: Tavistock Publications, 1951).

34. Thelen, Herbert A, *Dynamics of Groups At Work*, Un. of Chicago Press, 1954, pp. 114-115.

The following item appeared in the business section of *Newsweek*, March 22, 1954, under the heading, "How They Got More Done": "While the boss was away, some factory workers in Endicott, New York, switched jobs, just to break up the boredom. Result: it turned out to be just what the doctor ordered. By the time the switch was discovered, the men were all doing so much better that the boss decided to rotate jobs in his department—at an International Business Machines plant—as a matter of policy. That was a year ago. Since then manufacturing costs in the department have dropped about 19 percent. If nobody gets bored by the routine of rotation, everything will be dandy." Comment: If the boss maintains the kind of relationship that allows this spontaneous action of the workers to occur, he will keep production up. If he imposes rotation as a gimmick, the effect will be only temporary.

35. Coch, Lester, and French, John R. P., Jr., "Overcoming Resistance to Change," *Human Relations*, Vol. I, No. 4, 1948, pp. 512-532.

36. *Ibid.*, pp. 520-521.

37. *Planning and Training for Effective Leadership*. Seminar held jointly by the Society for the Advancement of Management, Cincinnati Chapter and the Foundation for Research on Human Behavior, February 1955, pp. 14-15. For another interesting example, see Mann, Floyd C., and Sparling, John E., "Changing Absence Rates," *Personnel*, January 1956, pp. 1-19.

38. Richardson, F. L. W., Jr. and Walker, Charles R., *Human Relations in*

An Expanding Company (New Haven: Labor and Management Center, Yale University, 1948), pp. 87-91.

39. Woodhead, E. A., "Job Break-Down Under Group Study Plan," *Electrical World*, Vol. 120, No. 124, 1943.

40. Thelen, Herbert, *op. cit.*, pp. 119-120.

41. Stogdill, Ralph M., and Koehler, Kathleen, "Measure of Leadership Structure and Organization Change," Studies in Naval Leadership, Personnel Research Board, (Columbus: Ohio State University, 1952).

42. Arensberg, Conrad M., and McGregor, Douglas, "Determination of Morale in an Industrial Company," *op. cit.*

43. Preston, Malcolm, and Heintz, Roy, *op. cit.*

44. Laurence, Lois C. and Smith, Patricia C., "Group Decision and Employee Participation," *Journal of Applied Psychology*, Vol. 39, No. 5, October 1955, pp. 334-337.

45. Lippitt, Ronald, and White, Ralph R., *op. cit.*

46. *Ibid.*, p. 487.

47. Gordon, Thomas, "Group-Centered Leadership and Administration," Chap. 8 in Rogers, Carl, *Client-Centered Therapy* (Boston: Houghton-Mifflin, 1951).

48. Whyte, William F., "Leadership in the Work Team," Mimeographed report, October, 1953. (Ithaca, New York: School of Industrial Relations, Cornell University).

49. Mann, Floyd, and Dent, James, "Appraisals of Supervisors," (Ann Arbor: Survey Research Center, University of Michigan), March, 1954, p. 5.

50. Zaleznik, A., "Worker Satisfaction and Development," (Boston: Dev. of Research, Graduate School of Business Administration, Harvard University, 1956), p. 127.

51. Baumgartel, Howard, "Leadership, Motivation, and Attitudes in Research Laboratories," *Journal of Social Issues*, Vol. XII, No. 2, 1956, pp. 24-31.

52. Katz, Daniel, "An Overview of the Human Relations Programs," in Guetzkow, (ed.) *Groups, Leadership and Men* (Pittsburgh: Carnegie Press, 1951), pp. 68-85.

53. Campbell, Clyde M., *Practical Applications of Democratic Administration*, *op. cit.*, pp. 107-108.

54. McGregor, Douglas, "Conditions of Effective Leadership in the Industrial Organization," *Journal of Consulting Psychology*, Vol. 18, 1944, pp. 55-63.

55. Turner, Arthur N., *op. cit.*

56. Bavelas, Alex, *op. cit.*

57. Nelson, Charles W., "Concepts and Measures of Leadership," in Argyris, Chris, *The Present State of Human Relations Research*, *op. cit.*, p. 228.

58. Kahn, Robert L., and Katz, Daniel, *op. cit.*, pp. 612-628.

59. Mann, Floyd C., and Dent, James K., *op. cit.*, pp. 103-112.

60. Likert, Rensis, "Motivation: The Core of Management," American Management Association, 1953, pp. 3-21.

61. —— Motivational Dimensions of Administration, Public Administration Service, Chicago, Ill., 1954, pp. 89-117.

62. Halpin, Andrew W., "The Leadership Behavior and Combat Performance of Airplane Commanders," *Journal of Abnormal and Social Psychology*, January, 1954, Vol. 49.

63. Laurence, L. C., and Smith, P. C., *op. cit.*, pp. 334-337.

64. Maier, Normal R. F., and Danielson, Lee E., "An Evaluation of Two Approaches To Discipline in Industry", *Journal Applied Psychology,* Vol. 40, No. 5, October, 1956, pp. 319-323.

65. Whyte, William F., *Pattern for Industrial Peace* (New York: Harper, 1951), pp. 166-172.

66. *Ibid.,* pp. 170-171.

67. Likert, Rensis, *op. cit.,* pp. 6-7.

68. Guetzkow, Harold, and Kriesberg, Martin, "Executive Use of the Administrative Conference," *Personnel,* March 1950, pp. 2-7.

69. Kriesberg, Martin, "Executives Evaluate Administrative Conferences," *Advanced Management,* Vol. 15, 1950, pp. 15-17.

70. This definition is used in leadership research at Ohio State, Survey Research Center and the Research Center for Group Dynamics, University of Michigan, See Argyris, Chris, *Present State of Human Relations Research, op. cit.,* pp. 18-20.

71. Snyder, Richard, and French, John R. P., *Experiments on Leadership in Small Groups,* Project No. 21-07-020, Contract Air Force (038)-14091.

72. The definition used by such researchers as Gordon, Tannenbaum, Knickerbocker, MacGregor, Bradford.

    a. Knickerbocker, Irving, "Leadership: A Conception and Some Implications," In S. Hoslett's *Human Factors in Management (rev. ed.* New York: Harper, 1951).

    b. Also Bradford, Leland, and others, *Exploration in Human Relations Training,* Report of the National Training Laboratory in Group Development, 1953; and Report of the Second Summer Session of the National Training Laboratory in Group Development, 1948.

73. Murphy, Gardner (ed.), *Human Nature and Enduring Peace* (Boston: Houghton-Mifflin, 1945), pp. 303-304.

74. Lippitt, Ronald, and White, Ralph K., *"The 'Social Climate' of Children's Groups,"* (ed) Barker, R. G., Kounin, J. S. and Wright, H. F. (New York: McGraw-Hill, 1943), pp. 485-508.

75. Lippitt, Ronald, and Bradford, Leland, "Building a Democratic Work Group," *Personnel, op. cit.*

76. Argyris, Chris, *Present State of Human Relations Research, op. cit.,* pp. 23, 24, 25.

77. Whyte, William F., *Leadership and Group Participation,* New York State School Industrial Labor Relations, (Ithaca: Cornell University), Bulletin No. 24, May, 1953.

78. Recent research in phychotherapy confirms Whyte's hypothesis that a pre-defined goal and some pre-defined structure (i.e., *not* an individual-need centered group) can accelerate therapy. See a) French, Thomas M., "Study of the Integrative Process," in *Feelings and Emotions* (New York: McGraw-Hill, 1950), pp. 111-113. b) Eldred, S. H. et al, *Psychiatry,* Vol. 17, 1954, pp. 337-346.

79. Jacobson, Eugene, "The Growth of Groups in a Voluntary Organization," *Journal Social Issues,* Vol. XII., No. 2, 1956, pp. 18-23.

80. Gordon, Thomas, *Group-Centered Leadership* (Boston: Houghton Mifflin, 1955), pp. 197-200.

81. Hood, Robert, "Effective Employee and Community Relations," (*Business Relations Department,* Chamber of Commerce, 1956), p. 6.

82. Hood, Robert, "Concern for Cost," Ansul Chemical Company. Mimeographed report 1956. Hood reports that two years passed before results became evident but that once the attitude for "cost concern" (not cost reduction) had been developed, the results continued to come long after the formal committees stopped functioning.

83. Richard, James, "Management Practices that Develop People," (Chicago: University of Chicago, Industrial Relations Center, 1955), p. 524.

84. ———— in Thomas Gordon's *Group Centered Leadership* (Boston: Houghton, Mifflin, 1955).

85. 1. Argyris, Chris, "Top Management Dilemma," *Personnel,* Vol. 32, No. 2, September, 1955, pp. 123-134..

86. 2. ———— "Some Characteristics of Successful Executvies," *Personnel Journal,* Vol. 32, No. 2, June 1953, pp. 50-63.

87. It is interesting to note the high degree of congruency between the above results and the earlier results of Henry, William E. (University of Chicago). He finds thàt executives tend to manifest characteristics as "high achievement drive," "strong upward mobility," "importance of the organization is paramount," "strong self-structure," "high aggressiveness," "strong reality orientation," quoted from *Present State of Human Relations Research, op. cit.,* pp. 232-233.

88. For definitions, see the writer's *"Top Management Dilemma," op. cit.,* pp. 123-134.

89. Morse, Nancy C., *Satisfaction in the White Collar Job* (Ann Arbor: University of Michigan, 1953), pp. 5-28.

90. Jacobson, E., et al, *op. cit.,* p. 8.

91. Mischler, Elliot G., "Personality and Social Structure: A Conceptual Framework with Implications for Research on the Psychological Consequences of Organizational Membership." (Princeton, N. J.: Princeton University, Organizational Project, 1954).

92. Argyris, Chris, *Executive Leadership, op. cit.*

93. Bailey, Joseph C., "A Classroom Evaluation of the Case Method," in *Human Relations and Administration,* (ed) Andrews, Kenneth C. (Cambridge, Mass: Harvard University Press, 1953), pp. 35-40.

94. Morse, Nancy C., and Reimer, Everett, "The Experimental Change of a Major Organizational Variable," *Journal of Abnormal and Social Psychology,* Vol. 52, No. 1, January, 1956, pp. 120-129.

95. Reimer, Everett, "Creating Experimental Social Change in an Ongoing Organization," American Psychological Association Symposium on "Change in Control Processes in Social Organization, New York, September 1954, pp. 7-12.

96. Likert, Rensis, *Motivational Dimensions of Administration, op. cit.,* p. 9.

97. Gordon, Thomas, *op. cit.*

98. Richard, James, *Management Practices That Develop People* (Chicago: University of Chicago Industrial Relations Center, 1955).

99. Singer, J. L., and Goldman, G. D., *Journal of Social Psychology,* Vol. 40, 1954, pp. 23-27.

100. Fiedler, Fred C., "Non-Fraternization Between Leaders and Followers and Its Effects on Group Productivity and Psychological Adjustment." Paper presented at Preventive and Social Psychiatry, Walter Reed Army Institute of Research, April, 1957.

101. Torrance, E. Paul, "Perception of Group Functionings as a Predictor of

Group Performance," *Journal of Social Psychology*, Vol. 24, 1955, pp. 271-282.

102. Cattell, R. B., "New Concepts for Measuring Leadership in Terms of Group Syntality," *Human Relations*, Vol. 4, 1951, pp. 161-184.

103. Martin, W. E., Darley, J. G., and Gross, N., "Studies in Group Behavior: II," *Educational and Psychological Measurement*, Vol. 12, 1952, pp. 533-553.

104. Berkowitz, Leonard, "Group Norms Among Bomber Crews," *Sociometry*, Vol. 19, No. 3, September 1956, pp. 141-153.

105. Vollmer, Howard M., and Kinney, Jack A., *Identifying Potential Supervisors* (Iowa City: Bureau of Labor and Management Research Service, University of Iowa, No. 12, 1956).

106. Directive leadership may also be necessary under extreme stress conditions (e.g., war) or when individuals are in new psychological situations.

106A. Case, Lynn M., *French Opinion on War and Diplomacy During the Second Empire*, University of Pennsylvania Press, 1954.

106B. Davison, W. P., Preliminary Findings reported in a paper identified as P-851 The Rand Corp., Santa Monica, California.

107. Roethlisberger, F. J., *Training for Human Relations* (Boston: Harvard University Division of Research, Graduate School of Business Administration, 1954). See especially pp. 115-142.

108. Argyris, Chris., "Research Trends in Executive Behavior," *Advanced Management*, March 1956.

109. Hemphill, John K., "Leadership Behavior Associated with the Administrative Reputation of College Departments," *Journal of Educational Psychology*, Vol. 46, No. 7, November 1955, pp. 385-402.

110. Consideration is similar to what we have been calling "employee-centered," and Initiating Structure is similar to "directive" leadership.

111. Halpin, A. W., "The Leadership Behavior and Combat Performance of Airplane Commanders," *Journal of Abnormal Psychology*, Vol. 49, 1954, pp. 19-22.

112. Cleven, Walter A., and Fiedler, Fred E., "Interpersonal Perceptions of Open-Hearth Foreman and Steel Production", *Journal of Applied Psychology*, Vol. 40, No. 5, October 1956, pp. 312-314.

113. Fiedler, F. E., "Assumed Similarity Measures As Predictors of Team Effectiveness" *Journal of Abnormal Social Psychology*, Vol. 49, 1954, pp. 381-387.

114. ——— "The Influence of Leader-Keyman Relations on Combat Crew Effectiveness", *Journal of Abnormal Social Psychology*, Vol. 51, 1955, pp. 227-235.

115. Kahn, Robert L., and Katz, Daniel, "Leadership Practices in Relation to Productivity and Morale," in (eds) Cartwright, D. and Zander, A. Group Dynamics Research and Theory (Evanston: Row-Peterson, 1953).

116. "Leadership Patterns and Organizational Effectiveness," Seminar Conducted by The Foundation for Research on Human Behavior," 1954, p. 11.

117. Bach, George R., "Pathological Aspects of Therapeutic Groups," *Group Psychotherapy* Vol. IX, No. 2, August 1956, pp. 133-148.

118. An example of the bickering that existed is the criticism by some social scientists that some human relations research is "management" oriented. All the critics know full well that there are no scientific grounds for criticizing something as "management" oriented. The only scientifically permissible argument is the question, "Is the research valid?" It is not the scientist's concern to judge on whose side valid results seem to fall.

The same argument expanded suggested that human relations researchers denied the constructive importance of industrial conflict. Let us hope that this argument is diminished by such excellent books as *Industrial Conflict* (ed) Kornhauser, A., Dubin, R., and Ross, A. (New York: McGraw-Hill, 1954). Ross (pp. 531-532) defines appropriately the organizational behaviorist's position.

CHAPTER VIII

1. Urwick, Lyndall F., *Management Education in American Business,* General Summary, American Management Association, 1954.

2. Ginsburg, Eli, *What Makes An Executive* (New York: Columbia University Press, 1955).

3. Rainio, Kullervo, *Leadership Qualities: A Theoretical Inquiry and an Experimental Study of Foremen,* Helsinki, 1955.

4. Stogdill, R. M., "Personal Factors Associated with Leadership: A Survey of the Literature," *Journal of Psychology,* Vol. 25, 1948, pp. 35-71.

5. Gouldner, Alvin, *Studies in Leadership* (New York: Harper, 1950).

6. Krech, David, and Crutchfield, Richard S., *Theory and Problems of Social Psychology* (New York: McGraw-Hill, 1948).

7. Gebb, Cecil A., "The Principles and Traits of Leadership," *Journal of Abnormal and Social Psychology,* Vol. 3, 1947, pp. 267-284.

8. Jennings, Helen Hall, *Leadership and Isolation* (New York: Longmans, Green, 1943).

9. Carter, Launor F., "Leadership in Small Group Behavior," in (ed.) Sherif, M., and Wilson, M. O., *Group Relations At the Crossroads* (New York: Harper, 1953), pp. 277.

10. Mace, Myles L., "Problems of Executive Development," *Social Science in Industry* (Stanford, California: Stanford Research Institute, May 11, 1954).

11. Stolz, Robert K., "Getting Back to Fundamentals in Executive Development," *Personnel,* May 1954.

12. Chapman, John F., "Thinking Ahead: Trends in Management Development," *Harvard Business Review,* Vol. 32, No. 2, March-April 1954.

13. Mann, Floyd C., "Studying and Creating Change: A Means to Understanding Social Organization," *Research in Industrial Human Relations* (New York: Harper, 1957).

14. Fleishman, Edwin A., "Leadership Climate, Human Relations Training, and Supervisory Behavior," *Personnel Psychology,* Vol. 6, 1953, pp. 205-222.

15. Mahler, W. R., and Monroe, W. H., *How Industry Determines the Need for and Effectiveness of Training,* Personnel Research Section, Report 929, Dept. of the Army, 1952.

16. For a series of case studies see Report of Seminar Conducted by the Foundation for Research on Human Behavior entitled *Training in Human Relations,* November-December 1954, Ann Arbor: Michigan.

17. Anshem, Melvin, "In Company vs. University Programs," *Harvard Business Review,* 1954, Vol. 32, No. 5, September-October, pp. 83-91.

18. Anshem, Melvin, "Better Use of Executive Development Programs," *Harvard Business Review,* Vol. 33, No. 6, November-December 1955, pp. 67-74.

19. For an interesting discussion of "human skill" vs. "technical" and

"conceptual" skills see Katz, Robert L., "Skills of an Effective Administrator," *Harvard Business Review*, 1955, Vol. 33, No. 1, January-February, pp. 34-36.

20. Nickerson, Albert J., "Climbing the Managerial Ladder," *Saturday Review*, November 21, 1953, p. 38.

21. Bakke, E. W., *The Fusion Process* (New Haven, Conn.: Labor and Management Center, Yale University, 1955).

22. Weschler, Irving R., Klemes, Marvin A., Shepherd, Clovis, "A New Focus in Executive Training," (Los Angeles, Calif.: University of California, 1955), Reprint 48, p. 2. See also Tannenbaum, Robert Kalejian, Verne, and Weschler, Irving R., "Training Managers for Leadership," *Personnel*, Vol. 30, January 1954, pp. 254-260.

23. Bradford, Leland, "Explorations in Human Relations Training," Washington, D. C.: National Training Laboratory for Group Development, 1954, pp. 13-14.

24. Roethlisberger, Fritz J., "The Administrator's Skill," *Harvard Business Review*, Vol. 31, No. 6, December 1953, p. 61.

25. Roethlisberger, Fritz, et al, *Training for Human Relations, op. cit.,* p. 14.

26. Fromm, Erich, *Escape From Freedom* (New York: Farrar and Rinehart, 1941).

27. ———— *Man For Himself* (New York: Rinehart, 1947).

28. *Ibid.,* p. 162.

29. Adorno, T. W., Frenkel-Brunswick, E., Levinson, B. J., Sanford, R. N. *The Authoritarian Personality* (New York: Harper, 1951). See also Gilbert, G. M., *The Psychology of Dictatorship* (New York: The Ronald Press, 1950); Roheach, M., *Prejudice, Concreteness of Thinking and Reification of Thinking, Journal of Abnormal and Sociological Psychology*, January 1951, pp. 83-91.

30. A defense mechanism by which the individual consciously denies unconscious needs.

31. These are the same requirements outlined in more detail in Chapter I.

32. Katz, Robert L., "Human Relations Skills *Can* be Sharpened," *Harvard Business Review*, Vol. 34, No. 4, July-August 1956, pp. 70-71.

33. Lewin, Kurt, and Grabbe, Paul, "Changing Behavior and Attitudes," *Journal of Social Issues*, December 1955, pp. 1-12.

34. Lippitt, Ronald, and Radke, Marian, "New Trends in the Investigation of Prejudice," *Annals of the American Academy of Political and Social Sciences*, March 1946, pp. 167-176.

35. Katz, Robert L., "Human Relations Skills *Can Be* Sharpened," *op. cit.,* pp. 65-66.

36. Thelen, Herbert, *op. cit.*

37. McGregor, Douglas, "The Staff Function in Human Relations," *Journal of Social Issues*, Vol. IV, No. 3, Summer 1948, pp. 5-22.

38. Gordon, Thomas, Memorandum (Chicago, Ill.: University of Chicago, Counseling Center), mimeographed, pp. 1-3.

39. For another interesting study see Kallejian, Verne J., Weschler, Irving R., and Tannenbaum, Robert, "Managers in Transition," *Harvard Business Review*, Vol. 33, No. 4, July-August 1955, pp. 55-64.

Klemes, Marvin A., and Kallejian, Verne J., "The Group Psychotherapist in Industry: A Preventive Approach," *The International Journal of Group Psychotherapy*, Vol. V, No. 1, January 1955, pp. 91-98.

Also, Rogers, Carl, "The Necessary and Sufficient Conditions of Therapeutic Personality Change," (Chicago, Ill.: University of Chicago, Counseling Center), Discussion Papers, Vol. 11, No. 8, April 4, 1956.

40. Thelen, Herbert, *op. cit.* See also Benne, Kenneth, and Muntyan, Bozedar, *Human Relations in Curriculum Change* (New York: The Dryden Press, 1951).

41. The next seven points are abstracted from Dr. Thelen's discussion of the role of the staff specialist. The reader is referred to the book for a more detailed and highly stimulating discussion.

41. Argyris, Chris. "Techniques of 'Member-Centered' Training," *Personnel*, Vol. 28, No. 3, November 1951, pp. 236-246.

CHAPTER IX

1. Sinnott, Edmund W., *Cell and Psyche* (Chapel Hill: University of North Carolina Press, 1950); "The Biology of Purpose," *American Journal of Orthopsychiatry*, Vol. XXII, No. 3, July 1952, pp. 457-468; "Biology and Teleology," *Bios*, Vol. XXV, No. 1, March 1954.

2. See Chapter II.

3. Bakke, E. Wight, *Bonds of Organization* (New York: Harper, 1950), pp. 191-196.

4. ———— "Properties of Activities," working paper, Fall 1953.

5. ———— *The Fusion Process* (New Haven: Labor and Management Center, Yale University, 1953).

6. ———— and Argyris, Chris, *Organizational Structure and Dynamics* (New Haven: Labor and Management Center, Yale University, 1954), pp. 7-8.

7. This proposition does not hold under certain conditions. See Proposition IX.

8. These problems may not arise for the subordinate who decides to become apathetic, disinterested.

9. In Chapter III, evidence is presented which suggests this may work. Another way may be to eliminate people altogether. This is not discussed, for once this action is taken, the analysis does not apply in changing the structure.

10. It is assumed that the pseudo human relations programs are easily eliminated.

11. How management controls may be modified is a crucial area that requires much exploration.

APPENDIX

1. Bakke, E. Wight, *Bonds of Organization* (New York: Harper, 1950). See especially pp. 191 ff.

2. Massarik, Fred, Tannenbaum, Robert Kahane, Murry, and Weschler, Irving R., "Sociometric Choice and Organizational Effectiveness: A Multi-Relational Approach," *Sociometry*, Vol. XVI, No. 3, August 1953.

3. Jacobson, E., et al (eds.) "Human Relations Research in Large Organizations," *Journal of Social Issues*, Vol. VII, No. 3, 1951, p. 19.

4. Newcomb, Theodore, *Social Psychology* (New York: Dryden).

5. Rohrer, John H., *Nursing Services in a Premature Infant Center: A Study of Social Organization and Function*, Urban Life Research Institute, Tulane University, 1953, pp. 22.

6. Blake, Robert H., and Ramsey, Glenn V., *Perception*, (New York: The Ronald Press, 1951). See especially Chapters 1, 5, 6, 10, 11, 12, and 13.

7. Bakke, E. W., and Argyris, C., *Organizational Structure and Dynamics* (New Haven: Labor and Management Center, Yale University, 1955).

8. Argyris, C., *Organization of a Bank, op. cit.*

9. Homans, George C., *The Human Group* (New York: Harcourt, Brace, 1950), p. 40.

10. Simon, Herbert, Smithburg, Donald, and Thompson, Victor, *Public Administration* (New York: Alfred A. Knopf, 1950), p. 205 ff.

11. Gardner, Burleigh B., and Moore, David G., *Human Relations in Industry* (rev. ed. Chicago: Richard D. Irwin, 1950), pp. 19-20.

12. Miller, Delbert, and Form, William H., *Industrial Sociology* (New York: Harper, 1951), pp. 342-379.

13. Bakke and Argyris believe this is one of the functions of the identification process. (See Bakke, E. W., and Argyris, C., *Organizational Structure and Dynamics, op. cit.*)

14. For an interesting discussion of internal stability problems see: Lysgaard, Sverre, "Some Problems In Connection With Informal Organization of Workers", in *Human Relations in Industry* (Paris: European Productivity Agency, January-February 1956).

15. Bernard, Claude, quoted by Homans, George, *The Human Group* (New York: Harcourt, Brace, 1950).

16. Chapter IV.

17. Hemphill, John K., and Westie, Charles M., "The Measurement of Group Dimensions," *Journal of Psychology*, Vol. 29, 1950, pp. 325-342.

18. Bakke, E. W., and Argyris, C., *Organization Structure and Dynamics, op. cit.*

19. Bakke's concept of *Bonds of Organization*, which is a more inclusive concept than *processes* of organization, would not be amenable to such analysis since he conceives of every bond being affected directly by and in turn affecting, the external as well as the internal environment.

20. Cattell, Raymond B., "Determining Syntality Dimensions as a Basis for Morale and Leadership Measurement," in (ed) Harold Guetzkow, *Groups Leadership and Men* (Pittsburgh: Carnegie Press, 1951), pp. 18-19.

21. Cattell, Raymond B., "Concepts and Methods in the Measurement of Group Syntality," *Psychological Review*, Vol. 55, 1948, pp. 48-63.

INDEX